Early English and Norse Studies

Professor A. H. Smith

EARLY ENGLISH
AND NORSE STUDIES

PRESENTED TO

HUGH SMITH

IN HONOUR OF

HIS SIXTIETH BIRTHDAY

Edited by

ARTHUR BROWN

AND

PETER FOOTE

1963

METHUEN & CO LTD

36 Essex Street · London WC2

First published 1963
© *1963 Methuen & Co Ltd*
Printed in Great Britain
by Butler & Tanner Ltd
Frome and London
Cat. No 2/2669/10

Dear Hugh,

A very happy birthday to you. You have from time to time expressed with some force your opinion of this kind of book; but you have also encouraged us at all times to think independently, and you have, therefore, no cause to complain if on this occasion we do not find ourselves in agreement with you.

If in the course of your countless activities you find time to read the book, you will recognize the names of many of your friends. Very many more would, of course, have wished to contribute to it, but even so generous and patient a publisher as ours has to draw the line somewhere. We have done our best to make the final selection of essays as representative as possible both of your scholarly interests and of those countries to which you have been a welcome visitor, or of which a number of scholars have particularly benefited from your influence. Our choice will not satisfy everyone – it may not even satisfy you – but it has been exercised with care and in good faith, and we ask you to accept the result as a token of the immense amount of goodwill with which the idea was greeted by your friends all over the world.

This is no occasion for sadness, but you will like to know that Benno Timmer was from the start an enthusiastic member of what was then an editorial trio. His death left a gap in all our lives, but his influence on this book will be found in the presence of a number of articles which he charmed, in his inimitable way, out of some of the more modest contributors. Another of our friends, F. T. Wainwright, also died before he could complete the article he had promised us.

It will please you to know that we are deeply indebted to Mr Ronald Versey of the Department of Geography, University College London, who was responsible for drawing the maps. Without the willing services of so able a cartographer we should indeed have been lost.

The book is now yours, in more ways than one. To the contributors we may say, adapting Caxton's words about his edition of *The Canterbury Tales*, 'this book we haue dylygently ouersen and duly examyned to thende that it be made accordyng vnto their owen makyng', and any faults that remain can only be ours. To our publishers we express our thanks for a full and cheerful co-operation at all times. To you, finally, the gratitude of all of us for many years of sound scholarship, wise counsel, and good friendship.

Yours ever,

ARTHUR BROWN
PETER FOOTE

Contents

vii

Contents

Illustrations

PLATES

LINE ILLUSTRATIONS

Abbreviations

(Notes to individual papers explain
additional abbreviations used in them)

AFr	Anglo-French
APhS	*Acta Philologica Scandinavica*
Bps.	*Biskupa sögur* (gefnar út af hinu íslenzka Bókmentafélagi, 1858–78)
(O)Dan	(Old) Danish
EETS	Early English Text Society
EPNE	A. H. Smith, *English Place-name Elements* I–II (EPNS XXV–XXVI, 1956)
EPNS	English Place-name Society
Flb.	(C. R. Unger and G. Vigfússon), *Flateyjarbok* I–III (1860–68)
Fritzner	J. Fritzner, *Ordbog over Det gamle norske Sprog* (1883–96)
ME	Middle English
MHG	Middle High German
Migne, *PL*	Migne, *Patrologia Latina*
ModFr	Modern French
ModI	Modern Icelandic
ModSw	Modern Swedish
NED	J. A. H. Murray and others, *A New English Dictionary* (1888–1933)
NoB	*Namn och Bygd*
(O)Norw	(Old) Norwegian
OE	Old English
OFr	Old French

OG	Old German
OHG	Old High German
OI	Old Icelandic
OLG	Old Low German
ON	Old Norse
OS	Old Saxon
PGmc	Primitive Germanic
PN	Primitive Norse
SnE	Finnur Jónsson, *Edda Snorra Sturlusonar* (1931)
SSON	*Sydsvenska ortnamnssällskapets årsskrift*
(O)Sw	(Old) Swedish
WGmc	West Germanic
WN	West Norse
WS	West Saxon
ZDA	*Zeitschrift für deutsches Altertum*

1 · Some Notes on Medieval Drama in York

1. Dating the York Cycle of Mystery Plays

It may be asserted without much fear of contradiction that the *York Memorandum Book*, edited by Maud Sellers for the Surtees Society in 1911, has never, perhaps understandably, been popular reading for literary scholars. This is a pity, for its contents, records and documents dealing with all aspects of civic activity in York, and especially those involving the crafts or trade guilds from 1376 to 1478, throw a great deal of light on the production of the York Cycle of Mystery Plays until they met their end for a variety of reasons in the sixteenth century. When Lucy Toulmin Smith edited the cycle in 1885 she did not, of course, have the Surtees Society edition of the *Memorandum Book* to help her. She relied to a great extent on material from Drake's *Eboracum* (1736), Robert Davies's *Extracts from the Municipal Records of York* (1843), and one or two extracts from the Historical Manuscripts Commission's Report on the Records of York. Although she examined the *Memorandum Book* for herself, she seems to have concentrated very largely on Roger Burton's lists of the various plays and the guilds responsible for them at various times.

It may have been this concentration which led Toulmin Smith to state (op. cit. pp. xxxi–xxxii) that 'the earliest notice of the Corpus Christi plays in York yet found is in 1378, when certain fines incurred by the Bakers were ordered to go, half to the city chamber, half "a la pagine des ditz Pestours de corpore cristi" ', a date which has apparently gone unchallenged ever since in books devoted to the Mystery Plays. It was accepted by E. K. Chambers in *The Medieval Stage* (1903), and has been

1

repeated more recently by Hardin Craig in *English Religious Drama of the Middle Ages* (1955), by Glynne Wickham in the first volume of *Early English Stages 1300–1660* (1959), and by Arnold Williams in *The Drama of Medieval England* (1961). Both Craig and Wickham specifically claim that the earliest record of a Corpus Christi play anywhere in England comes from Beverley in 1377.

Yet in 1376 the *Memorandum Book* from York has a laconic entry in a miscellaneous list of rents: 'De uno tenemento in quo tres pagine Corporis Christi ponuntur per annum ijˢ.' How long in fact the plays had been in existence in York before this date is still a matter for conjecture, and one which is unlikely to be cleared up without the discovery of further documentary evidence. It may be argued, however, that although the book contains no entries earlier than 1376, the very brevity of this one suggests that the item of rent concerned was one of fairly long standing; nothing but the barest details are given, as if it could be taken for granted that the situation was well enough known to all concerned to require no more.

At all events, it seems desirable to give this entry rather more publicity than it seems to have received hitherto, in literary fields at least, in the hope that York may receive the justice it deserves!

2. *Who were the 'Consules'?*

In four of the plays from the York Cycle, Toulmin Smith lists in the *dramatis personae* certain characters to whom she gives the name 'Consules', glossing this on its first appearance as 'King's Officers'. They appear with Pharaoh in the play on the Departure of the Israelites from Egypt, and with Herod in the Coming of the Three Kings to Herod, the Adoration of the Three Kings, and the Massacre of the Innocents. Unfortunately the manuscript of the plays does not help much in the interpretation of this word, since the scribe or scribes invariably abbreviate the speech headings to *Cons*, the final letter being a long *s* with a somewhat indeterminate mark of abbreviation through it.

An examination of parallel or similar plays in the Towneley Cycle does not bring a solution much nearer. In the Departure of the Israelites the corresponding characters are simply 'Milites'. But in the plays of Caesar Augustus, the Offering of the Magi, Herod the Great, The Scourging, and The Talents there are characters referred to as 1, 2, or 3 Consultus; this word is glossed by the editors of the Early English Text Society edition as 'Counsellor', and, if one is to trust these editors' use of italics to mark expansions in their text, the word was abbreviated in the manuscript in a variety of ways. Certainly the gloss 'Counsellor' seems appropriate, since this is the English word used by Caesar and Herod to address them, and they are specifically asked for counsel or advice, sometimes being told to consult their books for this purpose.

This situation does not, however, seem to arise nearly so clearly in the plays from York. These men are not addressed as Counsellors, nor is their advice sought so seriously. One solution to the difficulty may be found in the observance of the principle that it is never safe to ignore what your scribe has written and crossed out if there is the slightest chance of being able to decipher it. At one point in the Departure of the Israelites (on folio E2 of the manuscript) the scribe misassigned a speech to one of these characters; he corrected himself by crossing out the speech heading fairly heavily, but with a little trouble it is possible to see that he originally wrote *primus consolator* and did not use the normal abbreviation. It seems reasonable to suggest, therefore, that as far as the York Plays were concerned these men were not 'counsellors' in the sense that the Towneley Plays would suggest; still less were they 'consuls' or 'officers' as Toulmin Smith seems to imply. An interpretation of 'consoler' or 'comforter' with a very strong implication of 'flatterer' or 'yes-man' seems to fit both what the scribe wrote on this one occasion and what one can gather from their words and behaviour in the presence of Pharaoh and Herod.

3. *Other dramatic activities in York*

The earlier material published by Robert Davies and Maud Sellers has been augmented in a very important way since 1939 by the publication in the Yorkshire Archaeological Society's Record Series, under the editorship of Rev. Angelo Raine, of further material from York's civic records, taking us well into the sixteenth century. From these it is possible to see how the Mystery Plays fell on evil days: plague, civil strife, and religious controversy all played their parts in the cycle's decline and eventual disappearance. Yet the citizens of York were not to be deprived entirely of their dramatic entertainments. In the first place the records make it clear that the abolition of the Mystery Plays was not achieved without some opposition from the citizens: on 3 February 1579/80, the new mayor having taken his oath, 'the Commons did earnestly request of my L. Mayour and others this worshipfull Assemblee that Corpus Christi play might be played this yere, wherapon my L. Mayour answered that he and his Brethren wold consider of their request'. During the reign of Edward VI the plays had sometimes been allowed, provided that those concerned with the Virgin (the Dying, Assumption, and Coronation) were omitted; these were restored under Mary, and abolished again under Elizabeth. Changes were rung on the Creed Play and the Pater Noster Play, which always seem to have been a headache to the religious authorities.

By 1572 it seems that the texts of all these religious plays were in the hands of either Dean Hutton or the Archbishop 'for perusal', and little more is heard of them. Visits by travelling companies of players and the performance of the 'Midsummer Show' become more prominent in the records. Perhaps more significant, in view of dramatic developments elsewhere, is the request on 3 June 1584 by Mr Grafton, a schoolmaster, that 'for the furtherance of Midsomer shewe he may be licensed to get forth certane speaches, and also to have one pageant frame for that purpose, which speaches and matter is referred first to Mr Sheriffs to se and peruse . . .' Grafton was paid for 'the late pagiant or play' on 1 July 1584, and repeated his efforts the following year, the performance this time being referred to as an interlude. It is interesting to find that this interlude was to be played at stations round the city, just as the old Mystery Plays had been. It is also interesting to find that in 1585 the payments for the interlude included a Mr Wormall and his boys; Davies (*Extracts* p. 275), giving further details of the bill of charges but without any reference to his source, shows that Wormall's boys were choristers. It is tempting to think that they were from the Cathedral choir school and that they actually took part in acting the interlude, as was the case with the boys from St Paul's Cathedral and elsewhere, but the records are tantalizingly vague on this point. One remembers, however, that in 1571 Sebastian Westcott, Master of the Children at St Paul's, had visited York with a royal commission to 'take up' boys from the Cathedral choir for service in London, and that Westcott more than anyone was responsible for starting the Children of Paul's on their dramatic career (see *Modern Language Review*, January 1952, pp. 49–50). For all their importance in dramatic history Westcott and his immediate predecessor John Redford are still shadowy figures. The same is true of Grafton, Wormall, and their immediate predecessors in York, and much more research could profitably be devoted to such men who occupy so important a position between two great traditions of drama.

ARTHUR BROWN

B

2 · Place-names and the Geography of the Past

In the study of the changing English landscape, one category of place-names stands out as particularly relevant. It is the large group of descriptive names which have persisted long after the features they once described have ceased to exist. Such names provide a considerable body of evidence for reconstructing the primitive landscape of England, evidence that becomes all the more revealing when it is plotted on a map, and considered in relation to topography and soils. Full use has yet to be made of this material, but a number of studies have shown the way by using place-names in connexion with geographical themes.

As long ago as 1863, Isaac Taylor in his classic account of *Words and Places* spoke of what he called the 'geological significance' of many place-names, and one of his chapters is entitled 'Physical changes attested by local names'.[1] In the next decade, William Topley's remarkable studies of the Weald made use of place-name evidence in a discussion of the settlement of the area, and the method of his treatment anticipated much of our modern thinking about such matters.[2] Some years later, in 1887, Archibald Geikie again drew attention to the value of place-names as indicative of 'changes in the aspect of the country'.[3] In the years since then, others, in a variety of contexts, have pointed to place-names as indicating former geographical conditions, e.g. J. H. Round (1899) in his discussion of the Saxon settlement of Sussex,[4] Ellen Smith (1910)

[1] Isaac Taylor, *Words and Places* (1863), 3 and 235–55.
[2] W. Topley, 'On the relation of the parish boundaries in south-east England to great physical features', *Journal of the Anthropological Institute* III (1874), 32–56; idem, *The Geology of the Weald* (London, Mem. Geol. Survey, 1875).
[3] In an address from 1887, printed in A. Geikie, *Landscape in History* (1905), 10.
[4] J. H. Round, *The Commune of London and Other Studies* (1899), 1–27.

in her description of the Reigate district,[1] Sir Frank Stenton (1911) in his references to the one-time wooded character of northern Berkshire,[2] Charles Henderson (1935) in his study of former Cornish woodlands,[3] and P. A. Nicklin and E. G. Godfrey Faussett (1935) in their essay on the place-names of Sussex.[4] More recently, I. S. Maxwell (1958) has discussed the former distribution of vegetation over a part of Cornwall, 'as deduced from place-names'.[5]

Other writers have attempted detailed correlations of types of names with geological outcrops. Thus Sir Allen Mawer in 1920 essayed an interpretation of the distribution of 'ington' names in Northumberland and Durham in the light of the surface geology.[6] Such is the method of some of G. B. Grundy's studies, e.g. of the Saxon settlement of Worcestershire (1933); but, unfortunately, a number of his identifications are far from certain and some of his conclusions are open to question.[7] The method has also been used by L. W. H. Payling (1935) in his instructive study of 'Geology and place-names in Kesteven',[8] by S. W. Wooldridge (1935, 1936) in his interpretation of the phases of the Anglo-Saxon settlement in southeast England,[9] and by W. J. Arkell (1942) in his account of 'Place-names and topography in the upper Thames valley'.[10]

[1] Ellen Smith, *The Reigate sheet of the one-inch Ordnance Survey* (1910), 79–85.

[2] F. M. Stenton, *The Place-names of Berkshire: an Essay* (1911), 3–4.

[3] C. Henderson, 'An historical survey of Cornish woodlands', in *Essays in Cornish History* (1935), 135–51.

[4] P. A. Nicklin and E. G. Godfrey Faussett, 'On the distribution of place-names in Sussex', *Sussex Archaeological Collections* 76 (1935), 213–21.

[5] I. S. Maxwell, 'The former distribution of vegetation in Roseland as deduced from place-names', *Transactions and Papers, Institute of British Geography*, Publ. No. 25 (1958), 143–52.

[6] A. Mawer, *The Place-names of Northumberland and Durham* (1920), xvii–xix.

[7] G. B. Grundy, 'The Saxon settlement in Worcestershire', *Transactions of the Birmingham Archaeological Society* 53 (1931), 1–17.

[8] L. W. H. Payling, 'Geology and place-names in Kesteven', *Leeds Studies in English and Kindred Languages* 4 (1935), 1–13.

[9] S. W. Wooldridge and D. L. Linton, 'Some aspects of the Saxon settlement in south-east England considered in relation to the geographical background', *Geography* 20 (1935), 161–75. S. W. Wooldridge, 'The Anglo-Saxon settlement', ch. 3, H. C. Darby (ed.), *An Historical Geography of England before A.D. 1800* (1936), 88–132.

[10] W. J. Arkell, 'Place-names and topography in the upper Thames country: a regional essay', *Oxoniensia* 7 (1942), 1–23.

In the meantime, the English Place-Name Society (founded in 1922) had been well aware of this aspect – one might almost call it by-product – of its work. The county volumes of the Society are now making the evidence available in such a way that it can be used in a scholarly fashion, and brought into relation with other sources that bear upon the history of the English landscape. The volumes from 1933 onwards have included maps 'showing the distribution of those elements which

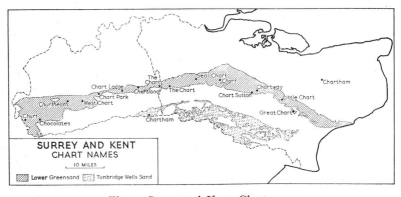

Fig. 1. Surrey and Kent: Chart names

Sources: (1) J. E. B. Gover, A. Mawer and F. M. Stenton, *The Place-names of Surrey* (EPNS XI, 1934); (2) J. K. Wallenberg, *Kentish Place-names* (1931); (3) J. K. Wallenberg, *The Place-names of Kent* (1934).

have a bearing on the history of the settlement' of each county. Some of the maps are of linguistic interest; others relate to the natural features and economy of the countryside. In the East Riding, for example, the elements 'holmr', 'kiarr', and 'mersc' provide a clue to the marshy condition of much of that countryside.[1] Or, again, in Essex we see that names containing the element 'wic' are very frequent along the coastal marshland; and they give us a glimpse of the dairying that was such a feature of this region and that was based upon the milk of ewes.[2] The villages along this coast in Domesday times had great

[1] A. H. Smith, *The Place-names of the East Riding of Yorkshire and York* (EPNS XIV, 1937), 314, 325, 326, 327.
[2] P. H. Reaney, *The Place-names of Essex* (EPNS XII, 1935), 569, 594.

stretches of 'pasture for sheep'; and about 1600, William Camden, in his account of Canvey Island, could write of the making of cheese from ewes' milk in 'those dairy sheddes of theirs, that they call there, *Wiches*'.[1]

One group of names shows how widespread was the former distribution of heath over the face of England. In Surrey, for example, names with the element 'chart' are restricted to the light soils of the Lower Greensand outcrop with the exception of Chartham, and even this lies on the light Tunbridge Wells Sand (Fig. 1). The element is derived from the Anglo-Saxon 'ceart', and denotes 'rough common, overgrown with gorse, broom, bracken'.[2] It is with surprise that we find the element concealed in 'Chocolates', the name of a wood in Thursley parish; this was known in the sixteenth century as *Chertelease*, compounded of 'ceart' and 'læs'. The element is also found in the place-names of the Kentish portion of the Lower Greensand belt.[3] Much of this tract of light soils was brought into tillage with the aid of the Norfolk Four-Course System, or of some variant of it; and other parts have been devoted to orchards and to hop-growing. These cultivated areas are often still known by names that recall their former condition. Thus to the east and west of Maidstone lie the orchard lands of Charing Heath, Lenham Heath, Barming Heath and Cox Heath. There are also other districts where heath names lie incongruously upon the present countryside. Such is the Oolitic Limestone belt to the south of Lincoln. This tract of heath and fern and gorse was brought under cultivation towards the end of the eighteenth century, but the heath names still remain as memorials of an older economy and landscape.

Another example of relict names is found on Dunsmore Heath to the west of Rugby (Fig. 2). This plateau area lies between

[1] For a discussion see J. H. Round in the *Victoria County History: Essex* I (1903), 368–74.

[2] J. E. B. Gover, A. Mawer, and F. M. Stenton, *The Place-names of Surrey* (EPNS XI, 1934), xix and 350.

[3] J. K. Wallenberg, *Kentish Place-names* (1931), *passim*; idem, *The place-names of Kent* (1934), *passim*.

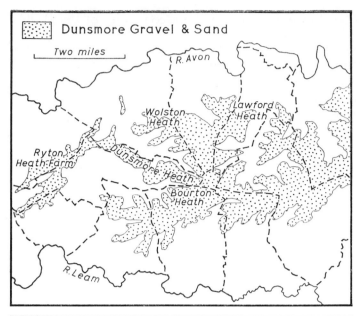

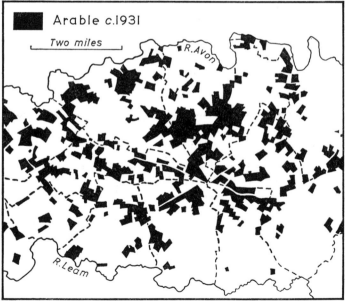

Fig. 2. Dunsmore Heath

Sources: (1) F. W. Shotton, 'The Pleistocene deposits of the area between Coventry, Rugby and Leamington and their bearing upon the topographic development of the Midlands', *Philosophical Transactions of the Royal Society of London*, Series B, vol. 237 (1954), 209–260; (2) Land Utilisation Map of England and Wales, Sheets 72 and 73. The heath names marked on the map are merely those on the seventh edition of the one-inch Ordnance Survey Map(1954). Parish boundaries are shown.

300 and 400 ft. above sea-level. The Lower Lias clays and
Keuper Marl are covered by spreads of glacial sands and
gravels that yield light soils favourable to the development of
heath. We hear of the heath of Dunchurch (*bruerie de Dunes-
cherch*) from the middle of the twelfth century; and, today,
portions of the nearby villages bear heath names.[1] Many
minor names also recall the former condition of this countryside. It is not surprising to encounter such names as Great and
Little Sandhill, or a number of localities called Small Thorns,
Cold Thorns, Thorn Hill, Broom Close, Broom Hill, and Ling
Hall. The names Rotton Hill and Starvehill indicates poor
land. That of Barn Heath is derived from 'burnt heath', and,
together with Pit Close and Marl Pit, suggests the effort of
bringing parts of the heath into cultivation. The village-name
of Ryton means 'rye farm', and the name Rye Hill is found in
the parishes of Bilton, Church Lawford and Thurlaston. All
these are reminiscent of Dugdale's comment in 1656: 'The soyl
here is of a light sandy disposition, and beareth Rye best of any
Grain.' In recalling these names we are, in a sense, looking at
the district through the eyes of those who saw it in an un-
reclaimed condition. The parish boundaries may also take us
far back into the early Middle Ages. The villages around seem
to have shared in this open uncultivated tract, and their
parish boundaries came to extend radially from the centre of
the heath. Anyone who walks today over this district of mixed
farming sees little to remind him of its former condition – to
which so many names bear testimony.

Of all the terminations that reflect the character of the
primitive landscape of England, those denoting the presence of
wood are the most frequent and the most important. This is
well illustrated by the place-names of Cambridgeshire.[2] On
the western claylands of the county, there are many names

---

[1] For the names in this paragraph, see J. E. B. Gover, A. Mawer, and F. M.
Stenton, *The Place-names of Warwickshire* (EPNS XIII, 1936), 128–9, 136–8, 146–7,
151–2, 178–9, 356–61.

[2] P. H. Reaney, *The Place-names of Cambridgeshire and the Isle of Ely* (EPNS XIX,
1943), xxvi–xxvii.

ending in 'leah', while the present-day names of Croydon Wilds and Hatley Wilds contain the Old English word 'weald'. Other evidence also shows the use of the word 'weald' elsewhere in this district, but the names have not survived on the modern map. It does seem as if this clay upland was once known simply as the Weald. On the eastern claylands of southern Cambridgeshire there is another group of parish and minor names denoting woodland, and it is clear that the great woodland of Essex once extended here. Finally, the clay islands of the Fenland also carried wood, and the southern part of the island of Ely contains examples of the use of 'weald' or 'walde' over a number of adjacent parishes.

The distribution of different types of names in Middlesex also provides a revealing supplement to any deductions from the surface geology of the county.[1] Upon the Valley Gravel and Brickhearth of the south of the county, names which do not indicate wood are common, e.g. those ending in 'ton' and 'cote'. The wood-names, on the other hand, lie on the intractable London Clay in the north of the county; here was a great expanse of wood, the memory of which is preserved by the name Enfield Chase. The contrast between the maps showing these two groups of names is a striking one. The wood-names register a stage in the process of clearing the northern part of the county; but even in the twelfth century, it could still be described as 'a great forest with wooded glades and lairs of wild beasts, deer both red and fallow, wild boars and bulls'.[2]

In the Scandinavian parts of England, strange-sounding terminations such as 'lundr', 'skógr' and 'viðr' are incorporated in the place-names; all three mean 'wood', and they occur intermingled with Old English words that also mean 'wood'. Along the Pennine valley of the Ure lies Wensleydale.[3] The

---

[1] J. E. B. Gover, A. Mawer, F. M. Stenton, and S. J. Madge, *The Place-names of Middlesex* (EPNS XVIII, 1942), xv.

[2] F. M. Stenton, H. E. Butler, M. B. Honeybourne, and E. Jeffries Davis, *Norman London* (1934), 27.

[3] A. H. Smith, *The Place-names of the North Riding of Yorkshire* (EPNS V, 1928), 246–69.

name Wensley itself means 'Waendel's clearing'. Higher up the valley there is a sequence of parish and other names that also imply the existence or former existence of wood. West Witton, for example, is 'the farm in the wood' (*wudu ton*); Ellerlands is 'alder wood' (*elri + lundr*); Aysgarth is 'the open space by the oaks' (*eik-skarð*); Lunds is 'wood' (*lundr*); Brindley is 'the clearing caused by fire' (*brende-leah*); Litherskew is 'the wood on the slope' (*hlíðar skógr*). Similar names are encountered in other Pennine valleys and in those around the North Yorkshire Moors.

In the Celtic parts of England there is another group of un-English names that indicate the former presence of wood. The exposed plateau surfaces of Cornwall are not very favourable for the growth of trees; but there was once a fair number in its valleys.[1] A common element in Cornish names is cognate with the modern Welsh word *coed*; and it appears in such forms as *cut, quite, coose*, and *coys*. Thus the name Trequite in the parishes of St Germans, St Mabyn, and St Kew is the same as Tregoose in the more westerly parishes of Probus, St Erth, Sithney, and the like. Penquite or Pencoose, meaning 'end of the wood', is another common Cornish name. But we shall be clearer about these matters when the Place-Name Society's publications include a volume on Cornwall.

The full bearing of such information upon the history and forms of settlement has yet to be investigated. A clear example comes from Warwickshire.[2] Anglo-Saxon place-names ending in *leah* or (*ge*)*hæg* show the former presence of wood, or of clearings in wood, and they lie almost entirely to the north of the River Avon (Fig. 3). In spite of some five centuries of clearing, there was still much wood there in Domesday times. Later documents show how the arable continued to expand at the expense of the wood, but the wood had far from disappeared even by the seventeenth century. Writers of that time were able to draw a distinction between the southern part of the county,

[1] C. Henderson, op. cit. 135–51.
[2] J. E. B. Gover, A. Mawer, and F. M. Stenton, *The Place-names of Warwickshire*, xiii–xv, 315, 316.

called Feldon or open country, and the northern woodland where lay the Forest of Arden. The earliest one-inch Ordnance map published in the 1830's show a contrast between the south, characterized by compact villages surrounded by open fields, and the north, characterized by dispersed houses, the dispersion resulting from scattered settlement proceeding piecemeal as the wood was cleared. The distinction between

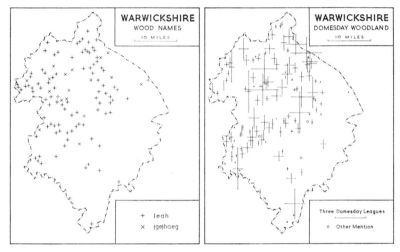

Fig. 3. Early Woodland in Warwickshire

Sources: (1) J. E. B. Gover, A. Mawer and F. M. Stenton, *The Place-names of Warwickshire* (EPNS XIII, 1936); (2) R. H. Kinvig in H. C. Darby and I. B. Terrett, *The Domesday Geography of Midland England* (1954), 292.

north and south is still important today, although industrial growth has complicated the picture.

Some of the difficulties of interpreting the evidence may be illustrated by the termination *den* or *denn*, meaning 'a woodland pasture, especially for swine'. We can assume that it was probably obsolete by the end of the Dark Ages because it is not found in Middle English field-names.[1] One difficulty arises from its late medieval orthographic confusion with *denu* meaning a valley. Essex, for example, has many major and minor

[1] A. H. Smith, *EPNE* I 129.

names that today end in *den*; but this is no reflection of the former heavily wooded clayland of the country, because the *den* in these names is almost always derived from *denu*. Only too frequently, however, it is impossible to be certain about both the earliest form and the meaning of a *den* name.

Doubt has been expressed about the use of *denn* outside the counties of Kent and Sussex and the adjoining parts of Surrey. Here, there are many names clearly derived from *denn*, although *denu* names are also frequent. The distribution of these *denn* names poses its own problems. Fig. 4 shows very many *denn* names in the eastern part of the Weald of Kent; the area of frequent occurrence stops abruptly at the Kent–Sussex border, although there is a number of *denn* names widely scattered throughout Sussex, and a few in Surrey. Why should this be so? Does the restricted distribution mean that swine pastures were frequent in the Kentish Weald but not in the Wealds of Sussex and Surrey? Or does it reflect the varying incidence of the available charter and other evidence? Or is it the result of a limited and local use of the word *denn* in Anglo-Saxon times?

The documents relating to the Canterbury estates in Kent are certainly very numerous, and this fact may be reflected on Fig. 4. Even so, it is likely that the most important single factor in this restricted distribution was that of the local use of the word *denn* by those who colonized the Weald from the north-east. Wealden swine pastures were not restricted to Kent, and the names of swine pastures recorded in pre-Conquest charters relating to Sussex and Surrey frequently do not end in *denn*.[1] Thus among the swine pastures belonging to Annington and Washington in Sussex in the tenth century, there were some whose names ended in *wic* and *hurst*; the names of a number of swine pastures in Kent itself also do not end in *denn*. The distribution of the element *den* reflects not only geographical and economic circumstances, but also local peculiarities in

[1] R. Lennard, *Rural England 1086–1135* (1959), 254. See also A. Mawer, F. M. Stenton, and J. E. B. Gover, *The Place-names of Sussex* (EPNS VI–VII, 1929–30), I 107, 160, 225, 226, 233; II 281.

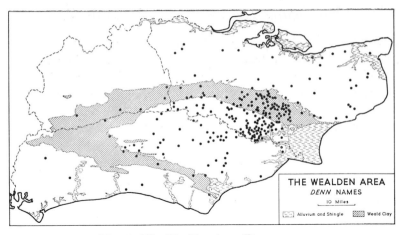

Fig. 4. The Wealden Area: Denn *names*

Sources: (1) J. E. B. Gover, A. Mawer and F. M. Stenton, *The Place-names of Surrey* (EPNS XI, 1934); (2) A. M. Mawer, F. M. Stenton and J. E. B. Gover, *The Place-names of Sussex*, 2 Pts (1929–30); (3) J. K. Wallenberg, *Kentish Place-names* (1931); (4) J. K. Wallenberg, *The Place-names of Kent* (1934).

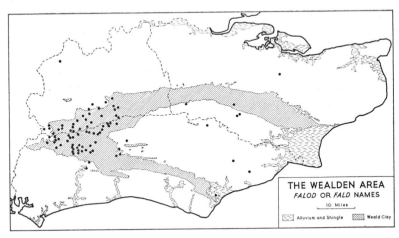

Fig. 5. The Wealden Area: Falod *or* Fald *Names*

Sources as for Fig. 4.

dialect. It implies the settlement of the southeastern peninsula by groups of people each with a nomenclature different from that of the other groups.

Some such similar explanation may also account for the restricted use of relatively early names ending in *falod* or *fald*, especially in parts of the Wealds of Sussex and Surrey (Fig. 5). The element means 'a small enclosure for animals', but we cannot assume that the animals were necessarily swine, especially in view of such place-names as Cowfold and Ramsfold. It is true that *falod* names are almost entirely confined to those clay areas where names indicating the former presence of wood are frequent. Might the word *falod* in this area have had a limited and specialized meaning? Or could the *falod* names belong to a later generation than the *denn* and other wood-names? In that case they would date from a period when the wood had been cleared from many parts of the Weald Clay, and when the grazing of cattle and sheep had replaced the herding of swine. The main period during which swine were pastured in the Weald may well have been over even before 1066, certainly before 1200. The earliest recorded dates of most *falod* names come from after 1200, but this in itself is no indication of the age when the element was in active use. *Falod* names are mostly those of minor features and, in general, record of them is not likely to date from earlier than the twelfth or thirteenth century. With these inconclusive speculations, we must leave the problem of the distribution of *falod* names.

In contrast to names ending in *denn* and *falod*, those ending in *hurst* are much more widely distributed over the three southeastern counties. But even they show local concentrations on parts of the Weald Clay belt (Fig. 6). The element *hurst* indicates 'a hillock, a wood or a wooded eminence', and in this area it can almost always be taken to imply the presence of wood. The distribution of a variety of other elements (such as *leah* and *field*) fill out the picture of the wooded Weald. We can, however, only guess at the variety within this wood-land, a variety ranging from the dense oakwoods of the heavy

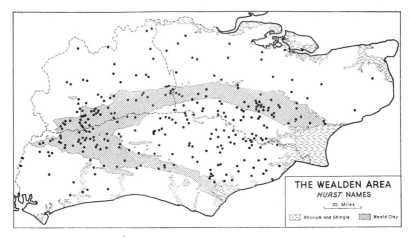

Fig. 6. The Wealden Area: Hurst *Names*
Sources as for Fig. 4.

claylands to the more open and more varied woods on the lighter soils.

Clearly many problems are involved in the use of place-names as evidence for the geography of the past. They must be considered side by side with other evidence – archaeological and historical, geological and topographical. In that way they may take their place as valuable clues in the unravelling of the history of our countryside.

H. C. DARBY

3 · Sir Gawain's Arrival in Wirral[1]

The most important scenes in *Sir Gawain and the Green Knight* [2] are at Camelot, the Castle, and the Green Chapel. Camelot is where Arthur lived, and the poet carefully places the Castle and the Chapel in some country of forest and crag a year and a day from Camelot. Although the scenery about the Castle and the Chapel might be recognizable in the district around Swythamley in northeast Staffordshire, near the Cheshire border and in the southwestern hills of the Peak district,[3] yet the poet's description of the location is allusive. While he is careful about natural features he uses no place-names. The landscape of these

[1] Abbreviations used:

Chester   *The Chartulary of Chester Abbey*, ed. J. Tait, 2 vols., Chetham Society, New Series lxxix (1920), lxxxii (1923).

ChFine   Palatinate of Chester, Fines and Recoveries, P.R.O. Chester 31, and *Twenty-eighth Report of the Deputy Keeper of the Public Records*, Appendix, 6–19.

ChGaol   Palatinate of Chester, Gaol Fines, Writs, etc., P.R.O. Chester 24.

Cl   *Calendar of Close Rolls*, P.R.O. (proceeding).

Court   *Calendar of County Court, City Court & Eyre Rolls of Chester, 1259–1297*, ed. R. Stewart-Brown, Chetham Society, New Series lxxxiv (1925).

Eyre   Palatinate of Chester, Eyre Rolls, P.R.O. Chester 17, and *P.R.O. Lists and Indexes 4* (1910), 129–130.

Fine   *Calendar of Fine Rolls*, P.R.O. (proceeding).

Harl.   Harleian Manuscripts in British Museum.

Ipm   *Calendar of Inquisitions Post Mortem*, P.R.O. (proceeding).

Pat   *Calendar of Patent Rolls*, P.R.O. (proceeding).

P.R.O.   Documents in, or calendars published by, the Public Record Office, London.

Sheaf   *The Cheshire Sheaf*, First Series (1878–1885), New Series (1895, 1 vol.), Third Series (1903–proceeding, Chester, at the office of *The Chester Courant*).

[2] Edited by J. R. R. Tolkien and E. V. Gordon, 1925, reprinted with corrections 1930, 1936.

[3] Cf. R. W. V. Elliott, 'Sir Gawain in Staffordshire, A Detective Essay in Literary Geography', *The Times*, May 21st, 1958. His topographical essay is only less interesting than his suggested association of the work or the poet with Swythamley, a grange of Dieulacres Abbey near Leek, Staffordshire, an abbey originally founded at Poulton, Cheshire, beside the R. Dee a few miles above Chester.

crucial scenes is not given a geography. The locations of Camelot, the Castle, and the Chapel, are traditional and imprecise, and
the audience is free to place them wherever it finds an allusion.

But at a juncture which is not important to the story, the
poet causes Sir Gawain to travel in a recognizable country,
geographically defined. In lines 697–702,

> . . . he neȝed ful neghe into þe Norþe Waleȝ.
> Alle þe iles of Anglesay on lyft half he haldeȝ,
> And fareȝ ouer þe fordeȝ by þe forlondeȝ,
> Ouer at þe Holy Hede, til he hade eft bonk
> In þe wyldrenesse of Wyrale; wonde þer bot lyte
> Þat auþer God oþer gome wyth goud hert louied.

The geography is discussed in Tolkien and Gordon's edition, 93,
note. It may prove to be more complicated than has been realized.

The text '*And fareȝ ouer þe fordeȝ by þe forlondeȝ, Ouer at þe
Holy Hede*' has hitherto been taken to refer to two localities, the
fords of Conway and of Clwyd, and a headland at the shore of
Dee. But the text also reads well if 'þe fordeȝ by þe forlondeȝ'
be taken as in apposition to 'þe Holy Hede', and the whole
allusion as referring to a crossing of Dee, or alternatively, to the
three crossings together, that of Dee being more precisely
identified as at 'þe Holy Hede'. This place could be read as a
point of departure or as a place of arrival.

Such a reading infers a crossing by a ford of the Dee estuary
at the very mouth, at the forelands, the seaward extremities of
the land, from Point of Air in Flintshire to the northwest
corner of the Wirral peninsula. The plural *fordeȝ* would suit the
two stages of such a crossing, that from Point of Air to Hilbre
Island, and that from the island to the Wirral shore at West
Kirby. The latter would be passable at low tide, but the former, a tidal channel once navigable and much deeper than
it now is, seems improbable. The improbability is demonstrated by the fact that the lowest ford of Dee below Chester
was that at Shotwick, guarded by Shotwick Castle (Nat. Grid
349704). By Edward I's time this was already of recognized

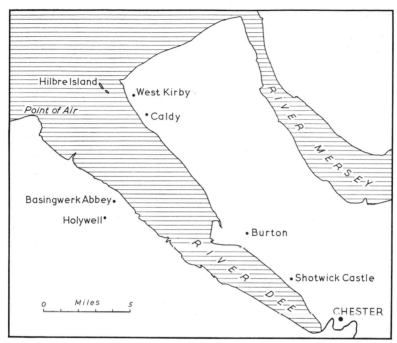

Fig. 7. The Dee Estuary in Sir Gawain

importance, both economic and strategic, cf. 'Salterway which is the kynges highway ner Chester for our lord the kynge to leide his hoost in the tyme of warr unto Shotwyk ford' (Sheaf, 3rd series, 50, No. 10041, and *Harl.* 2057, f. 130), alluding to a road from Chester. This ford is probably the unspecified place where Giraldus has Henry II crossing Dee in 1135, cf. Tolkien and Gordon, loc. cit. Other than this the only way of crossing the Dee estuary in the late-fourteenth century would be by the ferries at Caldy and Burton mentioned in 1357 (Palatinate of Chester, Forest Proceedings, P.R.O. Chester 33, 6, m. 4d) and the shipping at Hilbre in the roads of the medieval port of Chester.[1]

Improbability, however, is no discouragement of legend. The mouth of the estuary was indeed the site of a legendary ford. An account of this is given in stanzas 203–212 of Henry

---

[1] Cf. J. Brownbill, *West Kirby and Hilbre* (1928), 29 ff.

Bradshaw's *The Life of St Werburge of Chester*,[1] an English version made by this monk of St Werburgh's abbey, Chester, in 1513 (published by Pynson 1521), of an older, lost, Latin source then in his abbey's library.[2] Bradshaw recounts that Richard, earl of Chester (1101–1119), on a pilgrimage to the shrine of St Winifred at Holywell in Flintshire, was trapped, with the few retainers in his company, by the Welsh who blocked the road back to Chester. William fitz Nigel, constable of Chester, was called to the rescue and set off to meet the earl at Basingwerk (in Flintshire, north of Holywell). He went along the Wirral shore to Hilbre with his troops, expecting to find shipping there to ferry them across Dee. There were no ships. On the advice of an hermit of Hilbre (a cell of St Werburgh's was maintained there), he prayed to St Werburgh, offering gifts in return for her assistance. This procured a miracle forthwith,

> For like as to Moises deuided the redde see,
> And the water of Iordan obeyed to Iosue,
> Ryght so the depe riuer of Dee made diuision,
> The sondes drye appered in syght of them echone.

Whereupon 'They went into Wales vpon the sondes sure' and so rescued the earl and brought him home to Chester. Bradshaw then says (stanza 212)

> The said Wyllyam constable came to the monasterye,
> Thanked saynt Werburge with meke supplicacion,
> Fulfylled his promes made in extremite:
> Offred to the place the village of Neuton;
> Afterwards he founded the abbay of Norton.
> And where the host passed ouer betwix bondes
> To this day ben called 'the constable sondes'.

William fitz Nigel's grant of Newton near Chester to St Werburgh's was confirmed by charter in 1119 (Chester i, 40).[3]

The tradition of the constable's ford was obviously a cele-

---

[1] Ed. C. Horstmann, EETS 88 (1887), 179–81.   [2] Cf. ibid., xvi.

[3] For his foundation at Norton, see G. Ormerod, *History of Cheshire* (ed. T. Helsby, 1882), I 682, 690. For further commentary on the local history of the expedition, cf. Brownbill, op. cit. 29–30, 137.

brated part of the history of the house at St Werburgh's, which had a profitable memento of its discovery. It also seems to have been well enough known to the public for it to inspire a commemorative place-name and a pilgrimage. Allowing for the notorious shifting of the sands of Dee, the name of the sands survives as *Constable Bank*, a shoal off Chester Bar shown in the Ordnance Survey 1-inch map 1842, some four or five miles off Rhyl and Colwyn Bay on the North Welsh coast. Down to the Reformation, Hilbre Island appears to have been the place of a pilgrimage connected with the miracle.[1] If the poet knew about it, this legendary, miraculous, and locally famous ford might be alluded to in 'þe fordeȝ by þe forlondeȝ'.

The place West Kirby would be at the eastern end of such a ford at the mouth of the estuary, on the Wirral mainland opposite Hilbre. 'þe Holy Hede' might refer to this place. It calls to mind Holyhead in Anglesey. Geographically this is irrelevant, but the place-name seems significant. Holyhead is *Haliheved* 1315 Pat, *Holiheved* 1332 ib, et seq., 'the holy headland', so named from its being the site of a famous ecclesiastical centre associated with St Cybi. The Welsh name of the place is Caer Gybi, *gaer gybi* 959, *Kaer gybi c.* 1566 (cf. B. G. Charles, *Non-Celtic Place-Names in Wales*, London Mediæval Studies Monograph No. 1 (1938), 235–6). This appears in English records as *Castrum Cuby, -Cubii* 1288 Cl, -*Kuby* etc., 1318 Pat etc., but also as *Karkeby* 1316 Pat, *Kaerkeby* 1387, 1392 ib, 1411 Cl, *Caerkeby* 1390 Pat, *Kaerkuby* 1333 Fine, 1395 Pat, *Caercuby* 1382 Pat, *Caircuby* 1393 ib, *Carcuby* 1414 ib, *Kaerkyby* 1389, 1394, *Kayrkyby* 1399 ib.

Now the place-name spellings for West Kirby[2] in Wirral are *Ki-, Kyrkeby, (-in Wyrhale)* 1137–40 Chester, *Kirkby* 1237 ib, *Westkirk(e)by, -kyrk-, -kyrby, -kirby* 1285 ChFine, 1287 Court, etc., but there is also a variant series (*West-*) *Kerkeby* 1330 Ipm, 1355

---

[1] Cf. Ormerod, op. cit. II 501.

[2] The place-name means 'church-village', from ON *kirkju-bý(r)* (cf. A. H. Smith, *EPNE* II 4), and alludes to the ancient parish church of St Bridget. The affix *west* distinguishes this place from Wallasey, formerly *Kirkby in Waley* and the easterly of the two ancient centres of Norse settlement in Wirral (cf. J. McN. Dodgson, 'The Background of Brunanburh', *Saga-Book of the Viking Society* XIV (1953–7), 304–12).

Eyre, Kerkeby West 1347 *ChGaol,* etc.[1] If the poet knew West
Kirby as *Kerkeby* and Holyhead as *Kaerkeby* etc., then *þe Holy
Hede* could be a periphrasis for *Kerkeby* (West Kirby) by a
fancied analogy with the place-name Holyhead for *Kaerkeby*
(Caer Gybi). The drawing of this analogy might be prompted
by the holy and miraculous associations of the Hilbre passage.

Can the suggestion of such allusions be reconciled with the
context of the poem?

The geographical reference extends from the Anglesey
archipelago to Wirral, no farther. This seems deliberately intended for people who knew their country from Anglesey to
Wirral. Why, otherwise, need it have been introduced? There
is no other defined location in the poem, and the story does not
require Gawain to travel this way. Furthermore, the passage
seems to reflect a social estimation. The observation upon the
inhabitants of Wirral is in the same tradition of neighbourly con-
tempt as led nineteenth-century Chester folk to call the district
Gobbinshire, 'the country of simpletons' (Sheaf, 1st Series, iii, 10
and 211). It is intended for those who knew their men of Wirral.

If the itinerary is to lead through landscapes which are
familiar, but which must not seem an unsuitable background
for Gawain's adventures, the introduction of 'local colour' has
to be well managed. The poet would have had to be careful not
to allow the familiar to encroach upon the marvellous, or precise geography to contrast with imaginary locations. A journey
across North Wales into Wirral would not be marvellous to an
audience which knew the road. This familiar journey would
have to be made strange enough to be part of the road from
Camelot to the Green Chapel.

The crucial difficulty about landing Gawain in Wirral, once
the poet has committed himself to this, is that he provokes
speculation about the way of it. Whereas leaving all the isles of
Anglesey on the left hand does no more than set an easterly
course through North Wales in locations remote and not par-

---

[1] The spellings are from *The Place-names of Cheshire,* in preparation for the
English Place-Name Society.

ticular, in scenery wild and spectacular, an arrival in Wirral from North Wales is a particular transit. An audience which knew Wirral would know the crossings of Dee. It might seem very suitable, in the circumstances, for the poet to lead Sir Gawain's strange journey into familiar country not by any of the usual crossings but by a legendary ford, and to enhance the legend by giving a familiar place at that ford a strange and un-suspected venerability through associating its name with that of the more famous place in Anglesey. The place-name riddle and the allusion to the constable's ford would give the geo-graphy of the arrival in Wirral that element of mystery and unfamiliarity suitable for the scenery in a romance.

To justify these subtleties, it would have to be supposed that the poet or his audience or both knew the legend of the con-stable's ford, that they knew the two place-names well enough for the analogical allusion to be appreciated, that they had more than a general geographical knowledge of the districts named, and that they had a social estimation of some of the inhabitants. All this accepted, it would still have to be supposed that the poet felt it either necessary, advisable, or interesting to make these allusions as an appeal to very particular local associations. All this must wait upon the discovery of *facts* about the history and localization of the poet. The surmises of this essay, the detective topography of R. W. V. Elliott's essay,[1] lead only to conjectures. One is that the poet deliberately makes particular allusions to the topography and popular traditions of two districts, that of North Wales, the Dee estuary, West Kirby, Hilbre, Wirral, and that of Swythamley, northeast Stafford-shire, southeast Cheshire. Another is that the poet, or his patron, or both, ought to be sought amongst those whose personal, dynastic, institutional, or political associations touch these two districts. Nevertheless, where scholarship cannot yet penetrate the obscurity surrounding the facts, the moonshine of conjecture may still light up some reflection of the truth.

JOHN McNEAL DODGSON

[1] Elliott, op. cit.

4 · The Ending of Chaucer's *Troilus*

One of Chaucer's familiar pretences is that he is a versifier utterly devoted to simplicity of meaning—for the reason that he considers himself, apparently, utterly incapable of complexity. He defines his poetic mission as the reporting of facts in tolerable verse, and he implies that that's hard enough to do. True poetry may, for all of him, do something much better, but it is not clear to Chaucer exactly what it is or how it does it. He and *ars poetica* are, to be sure, on parallel roads, moving in the same direction; but the roads are a long way apart and are destined to meet, perhaps, not even in infinity. On the one hand, Chaucer, reciting his simple stories 'in swich Englissh as he kan'; on the other, poetry, penetrating regions of complex significance far beyond the grasp of a simple straightforward versifier.

Chaucer's pretended inferiority complex on the subject of poetry must have stemmed from something real in his own life, probably connected with his being a bourgeois writing for high-born members of the royal court. What interests me now, however, is not the origin of the pose, but its literary value. For I think that Chaucer discovered in the medieval modesty convention a way of poetic life: that, by constantly assuring us, both through direct statement and through implication, of his inability to write anything but the simplest kind of verse, Chaucer creates just that poetry of complex significance that he disclaims striving for. In this paper I shall focus attention on the last stanzas of *Troilus*, where it seems to me that a kind of dramatization of his poetic ineptitude achieves for him a poetic success that not many poets in any language have at-

26

tained. But I shall first consider briefly some characteristic Chaucerian 'ineptitudes' in his other works.

Modesty is endemic both with Chaucer in his own first person – whoever that is – and with his dramatic creations: none of them can do much in the way of poetry. Like the Squire, they cannot climb over so high a stile, or, like his father, they set out to plough, God wot, a large field with weak oxen; or, if they are not ploughing a field, they're gleaning it, like the author of the Prologue to the *Legend of Good Women*, and are full glad of any kernel that their talented predecessors have missed. Or else, like the Prioress, they are so afflicted by infantilism that they speak no better than a child of twelvemonth old, or less. Like the Merchant and the Franklin, they are rude men, 'burel' men, they cannot glose, they have no rhetoric, they call a spade a spade; they come after even such second-rate poets as that fellow Chaucer, bearing only *hawe bake* – pig food – and are reduced to prose, like the Man of Law in his Prologue. They can't even get the data down in the right order, like the Monk or like the narrator of the Prologue to the *Canterbury Tales*. Or, worst of all, as in the case of the pilgrim who recites the romance of Sir Thopas, their inability to frame a story of their own makes them resort to 'a rym I lerned longe agoon', and when that is shot down in mid-flight, they have to take refuge in one of the most anaesthetic sermons that ever mortified a reader. If it is dramatically appropriate that they be capable rhetoricians, like the Clerk, they comply at once with a decree that declares high style to be inappropriate to their audience. In short, they seldom admit to more than a nodding acquaintance with the Muse.

The normal function of the modesty convention is, I suppose, to prepare a pleasant surprise for the reader when the poem turns out better than he has been led to expect, or, at worst, to save him disappointment when the implied warning is fulfilled. This latter alternative is perhaps valid in some of Chaucer's tales, notably the Monk's. But the really important function of the modesty convention in Chaucer is to prepare a soil in which complexity of meaning may grow most fruitfully. That is, the narrator's assertion, implicit or explicit, of his devotion to the principle of simplicity, his denial of regard for possible complexity, results, by a curious paradox, *in* complexity; for the harder he tries to simplify issues, the less amenable to simplification they become, and, in artistic terms, the more complex and suggestive the poem becomes. To epitomize, the typical Chaucerian narrator begins by assuring you, either by a modesty prologue or by the notable simplicity of his manner – sometimes by both – that in what you are about to hear there will be nothing but the most straightforward presentation of reality: the narrator's feet are firmly on the ground, but he is no poet, and his control of anything but fact is weak. Subsequently the poet Chaucer, working from behind the narrator, causes to arise from this hard ground a complex of possible meanings, endlessly dynamic and interactive, amplifying, qualifying, even denying the simple statement: these draw much of their vitality from the fact that they exist – or seem to exist – either unknown to or in spite of the narrator; indeed, the latter sometimes betrays an uneasy awareness that the poem has got out of hand and is saying something he doesn't approve of or at least didn't intend, and his resistance to this meaning may well become an important part of it. That is, the ultimate significance of the poem derives much from the tension between the narrator's simple statement and the complex of implications that have arisen to qualify it.

The Chaucer who tells of the pilgrimage to Canterbury provides an obvious example of this tension between the simple and the complex. At the very beginning of the Prologue he lets us know exactly what we may expect of his narrative – namely, what he saw with his own two eyes, and not an adverb more. He does this, moreover, in one of the flattest, most prosaic sentences ever to have found its way into a great poem:

> But nathelees, whil I have tyme and space,
> Er that I ferther in this tale pace,
> Me thynketh it acordaunt to resoun . . .

and so on, down through

> And at a knyght that wol I first bigynne.[1]

This pedestrian matter-of-factness, supporting by example the limited poetic ideal that it is expressing, is intended to persuade the reader to expect no more than meets the eyes, if that. And it is because he has so persuaded the reader that, when a little later he comes to the portrait of the Prioress, the poet is able to reveal to us the profoundest depths of that rather shallow lady. The narrator, to be sure, describes her flatly as he saw her, and what he saw was attractive, and it attracted the warm fervour of his love; but what he did not see was that everything he did see amounted to a well-indexed catalogue of the Prioress's shortcomings, which seen coldly, would produce a kind of travesty of a Prioress. Only once in the course of his description does he have an uneasy moment: after spending twenty-four lines on pleasant irrelevancies, having nothing to do with her spiritual state, he suddenly recalls that she was, after all, a Nun, a Prioress, and he brings himself up short with a guilty 'But':

> But, for to speken of hire conscience,
> She was so charitable and so pitous, *etc.*[2]

Yet even here the blame for the lapse is made to fall upon the painter, not the subject. For if anyone had pointed out to the narrator the satirical potential of his portrait, he would have been horrified; if anyone had pointed it out to the Prioress, she would have been horrified; and even today when one points it out to some readers, they are horrified. And quite rightly, too, because of the great love that permeates the simple description. But the effect achieved by means of a narrator who resists complexity is of a highly complex strife between love and satire, between wholehearted approval and heartless criticism. These are factors which in logic would cancel one

---

[1] *Canterbury Tales* (= *CT*), A35–6, 42. All quotations from Chaucer are from F. N. Robinson's second edition of the complete works (1957).

[2] idem, A142–3.

another, as a negative cancels a positive; but in poetry they
exist forever side by side – as they also do in reality wherever
there are ladies at once so attractive and so fallible as the
Prioress. Indeed, the two factors, love and satire, unite with
one another to form a third meaning – one which both qualifies
and enhances the Prioress's own motto, *Amor Vincit Omnia*, by
suggesting something of the complex way in which love does
conquer all. This occurs because the narrator, incapable of
complexity, adheres rigorously to the presentation of simple
fact.

The ways in which Chaucerian narrators enhance the meaning of their stories by missing the point of them are various.
Occasionally, indeed, a narrator will rise up in the pulpit
sententiously to point *out* or at least to point *to* what he takes
to be his real meaning. The only trouble is that his aim is
likely to be poor: he will suggest a meaning which, while it
bears some logical relation to the ultimate significance, is at
best no more than gross over-simplification. For instance, the
Nun's Priest, at the end of his remarkably verbose epic of
Chauntecleer, solemnly addresses his audience:

> Lo, swich it is for to be recchelees
> And necligent, and truste on flaterye.
> But ye that holden this tale a folye,
> As of a fox, or of a cok and hen,
> Taketh the moralite, goode men.

He then goes on to quote St Paul in a way that suggests that
doctrine is produced every time a pen inscribes words on paper –
a thought most comforting to an author hard put to determine
his own meaning. With Pauline authority on his side, the
Nun's Priest exhorts us:

> Taketh the fruyt, and lat the chaf be stille.[1]

Now all this certainly bids us find a simple moral in the story;
but, so far as I know, no two critics have ever found the same
moral: most agree only in rejecting the Nun's Priest's stated

---

[1] idem, B²*3436–40, 3443.

moral about negligence and flattery. The reason for this disagreement is, as I have tried to suggest elsewhere,[1] that the
real moral of the Tale is in the chaff – the rhetorical ampli-
fications which make of Chauntecleer a good representative of
western man trying to maintain his precarious dignity in the
face of a universe and of a basic avian (or human) nature which
fail to co-operate with him. But the Nun's Priest, characteris-
tically, suggests this moral only by pointing towards another
which satisfies nobody.

Another Canterbury narrator, the Knight, similarly asks us
to take a simple view of a story which is really very complex.
After describing the languishing of Arcite in Theban exile and
of Palamon in Athenian prison, both of them quite out of the
running in their race for Emily, the narrator finishes off the
first part of his poem with a *demande d'amour*:

> Yow loveres axe I now this questioun:
> Who hath the worse, Arcite or Palamoun?[2]

With this tidy rhetorical flourish the Knight suggests that his
story is a simple one about a rivalry in love. The question
invites the reader to take sides in this rivalry, to feel sorrier for
one youth than the other, and hence to choose a favourite for
the contest that is to come. He appeals, that is, to our sense of
justice. Until recently, the majority of Chaucerian critics put
their money on Palamon; and since at the end of the story
Providence accords him Emily and lets him live happily ever
after, while it buries Arcite, this majority have naturally felt
that justice has operated in an exemplary manner, and nothing is pleasanter than to see justice behave itself. Yet there has
always been a noisy group – with whom I deeply sympathize –
who feel that Arcite is very badly treated by the story. This
disagreement represents a kind of protracted response to the
Knight's rhetorical question.

---

[1] See *Chaucer's Poetry: An Anthology for the Modern Reader* (1958), 940-4; also
'Patristic Exegesis in the Criticism of Medieval Literature. The Opposition', in
Critical Approaches to Medieval Literature (ed. Dorothy Bethurum, 1960), 16–20.
[2] *CT*, A1347-8.

The lack of critical agreement, however, once again suggests that there is something wrong both about the question and about the debate. If intelligent readers cannot agree on which of the two young men is the more deserving, then there is probably not much difference between them. And indeed, the way the poem carefully balances their claims bears this out. On temperamental grounds you may prefer a man who mistakes his lady for Venus to a man who knows a woman when he sees one, or you may not; but such preference has no moral validity. The poem concerns something larger than the young men's relative deserts, though it is something closely related to that question. Recognition of their equality leads to the conclusion that the poem does not assert the simple triumph of justice when Palamon ends up with Emily, nor the triumph of a malignant anti-justice when Arcite ends up in his cold grave, alone. What it does suggest – and I think with every syllable of its being – is that Providence is not working justly, so far as we can see, when it kills Arcite, nor, so far as we can see, unjustly when it lets Palamon live happily ever after. For no matter how hard we look, we cannot hope to see why Providence behaves as it does; all we can do is our best, making a virtue of necessity, enjoying what is good, and remaining cheerful.

But to most of us this is an unpalatable moral, far less appealing than the one which will result if only we can promote Palamon into an unchallenged position of deserving; and it is a very stale bit of cold cabbage indeed unless it is as hard-won as the Knight's own battles. The experience by which the individual attains the Knight's tempered view of life is an important part of that view, and renders it, if not palatable, digestible and nourishing. This experience must include our questioning of relative values, our desire to discover that even-handed justice does prevail in the universe, and our resistance to the conclusion that justice, so far as we can see, operates at best with only one hand. The emotional history of the ultimate conclusion makes it valid; and the way the Knight's question is framed, pointing at what we should like to believe, and through that at what we shall have to believe, causes us to share in that experience – leads us through the simple to the complex.

It is at the end of *Troilus* that Chaucer, employing the kind of devices I have been discussing, achieves his most complex poetic effect. His narrator has worked hard, from the very beginning, to persuade us of his simplicity, though from the very beginning his simplicity has been compromised by the fact that, apparently unknown to himself, he wavers between two quite different – though equally simple – attitudes towards his story. It is the saddest story in the world, and it is the gladdest story in the world. This double attitude appears strongly in the opening stanzas, when he tells us that his motive for writing is, paradoxically, to bring honour to Love and gladden lovers with a love story so sad that his verses shed tears while he writes them and that Tisiphone is his only appropriate Muse. Yet though he starts out firmly resolved to relate the double sorrow of Troilus

> . . . in lovynge of Criseyde,
> And how that she forsook hym er she deyde,[1]

as the story progresses he seems to forget all about the second sorrow. The historical perspective, which sees before and after and knows the sad ending, gives way to the limited, immediate view of one who loves the actors in the story, and in his love pines for what is not so desperately that he almost brings it into being. The scholar's motive for telling a sad story simply because it is true finds itself at war with the sentimentalist's motive of telling a love story simply because it is happy and beautiful. The optimism that one acquires when one lives with people so attractive makes a gay future for all seem inevitable. Once launched upon the love story, the narrator refuses to look forward to a future that the scholar in him knows to be already sadly past; at moments when the memory of that sad future breaks in on him, he is likely to deny his own sources, and to suggest that, despite the historical evidence to the contrary,

[1] *Troilus and Criseyde* (= *TC*), I 55–6.

Criseide was, perhaps, not unfaithful at all – men have been lying about her.[1]

For the greater part of the poem the intimately concerned, optimistic narrator is in full control of the story – or rather, the story is in full control of him, and persuades him that a world that has such people in it is not only the best of all possible worlds, but the most possible. When in the Fifth Book the facts of history force him back towards the historical perspective, which has always known that his happiness and that of the lovers was transitory, illusory, he does his best to resist the implications arising from his ruined story – tries to circumvent them, denies them, slides off them. Thus an extraordinary feeling of tension, even of dislocation, develops from the strife in the narrator's mind between what should be and what was – and hence what is. This tension is the emotional storm-centre which causes the narrator's various shifts and turns in his handling of the ending, and which also determines the great complexity of the poem's ultimate meaning.

So skilfully has Chaucer mirrored his narrator's internal warfare – a kind of nervous breakdown in poetry – that many a critic has concluded that Chaucer himself was bewildered by his poem. One, indeed, roundly condemns the whole fifth book, saying that it reads like 'an earlier draft . . . which its author lacked sufficient interest to revise'. According to this critic, Chaucer 'cannot bring himself to any real enthusiasm for a plot from which the bright lady of his own creation has vanished'. And, elsewhere, 'What had happened to the unhappy Criseyde and to her equally unhappy creator was that the story in which they were involved had betrayed them both.' [2] Now this is, in a rather sad way, the ultimate triumph of Chaucer's method. The critic responds with perfect sympathy to the narrator's bewilderment, even to the extent of seeming to suggest that the poet had written four-fifths of his story before he discovered how it came out. But in fact Chaucer's warmly sympathetic

[1] idem, IV 20-1.
[2] Marchette Chute, *Geoffrey Chaucer of England* (1946), 179, 180, and 178.

narrator has blinded the critic's eyes as effectively as he had blinded his own. It is not true that the bright lady of Chaucer's creation has vanished – Criseide is still very much present in Book Five. What has vanished is the bright dream of the enduring power of human love, and in a burst of creative power that it is not easy to match elsewhere.

For the *moralitee* of *Troilus and Criseide* (and by morality I do not mean 'ultimate meaning') is simply this: that human love, and by a sorry corollary everything human, is unstable and illusory. I give the moral so flatly now because in the remainder of this paper I shall be following the narrator in his endeavour to avoid it, and indeed shall be eagerly abetting him in trying to avoid it, and even pushing him away when he finally accepts it. I hope in this way to suggest how Chaucer, by manipulating his narrator, achieves an objective image of the poem's significance that at once greatly qualifies and enhances this moral, and one that is, of course, far more profound and less absolute than my flat-footed statement. The meaning of the poem is not the moral, but a complex qualification of the moral.

Let us turn now to that part of the poem, containing the last eighteen stanzas, which is often referred to by modern scholars, though not by the manuscripts, as the Epilogue. I object to the term because it implies that this passage was tacked on to the poem after the poet had really finished his work, so that it is critically if not physically detachable from what has gone before.[1] And while I must admit that the nature of this passage, its curious twists and turns, its occasional air of fecklessness, set it off from what has gone before, it also seems to me to be the head of the whole body of the poem.[2]

The last intimately observed scene of the action is the final, anticlimactic interview between Troilus and Pandarus, wherein

[1] The extreme exponent of detachability is W. C. Curry in his well-known essay, 'Destiny in *Troilus and Criseyde*', *Publications of the Modern Language Association*, XLV (1930), 129 ff., recently reprinted in his *Chaucer and the Medieaval Sciences* (second revised and enlarged ed., 1960): see especially pp. 294–8.

[2] I believe that this is the opinion of many Chaucerians. See, e.g., Dorothy Everett, *Essays on Middle English Literature* (1955), 134–8, and Dorothy Bethurum, 'Chaucer's Point of View as Narrator', *PMLA* LXXIV (1959), 516–18.

the latter is driven by the sad logic of his loyalty and of his pragmatism to express hatred of his niece, and to wish her dead. Pandarus' last words are, 'I kan namore seye,' and it is now up to the narrator, who is as heart-broken as Troilus and Pandarus, to express the significance of his story. His first reaction is to take the epic high road; by means of the exalted style to reinvest Troilus with the human dignity that his unhappy love has taken from him. The narrator starts off boldly enough:

> Gret was the sorwe and pleynte of Troilus;
> But forth hire cours Fortune ay gan to holde.
> Criseyde loveth the sone of Tideüs,
> And Troilus moot wepe in cares colde.[1]

But though the manner is epic, the subject is not: an Aeneas in Dido's pathetic plight is no fit subject for Virgilian style. And the narrator, overcome by the pathos of his story, takes refuge in moralization:

> Swich is this world, whoso it kan byholde:
> In ech estat is litel hertes reste:
> God leve us for to take it for the beste!

How true! And how supremely, brilliantly, inadequate! It has been said that all experience does no more than prove some platitude or other, but one hopes that poetic experience will do more, or in any case that poetry will not go from pathos to bathos. This moral, the trite moral of the Monk's Tale – Isn't life awful? – which the Monk arrives at – again and again – a priori would be accepted by many a medieval man as a worthy moral for the Troilus, and the narrator is a medieval man. But the poet behind the narrator is aware that an experience that has been intimately shared – not merely viewed historically, as are the Monk's tragedies – requires not a moral, but a meaning arrived at a posteriori, something earned, and in a sense new. Moreover, the narrator seems still to be asking the question,

---

[1] TC, V 1744–7. All subsequent quotations in this paper are from the lines intervening between these and the poem's end.

Can nothing be salvaged from the wreck of the story? For he goes on once more to have recourse to epic enhancement of his hero, more successfully this time, since it is the martial heroism of Troilus, rather than his unhappy love, that is the subject: there follow two militant stanzas recounting his prowess and his encounters with Diomede. But again the epic impulse fails, for the narrator's real subject is not war but unhappy love, for which epic values will still do nothing – will neither salvage the dignity of Troilus nor endow his experience with meaning. In a wistful stanza, the narrator faces his failure to do by epic style what he desires to have done:

> And if I hadde ytaken for to write
> The armes of this ilke worthi man,
>   [But, unfortunately, *arma virumque non cano*]
> Than wolde ich of his batailles endite;
> But for that I to writen first bigan
> Of his love, I have seyd as I kan, –
> His worthi dedes, whoso list hem heere,
> Rede Dares, he kan telle hem alle ifeere.

This sudden turn from objective description to introspection mirrors the narrator's quandary. Unable to get out of his hopeless predicament, he does what we all tend to do when we are similarly placed: he begins to wonder why he ever got himself into it. The sequel of this unprofitable speculation is likely to be panic, and the narrator very nearly panics when he sees staring him in the face another possible moral for the love poem he has somehow been unwise enough to recite. The moral that is staring him in the face is written in the faces of the ladies of his audience, the anti-feminist moral which is at once obvious and, from a court poet, unacceptable:

> Bysechyng every lady bright of hewe,
> And every gentil womman, what she be,
> That al be that Criseyde was untrewe,
> That for that gilt she be nat wroth with me.

D

> Ye may hire giltes in other bokes se;
> And gladlier I wol write, yif yow leste,
> Penelopeës trouthe, and good Alceste.

While anticipating the ladies' objections, the narrator has, with
that relief only a true coward can appreciate, glimpsed a possible way out: denial of responsibility for what the poem says.
He didn't write it in the first place, it has nothing to do with
him, and anyhow he would much rather have written about
faithful women. These excuses are, of course, very much in
the comic mood of the Prologue to the *Legend of Good Women*
where Alceste, about whom he would prefer to have written,
defends him from Love's wrath on the grounds that, being no
more than a translator, he wrote about Criseide 'from inno-
cence, and knew not what he said'. And if he can acquit himself
of responsibility for Criseide by pleading permanent inanity,
there is no reason why he cannot get rid of all his present ten-
sions by funnelling them into a joke against himself. This he
tries to do by turning upside down the anti-feminist moral of
the story:

> N'y sey nat this al oonly for thise men,
> But moost for wommen that bitraised be . . .

And I haven't recited this exclusively for men, but also, or
rather but mostly, for women who are betrayed

> Thorugh false folk; God yeve hem sorwe, amen!
> That with hire grete wit and subtilte
> Bytraise yow! And this commeveth me
> To speke, and in effect yow alle I preye,
> Beth war of men, and herkneth what I seye.

The last excursion into farce – in a poem that contains a good
deal of farce – is this outrageous inversion of morals, which
even so has a grotesque relevance if all human love, both male
and female, is in the end to be adjudged unstable. With the

narrator's recourse to comedy the poem threatens to end. At any rate, he asks it to go away:

> Go, litel bok, go, litel myn tragedye,
> Ther God thi makere yet, er that he dye,
> So sende myght to make in som comedye. . . .

(Presumably a comedy will not blow up in his face as this story has, and will let him end on a note like the one he has just sounded.) There follows the celebrated injunction of the poet to his book not to vie with other poetry, but humbly to kiss the steps of Virgil, Ovid, Homer, Lucan, and Statius. This is the modesty convention again, but transmuted, I believe, into something close to arrogance. Perhaps the poem is not to be classed with the works of these great poets, but I do not feel that the narrator succeeds in belittling his work by mentioning it in connexion with them; there is such a thing as inviting comparison by eschewing comparison. It seems that the narrator has abandoned his joke, and is taking his 'little book' – of more than 8,000 lines – seriously. Increasing gravity characterizes the next stanza, which begins with the hope that the text will not be miswritten nor mismetred by scribes and lesser breeds without the law of final -*e*. Then come two lines of emphatic prayer:

> And red wherso thow be, or elles songe,
> That thow be understonde, God I biseche!

It is perhaps inconsiderate of the narrator to implore us to take his sense when he has been so irresolute about defining his sense. But the movement of the verse now becomes sure and strong, instead of uncertain and aimless, as the narrator moves confidently towards a meaning.

For in the next stanza, Troilus meets his death. This begins – once again – in the epic style, with perhaps a glance at the *Iliad*:

> The wrath, as I bigan yow for to seye,
> Of Troilus the Grekis boughten deere.

Such dignity as the high style can give is thus, for the last time, proffered Troilus. But for him there is to be no last great battle in the West, and both the stanza, and Troilus' life, end in pathos:

> But weilawey, save only Goddes wille!
> Despitously hym slough the fierse Achille.

Troilus' spirit at once ascends into the upper spheres whence he looks down upon this little earth and holds all vanity as compared with the full felicity of heaven. The three stanzas describing Troilus' afterlife afford him that reward which medieval Christianity allowed to the righteous heathen. And in so doing, they salvage from the human wreck of the story the human qualities of Troilus that are of enduring value – most notably, his *trouthe*, the integrity for which he is distinguished. Moreover, this recognition by the plot that some human values transcend human life seems to enable the narrator to come to a definition of the poem's meaning which he has hitherto been unwilling to make. Still close to his characters, he witnesses Troilus' rejection of earthly values, and then, apparently satisfied, now that the mortal good in Troilus has been given immortal reward, he is willing to make that rejection of *all* mortal goods towards which the poem has, despite his resistance, been driving him. His rejection occurs – most unexpectedly – in the third of these stanzas. Troilus, gazing down at the earth and laughing within himself at those who mourn his death,

> . . . dampned al oure werk that foloweth so
> That blynde lust, the which that may nat laste,
> And sholden al oure herte on heven caste.

Up until the last line *Troilus* has been the subject of every main verb in the entire passage; but after he has damned all *our* work, by one of those syntactical ellipses that make Middle English so fluid a language, Troilus' thought is extended to include both narrator and reader: in the last line, *And sholden al oure herte on heven caste*, the plural verb *sholden* requires the subject *we*; but this subject is omitted, because to the narrator the sequence of the sense is, at last, overpoweringly clear. When, after all his attempts not to have to reject the values inherent in his love story, he finally does reject them, he does so with breath-taking ease.

He does so, indeed, with dangerous ease. Having taken up arms against the world and the flesh, he lays on with a will:

> Swich fyn hath, lo, this Troilus for love!
> Swich fyn hath al his grete worthynesse!
> Swich fyn hath his estat real above,
> Swich fyn his lust, swich fyn hath his noblesse!
> Swych fyn hath false worldes brotelnesse!
> And thus bigan his lovyng of Criseyde,
> As I have told, and in this wise he deyde.

But impressive as this stanza is, its movement is curious. The first five lines express, with increasing force, disgust for a world in which everything – not only what merely *seems* good, but also what really *is* good – comes to nothing in the end. Yet the last two lines,

> And thus bigan his lovyng of Criseyde,
> As I have told, and in this wise he deyde,

have, I think, a sweetness of tone that contrasts strangely with the emphatic disgust that precedes them. They seem to express a deep sadness for a doomed potential—as if the narrator, while forced by the evidence to condemn everything his poem has stood for, cannot really quite believe that it has come to nothing. The whole lovely aspiration of the previous action is momentarily re-created in the spare summary of this couplet.

The sweetness of tone carries over into the next two stanzas, the much-quoted ones beginning

> O yonge, fresshe folkes, he or she,
> In which that love up groweth with youre age,
> Repeyreth hom fro worldly vanyte,

And of youre herte up casteth the visage
To thilke God that after his ymage
Yow made, and thynketh al nys but a faire
This world, that passeth soone as floures faire.

The sweetness here adheres not only to what is being rejected,
but also to what is being sought in its stead, and this marks a
development in the narrator. For he does not now seem so much
to be fleeing away, in despair and disgust, from an ugly world –
the world of the Monk's Tale – as he seems to be moving volun-
tarily through this world *towards* something infinitely better.
And while this world is a wretched one – ultimately – in which
all love is *feynede*, 'pretended' and 'shirked', it is also a world
full of the young potential of human love – 'In which that love
up groweth with *oure* age'; a world which, while it passes soon,
passes soon as flowers fair. All the illusory loveliness of a world
which is man's only reality is expressed in the very lines that
reject that loveliness.

In these stanzas the narrator has been brought to the most
mature and complex expression of what is involved in the Christian rejection of the world that seems to be, and indeed is,
man's home, even though he knows there is a better one. But
the narrator himself remains dedicated to simplicity, and makes
one last effort to resolve the tension in his mind between loving
a world he ought to hate and hating a world he cannot help
loving; he endeavours to root out the love:

Lo here, of payens corsed olde rites,
Lo here, what alle hire goddes may availle;
Lo here, thise wrecched worldes appetites;
Lo here, the fyn and guerdoun for travaille
Of Jove, Appollo, of Mars, of swich rascaille!
Lo here, the forme of olde clerkis speche
In poetrie, if ye hire bokes seche.

For the second time within a few stanzas a couplet has undone
the work of the five lines preceding it. In them is harsh, exces-
sively harsh, condemnation of the world of the poem, including

gods and rites that have played no great part in it. In brilliant
contrast to the tone of these lines is the exhausted calm of the
last two:

> Lo here, the forme of olde clerkis speche
> In poetrie, if ye hire bokes seche.

There is a large imprecision about the point of reference of this
couplet. I do not know whether its *Lo here* refers to the five
preceding lines or to the poem as a whole, but I suppose it
refers to the poem as a whole, as the other four *Lo here*'s do. If
this is so, then the form of *olde clerkis speche* is being damned as
well as the *payens corsed olde rites* – by parataxis, at least. Yet
it is not, for the couplet lacks the heavy, fussy indignation of the
earlier lines: instead of indignation there is, indeed, dignity. I
suggest that the couplet once more reasserts, in its simplicity,
all the implicit and explicit human values that the poem has
dealt with, even though these are, to a medieval Christian,
ultimately insignificant. The form of old clerks' speech in poetry
is the sad story that human history tells. It is sad, it is true, it is
lovely, and it is significant, for it is poetry.

This is the last but one of the narrator's searches for a resolution for his poem. I have tried to show how at the end of
Troilus Chaucer has manipulated a narrator capable of only
a simple view of reality in such a way as to achieve the poetic
expression of an extraordinarily complex one. The narrator,
moved by his simple devotion to Troilus, to Pandarus, above
all to Criseide, has been vastly reluctant to find that their story,
so full of the illusion of happiness, comes to nothing – that the
potential of humanity comes to nothing. To avoid this – seem-
ingly simple – conclusion he has done everything he could. He
has tried the epic high road; he has tried the broad highway of
trite moralization; he has tried to eschew responsibility; he
has tried to turn it all into a joke; and all these devices have
failed. Finally, with every other means of egress closed, he has
subscribed to Troilus' rejection of his own story, though only
when, like Gregory when he wept for Trajan, he has seen his

desire for his hero's salvation confirmed. Once having made the rejection, he has thrown himself into world-hating with enthusiasm. But now the counterbalance asserts its power. For the same strong love of the world of his story that prevented him from reaching the Christian rejection permeates and qualifies his expression of the rejection. Having painfully climbed close to the top of the ridge he did not want to climb, he cannot help looking back with longing at the darkening but still fair valley in which he lived; and every resolute thrust forward ends with a glance backward. In having his narrator behave thus, Chaucer has achieved a meaning only great poetry can achieve. The world he knows and the heaven he believes in grow ever farther and farther apart as the woeful contrast between them is developed, and ever closer and closer together as the narrator blindly unites them in the common bond of his love. Every false start he has made has amounted, not to a negative, but to a positive; has been a necessary part of the experience without which the moral of the poem would be as meaningless and unprofitable as in the form I gave it a little while ago. The poem states, what much of Chaucer's poetry states, the necessity under which men lie of living in, making the best of, enjoying, and loving a world from which they must remain detached and which they must ultimately hate: a little spot of earth that with the sea embracéd is, as in Book Three Criseide was embraced by Troilus.

For this paradox there is no logical resolution. In the last two stanzas of the poem Chaucer, after asking Gower and Strode for correction, invokes the power that, being supra-logical itself, can alone resolve paradox. He echoes Dante's mighty prayer to the Trinity, 'that al maist circumscrive', and concludes with the lines:

> So make us, Jesus, for thi mercy digne –
> For love of mayde and moder thyn benigne.

The poem has concerned a mortal woman whose power to love failed, and it ends with the one mortal woman whose power to love is everlasting. I think it is significant that the prayer of the poem's ending leads up, not to Christ, son of God, but to his mother, daughter of Eve – towards heaven, indeed, but towards heaven through human experience.

E. TALBOT DONALDSON

5 · Some Continental Germanic Personal Names in England

In 1916 Thorvald Forssner published, as an Uppsala dissertation, what has remained the classic and in some respects definitive treatment of the Continental Germanic element in English personal nomenclature.[1] Forssner's book was based upon an extensive collection of material drawn from practically all the important records available in print at the time, and his analysis of etymological and phonological problems is thorough and well informed.

However, the past four decades have seen the publication of many additional sources for English medieval history as well as the appearance of new critical editions of earlier texts. The present paper treats a selection of Continental Germanic personal names found in English records but not known to or included by Forssner. Particularly abundant sources include the later Pipe Rolls, the Curia Regis Rolls and the volumes issued by the Selden Society. Re-examination of the Liber Vitæ of Hyde, which was known to Forssner only through the occasional forms listed by Searle, and of the medieval portions of the Liber Vitæ of Durham in the facsimile edition of 1923 has also yielded numerous additions.[2]

The vast material collected by Dr P. H. Reaney in his *Dictionary of British Surnames* (1958) includes a great many names

[1] *Continental Germanic Personal Names in England in Old and Middle English Times* (1916).

[2] Joseph Stevenson's printed edition, Surtees Soc. Publ. 13, 1841, is extremely unreliable and full of absurd misreadings, e.g. *Deudeuize* (Forssner 59) for *Deudune* (= Dieudonné), *Henaud* (ib. 146) for *Hersand* (< OG *Herisint*, ib. 152), *Ithrgunt* (ib. 168) for *Th[u]rgunt* (< ODan *Thorgun*, NPN 150), *Mergessent* (Forssner 190) for *Megessent* (ib. 183 f.).

of the category under notice, and such names have not been included in my list except in a few cases where I have not been able to accept the etymologies suggested by Dr Reaney.[1]

In establishing the Continental etyma of the ME names recourse has naturally in the first place been had to Förstemann's *Altdeutsches Namenbuch*, still an indispensable store-house of information but full of pitfalls for the unwary. Apart from J. Mansion's masterly analysis of Gent names (*Oud-Gentsche Naamkunde*, 1924), Schlaug's *Studien zu den altsächsischen Personennamen des 11. und 12. Jahrhunderts* (1955) and K. Bohn's *Untersuchungen zu Personennamen der Werdener Urbare* (1931) have proved most valuable for the Low German element.

On the whole, however, collections like these that deal with specific areas on the Continent are disappointingly few. This is particularly true of France where the works of Drevin, Michaëlsson and Jacobsson[2] cover only a small part of the field, geographically and chronologically. Hence the assignment of the supposed Continental etyma of ME names to their precise area of origin or dialect is often impossible, and it is inevitable that the majority of parent forms adduced should be described rather vaguely as Old German (OG). However, there can be no doubt that the Low German element was very important. A few name-bearers are explicitly described as Flemings or Saxons (cf. *Ailbodo*, *Thiedlef*) and some themes, such as *-lēf* (see *Brunlef*) and *Sūth-* (see *Sudhard*), point distinctively to that provenance.

The following names have so far not been recorded in Continental sources: *Brandhard*, *Brandred*, *Dagenild*, *Frumbald*, *Hugenild*, *Suthhard*, *Thegenfrid*, *Thruthward* (see *Druward*), *Wandard*. Some of these may after all be hybrid compounds formed in England with the productive suffixes *-hard* and *-hild*.

---

[1] It is much to be regretted that there is no list of names of OG origin, similar to those of OE and Scandinavian names (op. cit. xxi ff.).

[2] H. Drevin, *Die französischen Sprachelemente in den lateinischen Urkunden des 11. und 12. Jahrhunderts (aus Haute-Bretagne und Maine)* (1912); K. Michaëlsson, *Études sur les noms de personne français d'après les rôles de taille parisiens 1–2* (1927–36); H. Jacobsson, *Études d'anthroponymie lorraine* (1955).

Aikefrid 1197 P 58 (Y). – OG *Aigofred, Eicfred* F 48.[1]

Ailbodus *c.* 1155 DC 186, *Ailbodone* (abl.) Flandrensi Rich. I ib. 190, *Eilbode* de Scendelbi Hy II ib. 18, *Heilbode* de Schedelbi ib. 20 (all Li). – OLG *Eilbodo* F 31, Mansion 43, or possibly *Athalbodo* F 164. On the second element see Schramm 43.

Æilgild vidua 1087–98 (late 12) Bury 33 (Sf).[2] – Probably OG *Adalgildis* F 168; for the second element cf. Schramm 161. There is no safe evidence for an OE fem. element -*g(i)eld*.[3] The form *Segild* 11 (late 12) Vita Wulfstani 36 (var. *Segyld, Sigelda*) may represent an OE **Sigehild*, and *Wlfgilda* 12 (?) LVD 80, is probably a Continental loan, though an OG **Wulfgild(is)* is not on record.

Antelmo (abl.) priore 1151 FRC 32 (Ha).[4] – OG *Andhelm, Anthelm* F 103.

Atceman: Herueo filio *Atceman c.* 1155 DC 250 (Le),[5] *Aceman* fabro *c.* 1155 ib. 249 (Le). – OG *Azeman* F 222.

Berewin: Ric[ardus] filius *Berewini* 1167/68 P 161 (W). – OG *Berewin* F 265 f. Here may also belong the instances recorded by Reaney, DBS s.n. *Berwin*, and derived by him from OG *Bernwin*.

Bernesent: Siredus filius *Bernesent* 1168–75 Holme 166 (Nf). – OG *Berns(w)ind* f., F 271; for the second element, PGmc **swinþ-* or **sinþ-*, see Forssner 24, Schramm 166.

Blizot: Ricardo filio *Blizoti c.* 1200–7 StGreg 50 (K). – An AFr diminutive of OG **Blizo*, DB *Blize* (Forssner 50).

Botsardus *c.* 1121–2 Reg. ii. 1365 (Winch.). – OFr *Bozardus, Bociardus, Botzart* 11–12 Drevin 28. A secondary compound

---

[1] For a list of sources and abbreviations see p. 60. Cf. p. xi. above.

[2] Reaney, SMS xviii 85, takes this to be OE **Æðelgild* f. The other two examples from Bury quoted by him are irrelevant: *Æilild*, ib. 31, is from OE *Æðelhild*; *Aeilild*, ib. 32, is from OE *Æðelgýð*.

[3] A masc. element -*g(i)eld* occurs in *Eadgild, Feologeld, Ingeld, Þeodgeld* (native?), *Wiligeld* and *Wiðergyld* (mythological).

[4] Perhaps prior of the Austin canon priory at Porchester-Southwick; FRC loc. cit. (note by editors).

[5] There is no need to emend this to *Acceman* as Stenton suggests (DC loc. cit. note).

with -*hard* (cf. PNDB 16), the first element of which should perhaps be associated with Old Flemish *Butsa* (Mansion 33).[1]

Brandardus 12–13 LVD 64. – OG **Brandhard*; cf. the compounds in *Brand*-, F 333 ff. The element does not occur in OE.

Brandrede (abl.) 1155–64 Writs 503 (K). – OG **Brandrad*.

Brunlef 12 LVD 5. – OLG *Brunlef*, Bohn 284. The second element -*lēf* (OE -*lāf*) is very common in LG and Fris. sources; cf. Bohn 284 f., 291, 296 (15 compounds), Schlaug 236 (14 compounds), W. de Vries, *Friese Persoonsnamen* (1952), 183 f. With the possible exception of *Godlēof* (Reaney, SMS xviii 93), -*lēof* does not occur as a second element in OE masc. names.[2]

Burgund 12 LVH 133. – OG *Burgund* F 350.

Dagenild' que fuit uxor Godefridi juuenis 1202 Pleas i. 240 (E). – OG **Daganhild*; cf. the compounds in *Dagan*-, *Dagin*-, an extension of *daga*-, listed F 396 f.

Damesænt c. 1100 LVH 72. – A fem. name in -*s(w)ind*; cf. *Hærsæn* ib. from OFr *Hersent* (Forssner 152). First element obscure, possibly *Dan(a)*- as in the next entry.

Damfridum (acc.) de Talland 1201 Pleas i. 33 (Co). – OG *Danafrid* F 401.[3]

Druwardus miles de Federstan c. 1150 Gilb 104 (St or Y). – OLG **Thrūthward*, OHG **Drūdwart* (< **þrūð*-) or OLG **Drūtward* (< **drūt*-), neither of which is so far on record. On the first element see Mansion 107 f., Schatz *ZDA* 72 (1935), 140, and cf. *Thruwin* below.

---

[1] If the forms *Boszart* 1177 and *Bozard* 1258 quoted by Reaney (DBS s.n. *Buzzard*) have z for [ts], as seems likely, they belong here and should not be derived from OFr *busart*, 'buzzard'. The OFr examples should not be associated with OHG *bōz*-, F 330 ff., as Drevin thinks. Cf. perhaps also OHG *Butshardus*, *Buhzhardus* in thirteenth-century Basle records (A. Socin, *Mittelhochdeutsches Namenbuch* (1903), 136).

[2] *Cynelēof* (Searle 156) is a false reconstruction of the coin-spelling *Cunleof*, an error for *Gunleof* < ON *Gunnleifr* (Hild. 242 f.; cf. NPN 57). Cf. further the entries *Manleof*, *Redlef*, *Saxlef* and *Thiedlef* in the present paper.

[3] Cf. also *Tanfrido* (dat.) de Espanni 1079 (12) Recueil des actes de Philippe I, i (1908), 93 (Corbie).

Engelberga: *Yngelberga* uxor Petri de Alesbi 1202 LiAss 146. – OG *Engel-, Ingelberga* F 110.

Engelmunt filius Pagani 1180/81 P 144 (Sx). – OG *Engelmund* F 116.

Fastradus 1086 DB So 89. – The etymon is OG *Fastrad* F 501, f., Bohn 63, not, as Björkman (NPN 40) thinks, an unrecorded ON *Fastráðr.*[1]

Fladaldus villanus 1114–18 Burton Survey 244 (Db); *Fledaldus* a 1080 Round Studies 122,[2] Alano *Floaldi* filio 1100–8 (18) France 442, *Float* filius Alani dapiferi 1101–2 (contemp.) France 408, Alanus filius *Fladaldi* 1133 FRC 13, Alan *Flauudi* (for *Flaaudi*) Hy II (17) France 441, Alani filii *Flealdi* 12 (contemp.) Round Studies 126 n. 4; *Flawoldus* 1176 FRC 57 (Thanet); *Flaut c.* 1200 Seals 204 (Nth). – OG **Flādwald* (first element OG *flād-*, MHG *vlāt*; cf. F 509), which seems to be attested by the form *Fletuualdo* (dat.) presbiter 830 (orig.) Gent,[3] and which is in fact presupposed by the ModFr surname *Flahaut.*[4] The vowel variation in the first element is difficult to explain.

Fraricus de Bissopeston 1200 Cur 145, ∼ de Bissop' 1221 RJ iii. 366, *Fraricum* (acc.) de Bissaresdon' 1196 Cur (P) 89, ∼ de Bissopesdon 1200 Cur 145, *Fraericus* de Bissopesdon 1197 P 178, predicti *Fraerici* ib., *Frarii* (gen.) de Bisshopeston 1221 RJ iii. 23, *Frarinum* (acc.) de Bissopeston 1221 ib. [Bishopton, Wa].

Fraricus, Fraricum de Bosco 1221 RJ iii. 245.

Fraricum (acc.) de Burnham 1205 Cur 275, *Fraericum* (acc.) de Burnham 1204 Cur 224, *Frarius* de Burnham 1199 Pleas i.

---

[1] *Fastrethe* 12 (?) LVD 68 (transcript ib. 60: *Fastretha*) would seem to point to a Scand. **Fastríðr* f. On the specifically Sw element *fast-*, see E. Wessén, *Nordiska namnstudier* (1927), 99 ff.

[2] This and the following five examples refer to a well-known Anglo-Breton magnate, father of Alan FitzFlaald, on whom see J. H. Round, *Studies in Peerage and Family History* (1901), 120 ff.

[3] *Diplomata Belgica ante annum 1100 scripta* I (1950), 140. Mansion who discusses the form (pp. 55, 161, 193) hesitates between **flād-* and OS *flet*, 'floor'.

[4] A. Dauzat, *Dictionnaire étymologique des noms de famille et prénoms de France* (1951), 257.

200, *Frari* 1198 FF Nf 25, *Frarinum* (acc.) 1199 Pleas i, 172, *Fraer'* 1198 FF Nf 51–2 [Burnham, Nf].

Fraricus de Clopton 1199 Cur 86, *Frarinus* de Clopton 1221 RJ i. 519 [Clopton in Hill and Moor, Wo].

Fraericum de Darffeld 1225 Cur 43 (Wa).

Fraricum (acc.) de Dichford' 1221 RJ iii. 204 [Ditchford, Wa].

Fraricus 1204 Cur 95 (K).

This is a difficult name. The Bishopton man occurs once as *Fredericus* de Bisshopesdon 1221 RJ iii. 224, and Reaney (DBS s.n. *Frederick, Frary*) thinks that *Fraric* is a variant of *Frederic*. However, the persistent *a* or *ae* in the first element tells against this derivation, and *Fredericus* in the 1221 instance may after all be due to scribal association with a more familiar name. In Continental French sources OG *Frederic(us)* becomes *Frerricus* > *Ferricus* > *Ferri* in the twelfth century,[1] and the ME change of *er* + cons. to *ar* is too late to be considered here (Luick § 430). A possible clue to the interpretation of the first element may, however, be provided by the Continental forms *Fraericus* 9th cent. (11) Gesta SS. Patrum Fontanellensis coenobii (1936), 16, 17; *Fraorico* (abl.) 912 (18) Actes de Charles III (1949), 160; *Fraerius* de Lueris, Obituaires de la province de Sens iv (1923), 460 (MS *c.* 1290); *Fraric* 1037–52 Osnabrück (Schlaug 96). The last example is evidently a variant of *Froric* in the same document (Schlaug, loc. cit.). Hence, the first element should perhaps be connected with OLG *frā(h)*, *frāo*, *frō*, 'glad', or *frā(h)o*, *frō*, 'lord', which also seems to occur in ME *Frawin* (PNDB 252), *Fraaudus* 1075 Drevin 30 (unless < *Frōdwald*), *Frager* 12 Lüneburg (Schlaug, loc. cit.), *Frawara* 840–77 Mansion 44.[2]

---

[1] H. Jacobsson, *Études d'anthroponymie lorraine* (1955), 125 f. – OG *Frederic, Fretheric* usually appears as *Frethericus* in ME, e.g. 1170 St Greg. 143, 1216–50 Seals 380. Cf. also DB *Fredri* PNDB 254 and the forms *Fretherici, Fredrici, Fedrici* 1086 DB Nf 157b, 158, 161b, 165b. Other native and OG names in *Friðu-*, *Frethe-* show consistent *e* in ME; cf. Forssner 92 ff. and note also *Fre(e)burge* 1162/63–1166/67 P < OE *Friðuburh*.

[2] *Frari(c)* probably survives in the ModFr surname *Frary* (Normandy) which Dauzat, op. cit. 267, explains from OFr *frarie*, 'confraternity' (Tobler-Lommatzsch;

The phonetic value of the digraph *ae* in some Continental and ME instances is not clear. If, as seems probable, it indicated a diphthong, its use in the ME forms is difficult to account for. Loss of final [k] in *Frari(us)* is Anglo-Norman, whilst *Frarinus* exhibits a familiar pattern of latinization (PNDB § 148).[1]

Freðrica 12 LVH 131. – A Romanic fem. from *Frederic*.

Frumbaldus de Culeston 1175/76 P 51 (Nth), ∼ filius Godardi ib. 68 (Sf), *Frumboldus* de Haregraue 1180/81 P 126 (Bd).[2] – OG *Frumbald* (not recorded); for names in *Frum-* see F 545 f., Mansion 154.

Fulcomaro (abl.) de Bartona late 12 DC 263 (Li) – OG *Fulcmar*, *Folcmar* F 553, Bohn 213 f. *Fulc-* is a characteristic variant of *Folc-* in Frankish and Romance sources.[3]

Fulcmod: *Fulmotestuna* DB > Fulmodeston (Nf). – OG *Fulcmod* F 553 f.; DEPN s.n.

Fulcnod, *Fulnod, Folcnod* mon. Northumbria Eanred, Keary 151. – OLG *Folcnōth*; cf. OHG *Folcnand* F 554, and on OLG -*nōth* Bohn 104 ff.

Fulcoinus 1086 DB Ha 51, *Folcwine* mon. Sudbury Wm I (Brooke ccxl), ∼ 1185 Templars 64 (Ht), *Folcuuinus c.* 1100 LVH 74 (father of Teotselinus), *Folkwino* (abl.) de Fontanis uicecomite 1127–34 Holme 174,[4] *Fulquinus* de Alneto a 1186 Seals 198 (Li). – OG *Fulc-, Folcwin* F 558, Bohn 213, Schlaug 94. OE *Folcwine* is not found after *c.* 800.

Gisfrid: *Gysfreait* filius Morī 12 LVH 51. – OG *Gisfrid* F 645. The second element has Rom. -*freið-* < -*friðu-*.

---

cf. ME *frairie, frari, freri*, with the same meaning), or as a variant of *Fréry* < *Frederic*. In suggesting the latter alternative he apparently regards the *a* in the first syllable as due to the occasional interchange of pretonic *e* and *a* before *r* in OFr (PNDB § 1).

[1] Association with OFr *frarin* adj., 'poor, miserable', should also be considered. Cf. Girardus *Frarinus* 1095 *Cartul. noir d'Angers* (1908), 63.

[2] Perhaps identical with *Frumbardo* (dat.) de Haregrave 1222 Cur 329 (Bd), where the second *r* would be due to assimilation.

[3] There is no real evidence for an OE *Folcmǣr*. *Folcmerus* 968–970 BCS 1228, 1264, if genuine, may be the OG name. The reference is to an unidentified abbot in two spurious Westminster charters. ODan, OSw *Folkmar* is a loan from the Continent, cf. E. Wessén, *Nordiska namnstudier* (1927), 103.

[4] On him see Seals 277.

Gisulf: Rogerus filius *Gisulfi* 1201 Pleas i. 65 (Co) – OG *Gisulf* F 646.

Godold : Ohin filius *Godold* 1186–91 BuryS 45 (Sf). – OG *God-(w)ald* F 685, Drevin 32.[1]

Gonde: Bernardus filius *Gonde* 1114–19 Bury 110, 111 (Sf). – OG *Gundo* m., *Gunda* f., F 694 f.

Gyldewine mon. Canterbury Harold I–Edw. Conf., Hild. 343, 431, Grueber 308, 344–7 (var. *Gelde-, Gilde-, Gulde-*), ∼ 1038–50 OSF iii, 43; *Geldewinus, Geldewinum* filium Savarici 1156–8 Seals 434,[2] *Joldewinus* fil[ius] Sauar[ici] 1158/59 P 60; *Geldewinus* de Nereford 1175/76 P 62 (Nf), ∼ nepos *Geldewini* de Nereford 1184/85 P 31, *Joldewinus* de Nereford 1207 Cur 214; *Geoldewinus* de Palling 1199 Pleas i. 218 (Sx); *Joldewinum* (acc.) de Dowe 1201 Pleas i. 342 (W); ∼ de Angemere 1207 Cur 27 (Sx), *Jodewinum* ballivum 1214 Cur 149 (= the preceding). – As suggested by S. Holm, *Studier i Uppsala Universitets anglosaxiska Myntsamling* (1917), 43, the etymon is OG *Gild(e)win, Geldwin* (F 641, Drevin 33), which is common in French twelfth- and thirteenth-century sources, with the variants *Joldwin, Geduin*.[3] The first element is OG *geld-* (< **gelða-*), *gild-* (< **gelði-*), cf. Schönfeld 6 s.n. *Alagildus*, Bohn 180. In the OE forms above this has been identified with the corresponding OE word *g(i)eld, gyld*. The subsequent development is AFr; cf. *Holdebert* below. Ekwall ELPN 46, 191, who regards the name as native, connects the first element with OE *gylden, gold*, and Reaney (DBS s.n. *Jeudwine*) would explain it as an AFr variant of *Goldwine*. Both suggestions are inadmissible on phonological grounds.

Hargodus presbyter 1004 KCD 1300, *Hærgod, Haregod, Heregod*

---

[1] *Godwoldus* 1006 Twysden, *Historiæ Anglicanæ scriptores decem* (1652), 1781 (gift of land in Sturton to St Augustine's, Canterbury) may be OE *Godweald*. No other examples are known.

[2] Son of Savaric FitzCana; on this Norman family see Seals 304.

[3] In OLG sources the element appears as *Geld-* throughout. The forms *Gilduin : Gelduin* appear side by side in French records; cf. e.g. *Gilduinus : Gelduinus* 1075 (orig.) *Recueil des actes de Philippe I* (1908), 186 ff. Note also *Gelduinus*, var. *Jelduinus* ib. 268; *Geduinus* 1085–95 (12) *Cartul. de l'abbaye de Molesme* II (1911), 44, *Jolduinus* 1096–1107 ib. 137 (same person).

E

mon. Oxf. Edw. Conf. (Hild. 451, Grueber 421 f.), *Hargod*, *Hargo* mon. ib. Wm I (Brooke 52, 86, 87), *Hergodus* 12 LVD 16;[1] also in Haggerston, Mx (DB *Hergotestane*, ME *Heregodeston*, *Haregodeston*), DEPN s.n. – OG (OLG) *Heregod*, *Hergot* F 770 f., Schlaug 110, Bohn 306. OE -*god* does not occur as a second element.

Hawin: Godefř fiĺ *Hawini* 1169/70 P 16 (Lond), Godefridi filii *Hawini* 1175/76 P 16 (Mx), Reymundus filius *Hawini* 1175–86 Holme 117 (Nf). – OG *Hawin* F 722,[2] or perhaps rather *Hadwin* F 799 (cf. PNDB 282) with loss of the dental as in ME *Hawisa* from OG *Hadwidis* (Forssner 144).

Holdebert: Willelmus filius *Holdebert* late 12 DC 301, 302 (Le). – OG *Hildebert* F 823 f., with -*ol*- < -*el*- < -*il*- by an OFr sound-change on which see Forssner 154, M. K. Pope, *From Latin to Modern French* (1952), § 502. Cf. also *Ilbert*, Forssner 161 f.

Holdierdus, *Holdierdum* filium Henrici 1221 Cur 182 (Nth). – OG *Hildigard* m., F 828 f., *Hildiardus* 911;[3] for the form of the first element cf. the preceding entry.

Hugenild: Petrus filius *Hugenild* 1186–91 BuryS 11 (Sf). – OG **Hugenild* f.; cf. *Huginbald* F 926 with an *n*-extension of the stem *hugi*-, *hugu*-.

Hunaldus 1086 DB E 96, *Hunoldus* ib. E 96b. – OG *Hunold*, OFr *Hunaut* F 935, Drevin 40, Schlaug 116. OE *Hūnweald* occurs in LVD *c.* 800.

Inardus sacerdos 1185 Templars 38 (Sa), *Ynardi* (gen.) Parlarii ib. 32 (Wo). – This is not, as Reaney thinks (SMS xviii 96), a native compound with the rare and archaic element *In*-, but OG *Is(e)nard* F 976 f. with Rom. loss of pre-consonantal *s*. Both references are to the same man, the Wo landholder Isnardus Parler, whose name survives as the first element of Innerstone, Wo. See VCH Wo i, 330, and EPNS IV 157.

---

[1] Thus the facsimile. Stevenson prints *Heregodus*.

[2] First element probably *hāh*-; see Schatz, *ZDA* 72 (1935), 135, and cf. Schlaug 114.

[3] F. Æbischer, *Bull. du dict. général de la langue wallonne* xii (1923), 92 (from a Belgian cartulary).

Laudomar Ace 1121 Reg. ii. 1307. – OG *Laudomar* F 1014 f.; note also *terram Laudomari* 1142 (orig.), a property in Normandy.[1] This is evidently a traditional spelling, since we should normally expect *Lodmer*, *Lo(t)mer*; cf. Forssner 37 on *Aud-* : *Od-*.

Lecenta, *Lecentam* filiam Elflet 1209 FF Nf 239 (Nf). – OG *Leuts(w)ind* F 1047 f.; cf. *Damesænt, Tecent* (q.v.).

Letald: Johannes filius *Letaldi* 1142–54 YCh i. 450, *Letoldo* (abl.) 1125–35 ib. 357. – OG *Leudowald, Le(o)tald* F 1048, Jacobsson 169.

Linald 1186–91 BuryS 62 (Sf), *Linaldo* (abl.) ib. 63, Alexander filius *Linald'* 1207 FF Sf 477. – OG *Lindwald* F 1060; for the loss of *d* in the first element see PNDB § 103.

Manleof mon. Exeter, Harold I, Harthacnut (Hild. 346, 398). – OG *Manaliub* F 1091.

Manselinus 1203 Cur 145 (St). – A Romanic diminutive of *Manzo* F 1093 f.

Modbertus 1086 DB D 106, 106b, E 69b, *Motbertus* ib. D 106, 107b, Goisfridus filius *Modberti* 1087 InqAug 25 (K), *Modbert* 1121 Reg. ii. 1302 (So). – OG *Modbert* F 1129; cf. PNDB 328 n. 1, Tengvik 191.

Munold 1186–91 BuryS 67 (Sf). – OG *Munuald, Monald* F 1137.

Norðberd mon. Eadgar Hild. 12, *Norbertus* 1116–27 Burton Survey 245 (Db). – OG *Nordbert* F 1169 f.[2]

Odmer: Ricardus filius *Odmeri* 1184/85 P 49 (Nth). – OG *Odmar* F 198; cf. also *Odomer* mon. St. Eadmund, Forssner 199 f.

Odric Tederi 1087–98 Bury 26 (Sf), *Oðri* 12 LVD 55. – OG *Odric* F 200. *Tederi* is from OG *Theodoric* etc. (Forssner 232 f.).

Radgarus de Sapewica 1167/68 P 129 (D), ~ de Bolleham

---

[1] F. Lot, *Études critiques sur l'abbaye de Saint-Wandrille* (1913), 126.

[2] OE *Norð-* occurs in *Norðmann*; perhaps also in *Norðgar* mon. Eadred (Hild. 151), which may however be < OG *Nortger* F 1170. (Nafena ond) *Norwina* his broðor 989–990 (13) ASCh 63 (not in Searle) may be OE *Norðwine* (not previously recorded), but cf. OG *Nordwin* F 1171 f. *Norulf* mon. Stanford, Cnut (Grueber 294), quoted by Searle 359, is an error for *Morulf* ib. (Hild. 297) < OG *Morulf* (PNDB 330).

1175/76 P 147 (D). – OG *Radger* F 1212, Mansion 59, Schlaug 137.

Randwi: Willelmus filius *Randewi* 1199 Pleas i. 176 (Nth), ∼ *Randwi* 1200 Cur 117 (Nth), *Randwicus* cocus 1202 Pleas i. 235 (E). – OG *Randwig* F 1247, Schlaug 138.

Redlef: Ulmer *Redleui* filius 1087–98 Bury 39 (Sf). – OLG *Radlef* Schlaug 137, Bohn 285, Fris. *Redlef*,[1] OHG *Ratleif* F 1215 f. Tengvik 195 and Reaney (SMS xviii 99) derive this from an OE *Rǣdlēof. Cf. also *Brunlef* above.

Reingot de Hagwurdingeh[am] 1165/66 P 5 (Li), *Reingod* de Bærnest ib. 45 (Y), *Rengot* Barat Hy II DC 373 (Li), *Reingotus* late 12 Bury 176 (Sf), terram *Reingodi* Blundi 1186–1200 BuryS 168 (Li). – OG *Reingot* F 1229, Schlaug 139 f.

Richegard 1201 Pleas i. 38 (Co). – OG *Ricgard* m., F 1262. On OG masc. names in *-gard* see Schatz in *ZDA* 72 (1935), 157.

Richeman: Nicolaus filius *Richemanni* 1251 Rams i. 313 (Hu), Hawysia filia ∼ ib. 315. – OG *Ricman* F 1267; but cf. also ME *riceman* 1154 ASC etc., *NED* s.v. *richman*.

Ricolot 13 LVD 83. – An OFr diminutive of names in *Ric-*.

Riculf, *Ric(c)olf* mon. Chester, Shrewsbury Eadgar–Æðelred II (Hild. 84, 136, Grueber 183 f.), *Riculf(us)* 1086 DB K 11, D 112b, Ht 134, *Ricolf* ib. Le 235, *Riculfo* monacho (dat.) *c.* 1120 (Westminster),[2] *Riculf* 12 LVD 78, *Ricolf* 1165/66 P 25 (Nf or Sf), ∼ de Galmetona 1170–85 YCh ii. 702, *Riolfi* (gen.) de Saissun 1160/61 P 54 (Br), Simon filius *Riulfi* 1175/76 P 216 (Sr), Hugo f. *Richolfi* 1202 Li Ass 216. – OG *Riculf* F 1271. OE *Rīcwulf* is found once in LVD *c.* 800, the only other native names in *Rīc-* being *Rīcbeorht*, 7th cent., and *Rīcfolcyn*, *Rīcred*, *Rīcðrȳð*, all LVD *c.* 800.

Romilda mater ejus [scil. Hugonis] 1175 YCh i. 359, *Romild* 12–13 LVD 52. – OG *Romilda* F 884. First element probably OG *Rūma*, 'Rome', Schlaug 146 f.

Sadebert, a man of Spalding priory, 1116–22 Reg. ii. 1375. – OG *Sadelbert* F 1298.

---

[1] W. de Vries, *Friese persoonsnamen* (1952), 184; DGP s.n.
[2] J. A. Robinson, *Gilbert Crispin* (1911), 27.

Salemer 1185 Templars 15 (Lond). – OG *Salamar* F 1293.

Sasgarus 1086 DB Nth 227b. – OG *Saxger* F 1289, Bohn 99, Schlaug 147.

Saxlef 1086 DB Sf 446b. – OG *Sahsleib* F 1289.

Sigod mon. Bedford Wm I–II, Brooke 34, 44, 58, 226, 243. – OLG *Sigot* F 1325.

Sigrimus de Bada 1169/70 P 116 (So), *Sigrim* de Bada 1175/76 P 155 (So), 1180–81 P 5 (So), Osbertus filius *Sigrim* 1167/68 P 146 (So). – OG *Sigrim* F 1325, Bohn 187.

Sunnild Purre 1209 FF Nf 102. – OG *Sunnihilt* or *Sunhilt* F 1371 (perhaps two different names, on the first element of which see Schatz, $\mathcal{Z}DA$ 72 (1935), 130), or possibly a native *Sunnhild; cf. *Sunngifu* PNDB 378.

Sudhard: Andreas f. *Sudhard'* 1202 Li Ass 45, Albertus f. *Suttart*, ∼ f. *Suhard* ib. 206. – Cf. OFr *Suthardus* 1053, *Suhardus* c. 1053, 1100 Drevin 47. The etymon could be OLG *Sūthhard,[1] first element OLG *sūth*, 'south', as in *Sutire c.* 1050 Bohn 211, from *Suthheri. The corresponding OHG form *Sunthard* is on record, F 1369.

Suaneburg 1156/7 YCh i. 354 (p. 275) (Li). – OG *Swaneburg* F 1376, Bohn 201.[2]

Tecent late 12 DC 269, 271, Ricardo filio *Teiscant* ib. 273 (Nt, same person). – OG *Theuds(w)ind* F 1449, Rom. *Tetsindis, Tescenda, Tecindis*.[3]

Tedaldus 1086 DB Bk 144b, *Tædaldus* ib., Willelmus filius *Tedaldi* ib. K 1 (∼ *Theoldi* 1087 InqAug 24), *Tioldus* a 1186 Seals 198 (Li). – OG *Theodwald, Thedald* F 1449 ff.[4]

Teinfriþe (dat.) mine circwirhtan 1057–66 (14) AS Writs 87. – Probably, as suggested by Dr F. E. Harmer, *English*

---

[1] Evidently the source of the ModFr surname *Souhart, Suhard, Suard*, which Dauzat, op. cit. 558, would derive from an obscure OG *Sughard.

[2] ON *Svanbiǫrg* is found once in Iceland AD 1334. ON *Svanhildr*, ME *Swanhild* (ZEN 89, Reaney, DBS s.n. *Swannell*) is ultimately an OG loan (A. Janzén, *Personnamn* (1947), 91).

[3] e.g. 916 (orig.) *Cartul. de l'abbaye de Molesme* II (1911), 222; 929 *Cartul. noir d'Angers* (1908), 33; 12th cent. *Obituaires de la province de Sens* iv (1923), 409, 419, 429.   [4] Cf. also the material in Ekwall ELPN 66.

Historical Review li (1936), 98 note, from an OG * *Thegenfrid*; cf.
F 1406 ff. OE *þegn-* is found only in *þegnwine*. *Teinardo* fal-
conario 1130 (Reaney, SMS xviii 103) is of course OG
Theganhard (F 1407, Schlaug 82), not a native **þegnheard*.

Tescho 1086 DB E 106, a Colchester burgess. – OG *Thieziko*,
Tizeko F 1417, Schlaug 187 f., a hypocoristic form of names
in *Theod-*, *Thied-*.

Thiedlef: *Thiedleuo* (dat.), 'homo ducis Saxoniæ', 1175/76 P 11
(Mx). – OLG *Thiadlef* F 1438, Bohn 284, Schlaug 84.

Thruwin 12 LVD 78. – OG *Thrudwin* F 427; on the first
element see *Druwardus* above.[1]

Tidreda 12 LVD 6. – OG *Theodrada* F 1444 f., OLG *Thiderad*
f., Schlaug 85. Boehler 120 assumes an OE **Tīðrýð*.

Tuscelinus conuersus *c.* 1150 LVH 42. – Cf. OLG *Tucelin* 1133
Corvey (Schlaug 188), a variant of *Thiezelin*, from names in
Theod-, *Thied-*.

Walebrun *c.* 1155 DC 214 (Li). – OG *Walbrun* m. F 1502 (cf.
ib. 338), *Walebrun* 12th cent. Schlaug 154. First element *wald-*
or *walh-*; on the second see also Schramm 170.

Wandard: Willelmus *Wandard* 1169/70 P 20 (Le or Wa),
Robert ∼ *c.* 1240 Seals 261 (Wa). – OG **Wandhard* (cf. F
1525 f.) or OG *Wandrehard* F 1531 (Pol. Irm.) with dissimi-
latory loss of the first *r*.

Wideman mon. Wallingford Wm I (Brooke 88); *Withmannus*
abbas Rams iii. 173, *Wythmannus* (*Wytmannus*, *Withmannus*),
'Teutonicus natione', Chron. Abb. Rames. 121, 124, 125, 160,
abbot of Ramsey 1016–20. – OG *Widiman* F 1571. First element OG *wīd*, 'wide', or *widu*, 'wood'; cf. v. Feilitzen, *NoB*
30 (1942), 136 ff.

Widred mon. Edw. Conf., Grueber 456. – OG *Widred* F 1572,
Schlaug 159.

---

[1] The corresponding OE element is *þrýð-* in *Thrythred* LVD, *Thrythuulf* Bede HE,
and as a common second component in fem. names. Hence *Ðruðgar* cl[ericus]
879–909 (12) ASCh 15 (BCS 617), *Ðrudgar* cl[ericus] *c.* 900 ib. 20 (BCS 622),
þrudgar leuita *c.* 1030 LVH 25, may represent OLG *Thrudger*, *Thruthger* F 425,
Mansion 109, Bohn 273, unless this is a case of the occasional absence of *i*-mutation
in OE compounds, as in *Sā-* : *Sǣ-* (Luick § 199).

Winebaldus de Balam, *Winebaldi* de Balun 12th cent. (13) Mon ii. 73,[1] *Wynebald* de Baledon 1096 Reg. ii. 410; *Winebald* de Norton 1197 P 87 (Nth), Jordanus filius *Winebaldi* 1201 Pleas i. 110 (Co). – OG *Winebald* F 1611. Reaney DBS s.n. *Winbolt* (with additional material) takes the etymon to be OE *Winebeald*, which is found in LVD *c.* 800 and in BCS 404 (AD 831).

Winrichus 'transmarine nationis monachus' at Worcester, 11 Vita Wulfstani 14, *Winrichus* ib. 73. – OG *Winric* F 1616, Schlaug 165.

Wulfbern mon. Lincoln Æðelred II – Edw. Conf., *Wulbe(o)rn*, *Vlfbeorn* ib. (Hild. 96, 255), *Ulbern* 1087–98 Bury 38 (Sf), *Wlbern*, *Wlbernus* 1185 Templars 92, 87 (both Li). – OG *Wolfbern* F 1646, Schlaug 166. *-beorn* as a second element is not certainly attested in OE.

Wlfgot 1197 P 228 (Nf or Sf). – OG *Wulfgaud* F 1650, OLG *Wolfgot* Schlaug 166.

Sources and abbreviations

The abbreviations for sources and other works are those used in the publications of EPNS, in E. Ekwall's *Oxford Dictionary of English Place-names* (fourth edn., 1960) and in P. H. Reaney's *Dictionary of British Surnames* (1958). Full titles of some frequently quoted monographs are given above, pp. 46–7. The following abbreviations are also used:

Brooke	*A Catalogue of English Coins in the British Museum: The Norman Kings* (ed. G. C. Brooke, 1916).
Burton Survey	*The Burton Abbey Twelfth-century Surveys*, in *Collections for a History of Staffordshire* (1916; 1918).
Boehler	M. Boehler, *Die altenglischen Frauennamen* (1930).
Cur (P)	*The Memoranda Roll for the Tenth Year of the Reign of King John (1207–1208) together with the Curia Regis Rolls 1196, 1198* (Pipe Roll Soc. Publ. 69, 1957).

[1] On this Norman magnate, who came from Ballon in Maine, see J. H. Round, *Studies on Peerage and Family History* (1901), 189 ff.

DGP   *Danmarks gamle Personnavne* (1936–).
Ekwall ELPN   E. Ekwall, *Early London Personal Names* (1947).
F   E. Förstemann, *Altdeutsches Namenbuch* I (2. Aufl. 1900).
FF Li   *Feet of Fines for the County of Lincoln for the Reign of King John, 1199–1216* (Pipe Roll Soc. Publ. 67, 1954).
FF Nf   *Feet of Fines for the County of Norfolk for the Reign of King John, 1201–1215* (Pipe Roll Soc. Publ. 70, 1958).
FF Sf   ibid. for the County of Suffolk.
FRC   *Facsimiles of royal and other Charters in the British Museum.* Vol. i (1903).
Grueber   *A Catalogue of English Coins in the British Museum. Anglo-Saxon Series.* Vol. ii (1893).
Hild.   B. E. Hildebrand, *Anglosachsiska mynt i svenska kongliga myntkabinettet* (1881).
InqAug   *An Eleventh-century Inquisition of St. Augustine's, Canterbury* (ed. A. Ballard. British Academy Records 4b, 1920).
Keary   *A Catalogue of English Coins in the British Museum. Anglo-Saxon Series.* Vol. i (1887).
LiAss   *The Earliest Lincolnshire Assize Rolls 1202–1209* (ed. D. M. Stenton. Lincoln Record Society Publ. 22, 1926).
NPN   E. Björkman, *Die nordischen Personennamen in England in alt- und frühmittelenglischer Zeit* (1910).
OSF   *Facsimiles of Anglo-Saxon Manuscripts.* Vols. i–iii. (ed. W. B. Sanders, 1878–84).
Pleas   *Pleas before the King or his Justices 1198–1202.* Vols. i–ii. (ed. D. M. Stenton. Selden Soc. Publs. 67–68, 1952–3).
PNDB   O. von Feilitzen, *The pre-Conquest Personal Names of Domesday Book* (1937).
Reaney DBS   P. H. Reaney, *Dictionary of British Surnames* (1958).

RJ   *Rolls of the Justices in Eyre* ... [1–3] (ed. D. M.
              Stenton. Selden Soc. Publs. 53, 56, 59, 1934–40).
Schramm   G. Schramm, *Namenschatz und Dichtersprache*
              (1957).
Seals   *Sir Christopher Hatton's Book of Seals* (1950).
SMS   *Studier i modern språkvetenskap.*
SN   *Studia neophilologica.*
StGreg   *Cartulary of the Priory of St Gregory, Canterbury*
              (ed. A. M. Woodcock. Camden Soc. Publ. 88,
              1956).
Writs   R. van Caenegem, *Royal Writs in England from
              the Conquest to Glanvill* (Selden Soc. Publ. 77,
              1959).
ZEN   E. Björkman, *Zur englischen Namenkunde* (1912).

OLOF VON FEILITZEN

6 · Auðræði

Guðbrandur Vigfússon drew attention to the word *auðræði* in his introduction to *Biskupa sögur* I, published in 1858, when he noticed it as a rare word and one characteristic of the *Hungrvaka, Þorláks saga* and *Páls saga* in his collection.[1] By the time he published *An Icelandic-English Dictionary* in 1874 he had clearly become more used to the word, for in his article there he merely notes: 'not very freq., auðæfi is a more current word'. This present paper is chiefly intended to give a closer study of the word's distribution, with some concomitant remarks on the word's semantic background.

I

The following list of instances is hardly exhaustive, but it must represent a very large sample. It is based on the printed dictionaries, on the files of *Den Arnamagnæanske Kommissions Ordbog*, and on my own collection.[2]

    1. *Gammel norsk Homiliebog* (AM 619 4to, *c.* 1200): – iartæg-

---

[1] *Bps.* I xxxi. Apart from abbreviations listed p. xi above, the following are used here: *Acta SS.* – *Acta Sanctorum* (1863–); Blöndal – Sigfús Blöndal, *Íslenzk-dönsk Orðabók* (1920–24); Cleasby-Vigfússon – R. Cleasby – Guðbrandur Vigfússon, *An Icelandic-English Dictionary* (1874); Falk-Torp – H. S. Falk und Alf Torp, *Norwegisch-dänisches etymologisches Wörterbuch* (1910); *Hms.* – C. R. Unger, *Heilagra Manna Søgur* I–II (1877); Holtsmark – Anne Holtsmark, *Ordforrådet i de eldste norske håndskrifter til ca. 1250* (1955); Larsson – L. Larsson, *Ordförrådet i de älsta isländska handskrifterna* (1891); *Mar* – C. R. Unger, *Maríu Saga* (1871); *NgL* V – Ebbe Hertzberg, *Glossarium*, in *Norges gamle Love* V (1895), 57–834; *Post* – C. R. Unger, *Postola Sögur* (1874); de Vries – J. de Vries, *Altnordisches etymologisches Wörterbuch* (1961).

[2] I have discussed problems connected with this paper with several friends. I am especially grateful to Mr G. I. Needham, University College London, whose comments have greatly helped to clarify the argument. It should be noted that in the following quotations ligatures are freed and abbreviations not indicated.

nir menn þa er auð-ræðe hafa mykil. ok þessa hæims menn ero mycclir.[1] Cf. Matth. 13, 22 – hic est qui verbum audit, et sollicitudo saeculi istius et fallacia divitiarum suffocat verbum (cf. Marc. 4, 18–19, Luc. 8, 14).

2. *Homiliu-bók* (Stock. perg. 4:0 nr. 15, *c.* 1200): EN þriþia hlut auþrǽþa siNa. haofþo þav siólfom ser til atviNo.[2] Cf. Pseudo-Jerome, *Evangelium de nativitate Mariæ*: Nam omnem substantiam suam trifariam diviserunt . . . tertiam (*scil.* partem) suæ familiæ usibus et sibi reservabant.[3]

3. *AM 685 C 4to* (*c.* 1300, containing a translation of Prosper's *Epigrams* originally made in Norway in the twelfth century): þar davðinn skal þó taka frá mönnum avll þessa heims avðræði. þótt allir scaþarnir hlífiz við.[4] Cf. *Epigram.* LXXVIII: – Cui licet, adversis cessantibus, omnia parcant; Lege tamen mortis sit faciendus inops.[5]

4. From the so-called *Miðsaga* of St Olaf (date of origin *c.* 1200), the following text preserved in Uppsala Delegard. nr. 8[II] (*c.* 1250, *Den legendariske Saga*) and AM 61 fol. (late fourteenth century, *Den store Saga*): Gaf fe faður lausum auðræðe ækcium –.[6] (Cf. Deut. 26, 12.)

5. *Hungrvaka* (date of origin *c.* 1210; oldest manuscript of B-class, AM 380 4to, *c.* 1641, of C-class, AM 205 fol., *c.* 1644): ok hefir eigi annarr slíkr grundvǫllr verit auðræða (-rada B-class) ok hœginda í Skálaholti sem tíundargjaldit.[7]

6–7. *Þorláks saga* (between 1199 and 1211; Stock. perg. fol.

---

[1] ed. C. R. Unger (1864), 103[10]; ed. G. Indrebø (1931), 70[21].

[2] ed. Th. Wisén (1872), 127[32].

[3] Migne, *PL* 30, col. 298.

[4] Þorvaldur Bjarnarson, *Leifar fornra kristinna frœða íslenzkra* (1878), 17[8]. Cf. D. A. Seip, *The Arna-Magnæan Manuscript 677, 4to* (Corpus codicum islandicorum medii aevi XVIII, 1949), 18, 20.

[5] Migne, *PL* 51, col. 522.

[6] O. A. Johnsen, *Olafs Saga hins Helga* (1922), 27[34-35]; O. A. Johnsen and Jón Helgason, *Den store Saga om Olav den Hellige* (1941), 710[7]. Parallel texts in Tómasskinna, Bergsbók (*Den store Saga*, 709[20-21]) and *Flb.* III 247 do not have the word, but since the matter is demonstrably from Styrmir and the word is also in *Den legendariske Saga*, its origin in the *Miðsaga* is certain. Cf. Sigurður Nordal, *Om Olav den Helliges Saga* (1914), 90 (art. 26), 112, 131-3.

[7] *Bps.* I 68[10]; Jón Helgason, *Byskupa sǫgur* I (1938), 86[13]. On the basis of the form in -*ráða*, Fritzner includes a word *auðráð* – its existence must be counted uncertain.

nr. 5, *c.* 1360, AM 382 4to, fragmentary, first half of the fourteenth century, AM 383 4to I, fragment of two leaves, thirteenth century): En svá mikla stund sem hann lagði á um þá tilskipan, er til auðræða kom – (Stock. 5, cf. AM 382: En svá mikla stundan sem hann lagði á veraldlig auðræði –). Virðdi hann oc við þa eigi meiri varkvnn. at hepta sic eigi at vleyfþvm hlvtvm ær aðr hofþv bæþi mikit lan af gvði i avðræþvm oc mannvirþingvm (AM 383 I; í auðæfum, Stock. 5).[1]

8–12. *Páls saga* (soon after 1211; chief manuscript AM 205 fol., *c.* 1644): Herdís varðveitti bú þeirra . . . ok öll auðræði þeirra. – Auðræði urðu brátt ei mikil, en afvenslur þóttu varla með mikilli stillingu. – En allsvaldandi guð gæddi hann því meir, er ofarr var, bæði at auðræðum ok mannvirðingum. – sín efni, þau er hann hefði föng á, í auðræðum eðr í öðrum tillögum. – En við þat er oss at una . . . at hann hefir náliga öll þau gæði eptir sik leift, er menn megu eptir hafa góðs manns ok göfug[s]: . . . auðr gnógr ok allskyns staðarprýði . . . auðræði ok unaðsamar vistir, er hann ætlaði velflestum sínum nánum frændum; en hann man til þess hugt hafa, at guð muni þá hugga, er hann hefir eigi fé huggaða.[2]

13–14. *Jóns saga ens helga* (soon after 1200, extant in three forms, the chief manuscripts of each being AM 234 fol., *c.* 1325, Stock. perg. fol. nr. 5, *c.* 1350, Stock. papp. 4:o nr. 4, *c.* 1640): Hann lagði til stólsins Skálaholts land, ok mörg önnur auðræði í löndum ok lausum aurum (so also AM 235 fol., fragmentary, *c.* 1400; auðæfi, Stock. 5 and 4). – ok lagði (*scil.* Oxi) til þeirrar kirkju mikil auðræði (margar gersimar, Stock. 5; mikil audæfi, Stock. 4).[3]

15. *Gregorius saga* (twelfth-century work? The following text is from a small fragment in the Riksarkiv, Oslo, late thirteenth century): þeir tavlldv hann hava verit felogsmann mikin oc

---

[1] *Bps.* I 102[20], 277[6], 393[12], 107[13].   [2] *Bps.* I 129[7], 136[13], 137[10], 142[18], 146[11].
[3] *Bps.* I 158[28] (cf. 231[15]), 163[6] (cf. 235[9]). The text in Stock. papp. 4:o nr 4 is not printed; the readings are from fols. 227r, 229r. On the question of the relative dating of the versions, see Ole Widding, *Maal og Minne*, 1958, 4–5, Einar Ól. Sveinsson, *Dating the Icelandic Sagas* (1958), 109 note 1, P. G. Foote, *Íslenzk Tunga* I (1959), 39 note 38.

hava mioc eytt avðreþvm þeim, er lago til sto[l]s Petrs postvla.[1]
Cf. – cum calumniarum veterum incentores Gregorium pro-
digum dilapidatoremque multiplicis patriarchatus thesauri
perstreperent –.[2]

16. *Maríu saga* (before 1237–8; Stock. perg. 4:0 nr. 11, first
half of the fourteenth century, AM 234 fol., *c.* 1325, AM 232
fol., fourteenth century, AM 633 4to, *c.* 1700, transcript of an
original from *c.* 1300): ok tómir (*v.l.* hégómligir) munu verða
þeir er treystaz sínum auðræðum (so also in version of text preserved in Stock. perg. 4:0 nr. 1, first half of fourteenth century,
and related manuscripts).[3] Cf. Magnificat, Luc. 1, 53: et divites
dimisit inanes.

17. *Andreas saga I* (earliest text, fragmentary, in AM 645
4to, older hand, *c.* 1220; the following from AM 239 fol., end
of fourteenth century): Biðium ver nu sælan Andreas postola
oss arnadarordz, at hann arni oss i þessi verölldu ars ok audręda,
friðar ok farsęlu –.[4]

18–20. *Thómas saga erkibyskups* (first version from *c.* 1200;
following texts from no. 67a–d in the Riksarkiv, Oslo, early
fourteenth-century, Tómasskinna, *c.* 1400, and Stock, perg. fol.
nr. 2, *c.* 1425–45, respectively): hverr er þvi meirr skvllbvndinn
[við gvð sem] hann hefir meira lán af gvði i avðręðvm i þessi
[verolldv]; cf. quanto quis ab aliquo majora suscepisse dig-
noscitur, tanto ei obnoxior et magis obligatus tenetur.[5] – hann
resignerar – allt þat leen ok audrædi, er hann hafdi halldit

---

[1] *Hms.* I 395[29]. Several forms in the fragment suggest an old exemplar, doubtless
Norwegian. [2] *Acta SS.* Mart. II 200.
[3] *Mar* 24[4], 363[24–25]. The saga is attributed to Kygri-Björn Hjaltason, who died
1237 or 1238; he made use of an older vernacular source. See G. Turville-Petre,
Origins of Icelandic Literature (1953), 121–3.
[4] *Post* 343 note 4. It seems likely that the end of the text in AM 630 4to, from
which the main text is printed, has been abridged, cf. ibid. 382[32]–383[5], 404[3–7], the
end of *Andreas saga* II and III, which is more elaborate and more like AM 239 fol.
The invocation at the end is, however, doubtless a native addition; the text in
J. A. Fabricius, *Codex Apocryphus Novi Testamenti* (1719) I–II 515, ends at a point
corresponding to *Post* 342[35]. Note the identity of the formula here with that in no.
20.
[5] C. R. Unger, *Thomas saga erkibyskups* (1869), 533[22], Eiríkr Magnússon, *Thómas
saga erkibyskups* (Rolls Series, 1875–83), II 269[7]; cf. J. C. Robertson, *Materials for
the History of Thomas Becket* (Rolls Series, 1875–85), VI 565.

nærr ok firr af krununni.[1] – Bidium nu þa ok þenna enn dyrliga guds astvin, at hann arni oss fridar ok farsældar i heime þessum, ars ok audræda –.[2]

21. *Pétrs saga postola IIB* (AM 655 4to XIII, *c.* 1250–75; the following is part of an interpolation of uncertain date in the text of the saga): oc leggia til þess staþar [*scil.* í Skálaholti] a hveriom misserum slict, sem þeir ero scylldir til, i auþræþum –.[3]

22–23. *Stjórn* (this part of the text from leaves inserted in AM 226 fol.; they are Icelandic from the beginning of the fifteenth century, said to be based on a Norwegian manuscript from *c.* 1350–1400; date of origin uncertain, perhaps as early as the twelfth century, almost certainly before *c.* 1260): firir gnott allra audræda – firir fatækis sakir allra audræda.[4] Cf. Deut. 28, 47, 57: propter rerum omnium abundantiam – propter rerum omnium penuriam.

24–25. *Theophilus miracle* (oldest of the four versions of this miracle; AM 234 fol., 232 fol., 633 4to, see no. 16 above, and a fragment in the Riksarkiv, Oslo, from the first half of the fourteenth century?): þá tók hann öll þau auðræði (so AM 232, *v.l.* ráð, ræði) af Theophilo ok virðing, sem hann hafði haft. – Svá leiz honum þá, sem lítils væri vert hiá eilífum kvölum, þó at hann hefði bæði virðingar ok auðræði œrin nökkura stund.[5]

[1] Unger, *Thomas saga*, 316[38], Eiríkr Magnússon, *Thómas saga*, I 82[17].

[2] *Hms.* II 320[19]. These three passages are all likely to have been in the earliest Icelandic work on St Thomas, a translation made *c.* 1200 of a lost Latin life by Robert of Cricklade. See P. G. Foote, *Saga-Book of the Viking Society* XV (1958–62), 403–50.

[3] *Post* 215[19]. Ole Widding, *APhS* XXI (1952), 164, suggests that, given the date of the fragment, it is tempting to connect this interpolation with 'den kirke-politiske Situation omkring Aar 1250'. It could be older.

[4] C. R. Unger, *Stjorn* (1862), 345[15, 38]. On the date and source of the manuscript cf. ibid. v–vi, D. A. Seip, *Stjórn, AM 227 fol.* (Corpus codicum islandicorum medii aevi XX, 1956), 11; idem, *Palæografi* (Nordisk Kultur XXVIII: B, 1954), 134. The text on the inserted leaves has minor additions from Peter Comestor, so that the version it represents cannot as such be very early. These plain Biblical texts here translated could however have been taken over from the earliest version, which Seip dates at least as early as the first half of the twelfth century, see Seip, *Stjórn AM 227 fol.*, 11, 14–15, and his summary of the textual history, 18; cf. Finnur Jónsson, *Den oldnorske og oldislandske Litteraturs Historie* (1920–24), II 975–6.

[5] *Mar* 65[18] and note 5, 68[5]. In all the parallel texts, *Mar* 402 ff., 1080 ff., 1090 ff., the phrasing is different. At 406[3] and 1091[31] the word *vald* is used in the passage

Cf. Quid enim mihi profuit temporale commodum, et superciliositas vana hujus seculi? . . . Quid desideravi, propter vanam gloriam et vacuam opinionem tradere miseram animam meam in gehennam?[1]

26. *Margretar saga* (date of origin uncertain; AM 235 fol., *c.* 1400, AM 233 fol., fourteenth century): En audrędi (audæfvi, AM 233) þin veri i eilifri glatan med þer sialfum.[2]

27–28. *Antonius saga* (date of origin uncertain; AM 234 fol., *c.* 1325): Þat skolvm ver . . . skynia, at með lavgmali sialfs davðans verðvm ver navðgir fra slitnir þeim avðræðvm –. Cf. – illud perspicere debemus, quod etsi nostras velimus retentare divitias, lege mortis ab ipsis devellamur inviti –. – at eyddvm aðr hans avðræðvm. Cf. ejus opibus penitus dissipatis –.[3]

29–31. *Vitœ patrum* (date of origin uncertain; AM 225 fol., early fifteenth century, AM 234 fol., *c.* 1325, AM 232 fol., fourteenth century, both the last defective): en leitid eigi nöckut framarr, en skyllda krefr, eptir ydrum audrædum (so AM 232, naudsynium AM 225, auðæfum AM 234). Cf. nec

corresponding to *auðrœði* in no. 24, and this would appear to be a variant of *ráð*, *rœði*. This suggests that *auðrœði* here is an error (perhaps in some way connected with the preceding *þau*). The available Latin is not immediately helpful at this point, but a later passage would support a reading *ráð* or *vald*: præbuitque ei coram omni Clero et populo auctoritatem dispensationis sanctæ Ecclesiæ atque possessionum ei pertinentium, *Acta SS.* Feb. I 490. There seems no doubt about the authenticity of *auðrœði* in passage no. 25. On general grounds one would believe that the Theophilus legend was translated early, and the text here in which *auðrœði* occurs belongs with the oldest group of translated miracles of the Virgin, perhaps already in existence when *Maríu saga* itself was written (see note 15). Cf. Unger, *Mar* IV, F. Paasche, *Norges og Islands Litteratur* (ny utg. ved Anne Holtsmark, 1957), 296–7, Ole Widding, *Opuscula* II, 1 (Bibliotheca Arnamagnæana XXV, 1961), 3–5.

[1] *Acta SS.* Feb. I 490.

[2] *Hms.* I 476[19]. I have not found this sentence in the available Latin text, but St Margaret is here replying to the offer of *nog auðęfi* (*Hms.* I 476[14]) and this translates *multam pecuniam*, cf. e.g. B. Mombritius, *Sanctuarium* (1910), II 191[19–20]. The date of the translation cannot at present be determined; it is written in a simple style, which, at any rate, suggests the thirteenth century. St Margaret does not figure in church-dedications in Iceland until the beginning of the fourteenth century (*Diplomatarium Islandicum* II 409, 408 note 1 (cf. 119)), although the personal name Margaret is in use in Norway and Iceland in the twelfth century (E. H. Lind, *Norsk-isländska Dopnamn* (1905–15), 760–4), the period when her cult became generally popular in the West.

[3] *Hms.* I 63[19], 71[15]. Migne, *PL* 73, cols. 135, 140.

amplius quam stipendiis vestris debetur, aliquid requiratis.
– eignir ok audrædi. Cf. possessiones et prædia. – en bidr
sveinana veita öll sin audrædi rettum þurfamonnum. Cf.
præcepit pueris suis, ut omnia quæ superessent . . . pauperibus
erogarent.[1]

32–33. *Íslenzk Æventyri LXXXV:B, LXXXVII* (probably
recorded *c.* 1325–50; AM 657 B 4to, *c.* 1400): Nú skal ek
[eigi] þegar rjúfa . . . þat er ek játti þér, at nökkut auðræði
myndi af mér leiða. – Yfir auðræðum þersar veralldar er ok mjök
vakanda, hvat maðr á guði eða hvat mönnum á út at tæra –.[2]

To complete these instances from medieval texts Dr Jakob
Benediktsson has kindly sent me what the files of the Orðabók
Háskóla Íslands contain. There is one example in Lbs. 99 fol.,
written *c.* 1780–90 by Bishop Hannes Finnsson (1739–1796)
and containing his *Dictionarium Islandico–Latinum Littr. A–D*. He
has: '*audræde* s.n. – compendium operæ. 2. opes, copia rerum.
Þorlaks saga Helga.' I shall return to his first gloss later;
the second is avowedly from the early medieval *Þorláks saga*.
The files then have three other instances, two in works by
Hjálmar Jónsson (Bólu-Hjálmar, 1796–1875), written 1860 and
1867 respectively, and one in a translated story by Björn
Jónsson (1846–1912), published in 1892. These instances

---

[1] *Hms.* II 344[4], 351[14], 449[3]; the corresponding Latin text will be found on the
same pages. Finnur Jónsson, *Den oldnorske og oldislandske Litteraturs Historie*, II 875,
says that the translation of *Vitæ patrum* is 'næppe ældre end fra det 13. årh.s sidste
halvdel'; cf. Paasche, op. cit. 446. The same would probably be thought true of the
Antonius saga as well. Both translations are notably literal, however, and it seems to
me difficult to assign a date on stylistic grounds to a work which does no more than
stick close to the Latin, especially when one has regard to the fact that these translations are probably monastic productions. Such imitation of the Latin may be a
natural stage in the development of a native periodic and latinate style – but it may
represent no more than an exercise. This is not to say that the suggested date is
wrong, but to suggest that it needs a better basis, such as a study of the vocabulary,
for example, might provide.

[2] H. Gering, *Islendzk Æventyri* (1882–3), I 250[40], 266[3 24]. Gering, II xxv-vi, lxv,
thinks that these two tales belong to a collection made by one man and are to be
counted with the tales certainly connected with Bishop Jón Halldórsson, who died
in 1339. Absence of recognizable literary sources, elaborate periodic constructions
and a love of alliteration are characteristic of this author. One wonders if his use of
auðræði was an affectation.

appear after Guðbrandur Vigfússon had drawn attention to the word in the preface to *Biskupa sögur*, and to use Dr Jakob Benediktsson's words: 'Björn Jónsson var manna vísastur til að bregða fyrir sig fornum orðum, engu síður en Bólu-Hjálmar.' [1] It is reasonable to regard these last three instances as examples of literary resuscitation.

II

In the medieval texts cited above the word *auðræði* appears as the equivalent of a number of Latin words meaning 'wealth, substance, means'. Even in no. 12, where the word *auðr* has already been used and it might seem as if *auðræði* and *unaðsamar vistir* were nearly synonymous, the meaning is made almost brutally clear by the word *fé* in the following sentence.

The word normally appears as neuter plural (so also in the nineteenth-century instances mentioned above); it appears as a neuter singular in no. 32 (where *nökkut* would however be an easy scribal error for *nökkur*) and it might also be regarded as such in no. 19, though by no means necessarily.

All the medieval sources in which the word appears are of clerical provenance. Particularly noteworthy is the concentration of the occurrences in early texts. This is such that it would seem justifiable to include the word *auðræði* amongst the criteria that may be used in assessing the date of origin of a given work, although it obviously needs support of a general or particular kind.

As Guðbrandur Vigfússon remarked, *auðæfi* is a more current word. In the thesauri of the vocabulary of the oldest Norwegian and Icelandic manuscripts, this word occurs forty-two

---

[1] I am under great obligation to Dr Jakob Benediktsson for his information and comments, sent in a letter 13.10.59. Bólu-Hjálmar uses the word *auðræði* unnaturally as a concrete term: 'Grímur bóndi gekk . . . að sjá um auðræði sín', 'Maður gamall . . . vakti um nóttina yfir túni og auðræðum' (*Ritsafn* V (1949), 140, 231). The text by Björn Jónsson is a translation of a short story (*Najevska* by L. Sacher-Masoch): 'Eigi brustu hana nokkurs konar auðræði, og lét hún hvern mann undir sig stjana, svo sem drottning væri' (*Sögusafn Ísafoldar* V (1892), 251, reprinted in *Sögur Ísafoldar* II (1948), 193).

F

times, *auðræði* only twice.[1] The comparatively high number of variants found with the instances recorded above (cf. nos. 4, 7, 13, 14, 26, 29) suggests that scribes tended to find *auðræði* an unfamiliar or troublesome word. It may be noted in passing that both the words seem peculiar to West Norse.

It has been held that the first element in *auðræði* is the substantival stem found in the simplex *auðr* m., 'wealth, riches', OE *ēad*, OSax *ōd*, etc. It is apparently taken to be in object relationship to the second element, *-ræði* being thought to have the sense of 'rule, control' which is found as one of the meanings of *ráð* n., *ráða* vb.[2] The compound might thus be glossed 'wealth-control, command of wealth', and hence 'wealth, resources'. A comparative study suggests that this analysis is hardly tenable.

Other compounds in *-ræði* are common in ONorw and OI: *á-, bráð-, ein-, fals-, fjǫr-, flá-, for-, full-, goð-, glap-, glæ-, gǫr-, hag-, harð-, heil-, hjálp-, holl-, hvat-, hæg-, ill-, jafn-, kval-, mikil-, mis-, óð-, ór- (úr-), sam-, sjálf-, skað-, skjót-, skyndi-, snar-, snjall-, stór-, svik-, til-, um-, ú-, vand-, vél-, vin-*.[3]

---

[1] 23 in Larsson, 19 in Holtsmark.

[2] So apparently F. Holthausen, *Vergleichendes und etymologisches Wörterbuch des Altwestnordischen* (1948), s.v. *ræði* and de Vries, s.v. *ræði*; Ekwall relates the second element to *ráð*, 'förråd' ('supply' – a doubtful sense of the word) and glosses 'godt förråd af egendom' – see E. Ekwall, *Suffixet ja i senare leden af sammansatta substantiv inom de germanska språken* (Uppsala Universitets Årsskrift 1904, Filos. 3), 67.

[3] I have omitted *afræði*, cf. Falk-Torp, s. v. *Ævret* (where the second element is connected with *reiða*). I have also omitted the doubtful *folkræði*, hap. leg., in *Brot* 9: er hann fimm sono / at folcroþi / gvnnarfvsa / getna hafþi (S. Bugge, *Norrœn Fornkvæði* (1867), 239 and note, 418; the manuscript has *folc róþi*). Bugge's suggestion that it be read *folkræði* and means 'til at herske over Folket' has been widely accepted, cf. e.g. H. Gering, *Vollständiges Wörterbuch zu den Liedern der Edda* (1903), s.v., less confidently by Finnur Jónsson, *Lexicon Poeticum* (1931), s.v. The word does not fit happily into the series discussed above. It may be the word *folk(h)roð*, cf. Bugge and Finnur Jónsson, loc. cit. (*ó* for *æ* occurs otherwise once in the Codex Regius, but *ó* for *o* is found 83 times, see G. Lindblad, *Det isländska Accenttecknet* (1952), 102, 106.) Another possibility is that the origin of the word in *Brot*, if it is to be accepted as *folkræði*, is to be sought in WGmc, cf. OS *rādand*, OE compounds in *-rædend*, *-ræden*, and e.g. the discussion surrounding *worold rædenne*, *Beowulf* 1142.

It should be noted that some at least of these compounds in *-ræði* were originally fem. *-in* derivatives, not (or as well as) n. *-ia* derivatives, although few traces of fem. conjugation remain; on this see W. Cederschiöld, *Studier över genusväxlingen i fornvästnordiska och fornsvenska* (1913), especially 82–6.

Although not all of these occur frequently, it was clearly a productive type of compound. It will be observed that in many cases the first element is adjectival or adverbial, and that in other cases, where it consists of a substantival stem, the function of this in the compound is also adjectival or adverbial. In almost all the cases the second element, *-ræði*, can be given the sense of 'proposal, undertaking, action', and the first element acts as a definer. An obvious exception is *forræði* (= *forráð*), cf. *ráða fyrir*,[1] where the verbal element is 'rule, control'; the same is probably true of *sjálfræði*. Neither of these can, however, be analysed in the same way as is postulated for *auðræði*. It may be noted that compounds in *-ráð*, many of which of course have synonymous forms in *-ræði*, show the same features: the verbal second element is modified in some way by the first element. A word in *-ráð* which might appear to be different is *landráð*, but even here the basic sense seems to be not 'rule *of* the country', but 'counsels, decisions, courses of action affecting the country'. This conclusion seems strongly supported by the fact that *landráð* can also mean 'high treason'.[2] No word *landræði* is known.

It would hardly be possible either to conclude from the examples given above that the element *-ræði* had become reduced to a mere abstract suffix. The only case where this might be fully accepted is in *vinræði* = *vinsemd* (so Cleasby-Vigfússon), but this word is extremely rare and perhaps in a sense erroneous.[3] But a development in the direction of an abstract

[1] Cf. T. Johannisson, *Verbal och postverbal partikelkomposition i de germanska språken* (1939), 178.

[2] Even the rare *fjárráð* does not mean 'command of wealth', but 'anstiftelse af eller samraad om en forbrydelse mod en mands ciendclc', *NgL* V, s.v. But in ModI it is glossed by Blöndal as 'Finansbestyrelse; Finansministerium'.

[3] Cleasby-Vigfússon and Fritzner note only the one instance, *Flb.* I 163[18]: Palnatoki ferr ór lande... hann setr eptir Aka son sinn at rada firir buum sinum... ok bad hann vinræda vid Suein konung. ok þui het hann ok þat ende hann uel. The older text in AM 291 4to reads: ... oc baþ honom virkta viþ konvngiN... oc heit konvngr þvi ... at haN scyllde veita aka ena beztv vm sia oc þat sama eNdi haN (C. af Petersens, *Jómsvíkinga saga* (1882), 57[11-14]; the text in Stock. perg. 4:o nr. 7 also has *virkta*, G. Cederschiöld, *Jómsvíkinga saga* (1874), 12[31-32]). The word *vinræða* in *Flb.* thus probably results from a misreading, but in any case the context makes it reasonable to interpret it as 'friendly counsels, friendly actions' rather than as abstract 'friendship'.

sense in the element may be found in a natural extension of
meaning given to *vandræði*. This is used of a difficult proposal or
undertaking, of a difficult position or state, and so of trouble
generally. It is not uncommon in the plural in this generalized
sense, to be in difficulties and so forth, although, like the other
compounds in *-ræði*, it is never used so consistently in the plural
as *auðræði*. The rare *hægræði* could be regarded as formed on the
model of this extension of *vandræði*: it is glossed as 'Stilling
hvori man har det godt og behageligt'.[1] It is of course also
possible to regard *-ræði* in such compounds as directly connected with *ráð* in the sense of 'Stilling hvori et Menneske er
stedt eller befinder sig, Forhold hvori en lever eller kan komme'.[2]

If *auðræði* is to be fitted into this general background, it is
easiest to interpret the first element not as the substantive
stem but as the not uncommon prefix *auð-*, 'easy, easily'.[3] A
straight-forward interpretation of *auðræði* n.sg. would be 'easy
proposal, easy undertaking, easy action'. By similar extension
as in the case of *vandræði*, it could mean 'easy matters, easy circumstances, a state of ease', a sense which the regular use in the
plural might serve to underline. It could be regarded as basic-
ally synonymous with *auðveldi* n.sg., which occurs early as a
translation of *facultas*.[4] And just as *auðfenginn*, *auðfærr*, *auðsénn*
occur as antonyms of corresponding compounds with *vand-* as
first element, so *auðræði* could be taken as the antonym of
vandræði.[5] This explanation would also mean that there is no
need to dissociate *auðræði* from *auðráðr* ('easily managed'),
auðráðinn ('easily solved, easily steered'), any more than we
need dissociate *samræði*, for example, from *samráðr*, *samráðinn*.

[1] Fritzner, s.v. In *Hms.* I 292[33], the only reference, it translates *commodum*, cf.
e.g. B. Mombritius, *Sanctuarium* (1910), I 639, *v.l.* to 340[23]; cf. no. 25 above.

[2] Fritzner, s.v. *ráð*, art. (11), cf. also arts. (10) 'Levemaade' and (12) 'huslige
eller hjemlige Forhold'.

[3] On the prefix, see e.g. Falk-Torp, s.v. *Ydmyg*; *NED* s.v. *eath*. Relationship with
auðr adj. 'empty, deserted', is uncertain. On *auðr* m. (1) 'wealth' and *auðr* m. (2)
'fate' etc., see the recent work of O. Szemerényi, *Glotta* XXXIV (1955), 277–86.

[4] Larsson, s.v., cf. Fritzner. Note *auðvaldr ok auðráðr*, *Bps.* I 357[26].

[5] Prefix *tor-* is the more frequent antonym of prefix *auð-*, but it would be difficult
to distinguish between *torfenginn* and *vandfenginn*, *torfærr* and *vandfærr* as opposites of
auðfenginn, *auðfærr*.

The commoner word *auðæfi* is held to be from older *auðhæfi*, *auðhæfi*.[1] The second element here is rare.[2] The only common word in *-hæfi* is *athæfi* n., 'conduct, behaviour', where the sense is clearly related to constructions with *hafa(sk)* and *at*.[3] Late and unusual is *handhæfi*, 'hvad en har i Haanden', where the verbal sense of 'holding' is clear. It might thus be argued that in *auðhæfi* the second element is to be regarded as a verbal abstract, 'having, holding', and the first element as the substantival stem found in *auðr*. On the other hand, neither *athæfi* nor *handhæfi* would present an exact parallel to *auðhæfi* analysed in this way, and both these words have synonyms in *-hǫfn* while *auðhæfi* has not.

The word *athæfi* in its oldest forms regularly has *-hæfi* as the second element, but the compound with *auð-* mostly shows *-hœfi*.[4] It is difficult to keep these forms apart etymologically, but if *-hœfi* is aligned with the obvious words showing the same grade-vowel, *hóf* n., *hœfa* vb., *hœfr* adj., and if we regard *auð-* as the prefix 'easy, easily', the compound *auðhœfi* could be taken to mean 'something easily put into a proper state or position' (hence, 'something easily hit or fitted', so 'something easily perfected or done'). If *-hæfi* need be kept distinct from *-hœfi*, it could be taken as giving the compound the meaning of

---

[1] Alexander Jóhannesson, *Isländisches etymologisches Wörterbuch* (1956), 86, relates it to *œfr* adj., 'gewaltig, heftig', and compares it with Latin words with *op-*. It is true that none of the forms in Larsson and Holtsmark is spelt with *-h-*, but its loss after *-ð* is readily acceptable. The suggestion does not explain the forms that do appear with *-h-*, nor the early forms in *-œfi* (but cf. note 4 below).

[2] On *ørhæfi* see de Vries, s.v., with reference; *augnahæfi* = *augnaskot*, 'øiemaal', *NgL* V s.v.; *miðhæfi* (spelt *miðhæfui*), *Flb.* II 487³³, is supposed to render a foreign word, but may be equated with Norw *midhæve* n., 'Midte, Middelpunkt', cf. *midhæves* adv., 'i Midten', see I. Aasen, *Norsk Ordbog*, s.v. On *vandhæfi, torhæfi* (?), see below.

[3] Cf. e.g. E. Olson, *De appellativa substantivens bildning i fornsvenskan* (1916), 384–5.

[4] Of *auðhœfi* Larsson has 22 examples in *-œfi*, 1 in *-æfi*, Holtsmark 7 in *-œfi*, 11 in *-æfi* and 1 uncertain. Later the form *athæfi* is also found, but it is explained as a labialization, D. A. Seip, *Norsk Språkhistorie til omkr. 1370* (1955), 155. On *-hœfi* and *-hæfi* as ablaut variations, see A. Noreen, *Altisländische Grammatik* (1923), § 170, Anm. 1. The possibility might also be considered that *-æfi* in the early forms of *auð(h)œfi* represents a delabialized form, cf. Seip, op. cit. 154, J. Brøndum-Nielsen, *Gammeldansk Grammatik* I (2 udg., 1950), § 141.

'something easily held or handled'.[1] In either case, the sense would be close enough to *auðræði* in the interpretation of it given above. Moreover, just as it was possible to set *auðræði* beside *vandræði*, so one can also point to the existence of *vandhœfi*, which must be counted practically synonymous with *vandræði*.[2]

It thus seems most likely that both in *auðræði* and in *auðhœfi* (*-hœfi*) we have to do with some basic idea of 'easiness, ease, easy state'. The development of such expressions into abstract terms for 'wealth, substance' is not difficult to realize. We can in English talk of being 'in easy circumstances'. It is difficult to regard either of these compounds, however, as a popular word, and they seem rather to belong to a learned and literary style. It might then also be possible that their fixing in the sense of wealth was assisted by the common Latin *facultas*, also used, especially in the plural, in the same transferred sense of 'wealth'. The *Thesaurus linguae latinae* has meanings: I – possibilitas, potestas, etc.; II – vis, potestas . . . qua aliquid efficitur; III – opes, possessiones, divitiae; and notes: 'fere usque ad Constantinum significationes sub I–III tractatae in pari usu sunt, deinde significatio sub III tractata praevalere videtur'. The *Totius latinitatis lexicon* has: '*Facultas* – Proprie est facilitas agendi . . . *Facultas* sumitur sæpe pro copia et abundantia . . . *Facultates* sunt bona, patrimonium –.[3] Comments of classical grammarians on the relationship and distinction between *facilitas* and *facultas* were also remembered in medieval times.[4]

---

[1] Cf. *hæfr*, 'have-able, usable'; an adj. *hœfr*, 'usable' and an adj. *hæfr*, 'suitable' (cf. L. Heggstad, *Gamalnorsk Ordbok* (1930), s.v.), would be hard to keep apart.

[2] On *vandhœfi* see e.g. Cleasby-Vigfússon, Fritzner and Blöndal, s.v. Cf. also *NgL* V 685, where in the passage cited *vandhœfi* appears as a variant of *vandræði*. The form *van(d)hóf* also appears as a variant there and is accepted by Hertzberg, but it does not seem to occur elsewhere. (Fritzner's *auðhóf* has been dismissed by Jón Þorkelsson, *Anmærkninger til Fritzners Ordbog* (1913), 5.) The word *torœfi*, see *NgL* s.v., appears as a variant of *torrek*; Hertzberg suggests it may be for *torhœfi*, which certainly appears a possible word and not so far from *torrek*, if this word's original sense is 'something difficult to follow up' (not specifically of vengeance perhaps, as Árni Pálsson would have it, *Á við og dreif* (1947), 291–2, although this would follow naturally from the basic sense).

[3] The word came into French and Italian in this sense, as well as in others, *les facultés* (pl. in ModFr, pl. and sg. in OFr), *le facoltà*.

[4] Cf. the passages cited in *Totius latinitatis lexicon* III (1865), 13, s.v. *facilitas*.

The reason for the small use and rapid disappearance of *auðræði* doubtless lies in its ambiguity. As was seen above, the other numerous compounds in *-ræði* have a sense which places emphasis on the verbal element. The first suggestion of *auðræði* must have remained 'something easily undertaken' – not so very far from what was quoted above of *facultas*, 'Proprie est facilitas agendi', and doubtless the same as Bishop Hannes Finnsson intended when he gives the first meaning of *auðræði* as 'compendium operæ', a paraphrase which presumably means 'sparing of labour'. The compound *auðhæfi* (*-hæfi*) was much better placed to acquire and retain a specific sense divorced from its etymology. The second element was rare and, when reduced to *-æfi*, would have no specific semantic content. In such a case, it would not be difficult to associate the first element with substantive *auðr* rather than with prefix *auð-*. In the pair *vandræði – vandhæfi* the opposite tendency would operate. The compound acquired no extension of meaning to make the rarer form preferable, and association with other words in *-ræði* has ensured the solid predominance of *vandræði*.

It is finally interesting to note that modern Icelandic (or perhaps only the dictionaries) has a word *auðræði*, formally identical with the old word considered above.[1] It means 'plutocracy, capitalism', and is a neologism based on the simplex *ræði* in the sense of 'control, authority'. (This simplex occurs rarely in later medieval sources and is best explained as detached from compounded forms like *forræði*.[2]) This is compounded with the substantive stem of *auð(u)r*, 'wealth', and the whole thus means '(political) control by wealth'. It forms one of a group, *lýðræði*, *þjóðræði* (democracy, republicanism), *skrílræði* (mob-rule), formed on foreign models. Related types are *lýðveldi*, *þjóðveldi* (republic, republican or democratic state), *skrílveldi*, where the second element has an older independent history than *ræði*. The more usual term for the 'power of money, capitalism, plutocracy' seems to be *auðvald*, but *auðveldi* also

---

[1] See Jón Ólafsson, *Orðabók íslenzkrar tungu* (1912–15), and Blöndal, s.v.

[2] Or on the analogy of *ræði* == *ráð* in compounds; cf. Ekwall, op. cit. 67.

exists – we recall that a formally identical word meant 'ease, easiness' in medieval times and was used to translate *facultas* in an early text. These two new compounds, *auðvald, auðveldi,* exist also beside the old and common adj. *auðveld(u)r,* 'easy, easily done', but context and stress are likely to make their semantic distinction easy.[1] The word *auðrœði,* however, insofar as it seems to remain in its modern sense a 'possible' rather than an 'actual' word, may perhaps still be thought to present some difficulty for Icelandic idiom as long as the first element is divorced in meaning from prefix *auð-.*

PETER FOOTE

[1] My recollection is that distribution of stress between the components in words like *auðvald, auðveldi* is more or less even, while in *auðveldur* adj. (commonest in n.sg. *auðvelt*) the stress on the prefix is stronger than that on the second element.

7 · A Middle English Metrical Life of Job

In the Henry E. Huntington Library MS HM 140 (ff. 93b–96b), a fifteenth-century miscellany of prose and poetry, chiefly by Chaucer and Lydgate,[1] is to be found an anonymous metrical life of the Old Testament patriarch, Job. It is written in a clear, bold hand of the third quarter of the fifteenth century on paper bearing a watermark in use about the year 1473.[2] Frequent quotations from the Vulgate appear in the right-hand margins opposite the relevant passages of the English text. It has been suggested by H. N. MacCracken[3] that the author, in imitation of John Lydgate, was supplying verses 'to describe scenes painted in miniature on some fine MS of vellum, for some well-born person's moral edification. The original MS has long since disappeared, and the legend alone remains, the first extended notice of Job in English verse.'[4] In our MS passages from the Vulgate have replaced the miniatures,[5] to

---

[1] For a full description of HM 140, see J. M. Manly and E. Rickert, *The Text of The Canterbury Tales* (1940), I 433–8. The manuscript was formerly Phillipps MS 8299.

[2] Briquet 14261 (Tête de Bœuf).

[3] *Archiv für das Studium der Neueren Sprachen und Literaturen* CXXVI (1911), 365. MacCracken saw the MS in England before it went to the Huntington Library, but the transcript he made has many inaccuracies and misunderstandings, which justify a re-edition.

[4] MacCracken, op. cit. 365.

[5] For a full list of Western illustrations of Job see L. Réau, *Iconographie de l'Art chrétien* II, *Iconographie de la Bible* I, *Ancien Testament* (1956), 311–18. Miniatures illustrating Pierre de Nesson's *Paraphrase des IX leçons de Job* are to be found in BM MSS Harley 3999 fols. 25r–65v and Landsdowne 380 fols. 39v–73v. M. R. James, *Apocrypha Anecdota*, Second Series (1897), lxxxii, says that the Eastern Church has illustrated the Book of Job far more copiously than the Western. Three MS illustrations of the Testament of Job, i.e. Vat. Pal. gr. 230, ff. 46r, 47v, 53r (10–11 cent.), Oxford, Bodl. Libr., Barocci 201, ff. 36r, 39v (12–13 cent.), Vat. gr. 751, ff. 28r, 32r (13–14 cent.), are mentioned by C. O. Nordström, 'Some Jewish Legends in Byzantine Art', *Byzantion* XXV–XXVII (1955–1957), 487–508.

which the directions in the opening words of several of the stanzas originally pointed (*Here, lo, holy Iob his children doth sanctifie* 15, *Lo, here, the envy of this serpent* 29, *Here immediat begynnyth Iob* 36, *Here the blessid Lorde of hevyn* 113, *Nowe blessid Iob here makyth a ryall feest* 162). It is possible that the 'stages' of medieval pageant processions[1] may have suggested this kind of presentation to the author, who might have seen a religious pageant on Job (perhaps in the Low Countries or France where there was more interest in Job), or possibly he was writing a mumming poem[2] on the subject. However, it must be confessed that it does not read much like a dramatic vehicle, and is more likely to have been a tapestry poem, either by Lydgate or one of his school. Could our piece be an early example (perhaps the earliest example?) of emblem poetry[3] composed by a Quarles *au moyen-âge?*

The author's concern is more with circumstantial detail and melodramatic incident than with close characterization and philosophical argument. Thus he simply chronicles the vicissitudes of Job's career, almost entirely disregarding the dialogues on the nature of good and evil, which comprise nearly eighty per cent of the Biblical account and embody its whole *rationale*. In consequence of this procedure, Job's patience and his tenacious belief in the ultimate justice of Divine Providence receive particular prominence. In this respect our poem resembles the *Bible Historial*, which, as M. R. James[4] points out in his introduction to the Greek pseudo-Job, in its fullest form usually contains a version of the complete Book of Job from the Vulgate, and, in addition to this, a résumé of the story, omitting

[1] See Glynne Wickham, *Early English Stages* I, cap. III, who incidentally mentions (p. 78) a tableau of 'Deborah the Judge and restorer of Israel' in Fleet Street in Elizabeth I's reign.

[2] Cf. Glynne Wickham, op. cit. cap. VI for a discussion of Lydgate's mumming poems and also of the well-known passage in Lydgate's *Troy Book* (EETS II 169).

[3] Cf. Rosemary Freeman, *English Emblem Books* (1948) *passim*. [The sentence comes from one of R. R. R.'s letters which arrived two days after Professor Geoffrey Bullough had made a similar suggestion to me in conversation. G. N. G.]

[4] op. cit. xcvi.

the dialogues. These two documents are entitled respectively 'le grand Job' and 'le petit Job'.

'The frequent miseries of human life and the seeming indifference of the Gods to the sufferings of good men were topics of the Wisdom literature of the Near East before the earliest date that can be assigned to the Biblical poem of Job.' [1] Discussions in dialogue form from Egypt and ancient Babylon speak of the vicissitudes of fortune and the benefits of faithfulness to God, and the author of the Biblical poem of Job has inherited the tradition and outlook of such writings. However, it appears certain that a folk-tale of the Job story was already current before the composition of the Biblical Book of Job, which is held by most scholars to be post-exilic and by many to date from about 400 B.C. It is likely that the folk-tale provided the Biblical poet with a framework for the beginning and end of his poem, and that he found there the names and figures of Job's three friends and shaped from them the characters of his dramatic poem. However 'he has drastically altered the behaviour and final fortune of its principal character: for the Biblical poet leaves Job reconciled to his fate but still a sufferer, quite distinct from the vigorous, prosperous, and happy Job of the folk-tale'. [2]

This folk-tale with many variant details was popular for many centuries in various languages and countries: it was known to the Christian Greeks and to the Arabic Moslems, and travelled with the Arabs to Spain, and presumably from thence to Italy, [3] France, and England. The most important deposit of this folk-tale is the Greek 'Testament of Job' which is dated not later than the end of the fifth century A.D.

---

[1] W. B. Stevenson, *The Poem of Job*, a Literary Study with a New Translation (The Schweich lectures of the British Academy 1943; 1947), 73. For the literary history of the Biblical Book of Job we are indebted to this book, and also to H. H. Rowley, 'The Book of Job and its Meaning', *Bulletin of the John Rylands Library* XLI (1958-9), 167-207, with its comprehensive bibliography.

[2] W. B. Stevenson, op. cit. 85.

[3] See F. Harth, 'Carpaccio's Meditation on the Passion', *The Art Bulletin* XXII (1940), 25-35, for some pertinent material on the medieval attitudes to Job and on the veneration of Job in Venice.

It has been edited and translated with introductory and exegetical notes[1] by the Rev. Dr K. Kohler who describes it (p. 272) as 'perfectly Jewish in conception and spirit. It has many traits in common with the Rabbinical tradition, but it reflects a stage of Gnostic, or mystic, reasoning and practice which is peculiarly un-Talmudical and reminds the reader more of Christian views and practices ... it is an Essene Midrash on Job.' Since elements in our English poem are borrowed either from the Testament or its derivatives, it will not be out of place to give a summary of its contents.

The *Testament* gives the story of Job in the form of an address of the dying patriarch to his children.

Job was a rich king living in the East in the land of Uz. Near his house there was an idol to which the people were offering sacrifices. A prophetic voice disclosed to Job in a dream that the idol was the work of Satan, and when he resolved to destroy it, an archangel warned him that he would incur Satan's displeasure and be visited by many severe plagues. No sooner was the idol destroyed than Satan conspired to make Job's greatest virtue, his charity, the means of exerting his malign influence upon him. He came as a beggar asking for bread, which Job declared forbidden to him, and sent him burnt and stale bread instead, at which Satan spoke the curse, 'As thou seest this bread all burnt, so shall I soon burn thy body and make it like this.'

Job entertained lavishly and took especial care of orphans and widows. He had 130,000 sheep, 340,000 asses, and 305,000 yokes of oxen; the wool of 7,000 sheep he set aside for orphans and widows, and had 500 oxen plough land for crops for them. He had nine mills and fifty bakeries as well as ships to carry produce into every city and village to the feeble, the sick and the unfortunate. The four doors of his house were always open, and thirty fixed tables stood laid at all hours for strangers,

---

[1] *Semitic Studies in Memory of Rev. Dr Alexander Kohut* (ed. by G. A. Kohut, 1897), 264–338. A French translation of the *Testament* is printed in Migne, *Dictionnaire des Apocryphes*, II 403.

and twelve tables were spread for widows. So zealous was he in his philanthropy that his slaves grumbled as they toiled, and his own sons had to wait at table. While he feasted the poor, he made them offer praise to the Lord to the sound of music, musicians being employed all day for this purpose, and when they were tired he himself took the cithara and played.

However, Satan led a Persian army against Job, pillaged and burnt his house, killed all his children, and afflicted him with boils and worms. He left his city in terror, and went outside its walls to a dunghill where he sat for seven years. His wife, however, remained faithful to him, and worked as a slave in order to earn bread for her husband and herself. When the city rulers withheld bread, Satan in disguise appeared to her and gave her three loaves in exchange for her hair; when she brought these to Job she reproached him, telling him to curse God and die. Job rebuked her, and seeing Satan behind her, taunted him for a coward; whereupon Satan retreated discomfited.

On another occasion three kings visited Job and gazed in consternation at his plight; they were angered when Job refused the attention of their physicians and scorned their pity, pointing to the greater glory that awaited him in a higher world than this. Before their eyes, Job's wife was granted a vision of her children crowned in glory, and went back to her master and died of exhaustion in a cattle-shed.

Thereafter Job recovered his health, was welcomed back to the city and took a second wife, who, like the first, bore him three daughters and seven sons. At his death Job gave each of his daughters a three-stringed girdle which flashed with supernatural light and enabled them to see the wonders of the angelic world at the time of his passing. To one daughter he gave a cithara, to another a censer, and to the third a timbrel, and 'at his burial the three daughters marched ahead having put on their girdles, singing hymns in praise of God'.

A Moroccan Spanish version of the folk-tale based on an

Arabic original is the fullest and purest published form[1] of the tale, while in France its influence appears in mystery plays on Job, preserved in manuscript or in early printed editions,[2] and in stained-glass windows.[3] It would appear from the present state of the evidence that the French biographers of Job divide into those who keep fairly closely to the Biblical narrative, e.g. the dramatist of the *Vieux Testament*,[4] and, too, the composers of the many *dirige*-poems like Pierre de Nesson,[5] and those who were rather concerned with the sensational and comic apocrypha that became associated with his *vita*.

It will be observed that the folk-tale version of the story presents Job as an almost fanatical philanthropist. He kept open house, and his time was entirely occupied with works of charity. His mills, ships and bakeries were solely occupied in the service of the poor, and his slaves would often rebel against the great burden of work which Job imposed on them. Kohut (p. 276) describes him as 'the type of a philanthropic receiver of stran-

---

[1] 'La estona y recontamiento de Ayub, de sus pruebas y de su paciencia', ed. by F. Guillen Robles in *Leyendas Moriscas* (1885), I 225–63.

[2] See J. de Rothschild, *Mystère du Vieuil Testament* (*SATF*, 1878–91), V iii–xii, who lists various 'pièces anciennes et modernes dont l'histoire de Job a fourni le sujet', beginning with B. N. MS f. fr. 1774 and another MS, 'qui devait contenir la même pièce que le précédent', appearing, about 1490, in a catalogue of a library of Tours. Then follows a list of the various printed editions of *La Patience de Job* in Latin, French, Spanish and Italian. A French version printed in Paris about 1570 and again at Lyons in 1603 has 'au titre, un bois grossier représentant Job près de qui deux hommes jouent du tambour et de la trompette'. The editor does not seem to have examined all the editions of Job and it is therefore likely that similar representations are to be found in the others. For a summary of *La Patience de Job*, see Le Comte de Doubet, *Dictionnaire des Mystères* (1854), 474–7. There is a copy of the Lyons 1603 edition in the British Museum (1072 a 28). Cf. also Hardin Craig, *English Religious Drama* (1955), III 365.

[3] e.g. the magnificent windows in the churches of S. Patrice and S. Romain in Rouen. The former window has (bottom left) the inscription

> Satan réduit le bon Job en grand misère
> Et sa femme en sa colère
> Insulte méchamment à sa simplicité.

[4] Printed in J. de Rothschild, op. cit. V. 1–51.

[5] *Neuf leçons de Job ou Vigiles des morts*, a paraphrase of verses from the Book of Job in the Office of the Dead written *c.* 1424 as a *consolatio* for the imprisoned Duke of Bedford, see A. Piaget and E. Droz, *Pierre de Nesson et ses Œuvres* (1925).

gers, the pattern of a Bedouin prince of hospitality in the popular tradition, long before Abraham was rendered such'. Further, Job is depicted as a musician and as a great patron of music.[1] In the *Testament* III 34 ff. he tells how he had six harps and six slaves to play the harps, and also a cithara, a decachord, and

> I struck it during the day [35] And I took the cithara, and the widows responded after their meals. [36] And with the musical instrument I reminded them of God that they should give praise to the Lord. [37] And when my female slaves would murmur, then I took the musical instruments and played as much as they would have done for their wages, and gave them respite from their labour and sighs.

While the three musicians of the English poem may derive from a transmutation of Job's three comforters, they may also have been suggested by the three daughters of Job who after his restoration to prosperity sang to cithara and timbrel, which he had given them, that they might bless the holy angels who came for his soul (*Testament* XII 5, 6). It is also possible that a western iconographer saw a representation of the slaves and mistook it for a representation of musicians. In ll. 57–63 where our poem describes the destruction of Job's children, Job is represented as being present and no doubt as contributing to the 'armony at the fest'. This is certainly apocryphal, for although the poem places the feast at the elder brother's house (in common with Job I, 18–19), in the *Testament* Job's children live under their father's roof and 'take charge of the service'; the society is patriarchal, and accords with the oldest popular view of Job 'as a type of generous Bedouin saint whose nomadic tent is the joy of God and men'.[2] Our English poem does not

---

[1] See Kathi Meyer, 'St Job as a Patron of Music', *The Art Bulletin* XXXVI (1954), 21–31, for a fully documented and illustrated article on this aspect of the patriarch. Miss Rosemary Jackson has pointed out to us that the Great Bible (1539) begins Job XV with a miniature of two musicians, one with pipe, the other with drum, playing before the patriarch on his dunghill. See also Erwin Panofsky, *Albrecht Dürer* (1943), I 93–4.   [2] Kohut, op. cit. 272.

follow the folk-tale version exclusively,[1] but some of its details derive from apocryphal material:

(1) ll. 99–105, in elaboration of a rebuke by Job to his friends, 'As for you, you whitewash with lies; worthless physicians are you all' (Book of Job XIII, 4), a scene is introduced where doctors offer to restore him to health 'by crafte artificiall'. This derives from the *Pseudo-Job* VIII, 24–26,[2] which says:

> [24] Then Sophar rejoined and said: 'We do not inquire after our own affairs, but we desire to know whether thou art in a sound state, and behold, we see that thy reason has not been shaken. [25] What now dost thou wish that we should do for thee? Behold we have come here and brought the physicians of three kings, and if thou wishest, thou mayest be cured by them.' [26] But I answered and said: 'My cure and my restoration cometh from God, the Maker of physicians.'

It is likely that the Middle Ages with its sceptical attitude to the medical profession[3] would relish this elaboration of the episode.

(2) ll. 113–119, God surprisingly berates Job for his stern reproof of his wife's despairing counsel. This derives neither from the Biblical Job nor from the *Testament*, and the origin of the rebuke is obscure. It is possible that the poet wishes to stress Job's customary supreme patience under provocation (ὑπομονή) by this momentary departure from it. Testament literature generally shows a 'tendency to dwell on a particular virtue or vice which was illustrated by the life of the supposed author. Hospitality and mercy are the leading features of the Testament of Abraham, and in the Testament of Job the keynotes are ὑπομονή and ἐλεημοσύνη'.[4]

(3) ll. 120–133, minstrels play before Job as he sits on the dunghill. Destitute, he cannot reward them except with 'the brode scabbes of his sore body' which immediately turn to gold.

---

[1] e.g. the enemies of Job, the Sabaeans and Chaldeans (str. 6) are replaced in the *Testament* by a Persian army led by Satan himself in the guise of a Persian king.

[2] Kohut, op. cit. 330.

[3] See the note by R. R. Raymo on *Speculum Stultorum* 89 (ed. R. R. Raymo and J. H. Mozley, 1960), 143–4.   [4] M. R. James, op. cit. lxxxv.

PLATE I   Paris B.N. f. fr. 1226 fol. 40r

PLATE II Centre panel of the altar of St Job by the Meister der Barbara-legende. Wallraf-Richartz Museum [WRM 412], Cologne

PLATE III   Hours of the Virgin, with Calendar. French manuscript
(Paris?). Reproduced by the courtesy of Philip C. Duschnes, New York

Before they take their leave, the minstrels display their wealth to Job's wife, provoking her anger. She confronts her husband and reviles him for his apparent dissimulation of poverty. Contrary to his behaviour on the previous occasion, Job now endures her rebukes in silence, thinking it wiser 'to observe pacience and so to leve in rest'.[1] In *La Patience de Job* it is Satan who, having failed in all his attempts to confound Job, disguises himself as a beggar, and asks Job for alms. Job gives him the worms from his wounds, which appear like pieces of gold when Satan shows them to Job's wife. There is every likelihood that the story derives its origin from folklore, for several tales in popular tradition describe the magical transformation of worthless objects (scabs, spittle, shavings, dead leaves, hair, etc.) into gold.[2] Significantly, the motif is sometimes brought into association with ascetics and anchorites who, like Job, expiate their guilt by mortification of the flesh. It is tempting to think that it may have come from the life of some Job-like, scab-ridden medieval saint or desert father.

We are particularly grateful to Father Paul Grosjean for drawing our attention to the prevalence of this motif in Irish

[1] The representations, one, Plate I, from Paris B.N. f. fr. 1226 fol. 40r and the other, Plate II, from the centre panel of the Altar of St Job by the Meister der Barbara-Legende in the Wallraf-Richartz Museum [WRM 412] in Cologne, dated c. 1485, illustrate this episode; in fact the latter tells the whole story by its separate groupings of figures. Another representation, Plate III, is to be found in a sixteenth-century French MS (Paris?) sold by Philip C. Duschnes of Lexington Avenue, New York (from Catalogue 40), to a private collector in California. It was originally listed in C. W. Traylen of Guildford's Catalogue 50 (1959) as Hours of the Virgin, with Calendar, and contained 14 full-page miniatures of which the last but one, an Office of the Dead, showed (to quote the catalogue) 'Job seated on a dung heap outside a city wall; his friends, richly dressed and playing pipe and lute, approach at a stately pace from the left; in an architectural frame, at the foot a putti balances on a branch; below a canopy on the right are three naked male figures wearing Oriental head-dress.' We are greatly indebted both to Mr Duschnes and the present owner of the MS for the reproduction which they so kindly arranged to have made for us.

[2] S. Thompson, *Motif Index of Folk-Literature* (1933), II 37–9; R. S. Boggs, *Index of Spanish Folktales* (1930), 181; C. A. Williams, *Oriental Affinities of the Legend of the Hairy Anchorite* (1925), 11; J. Grimm, *Deutsche Mythologie* (1875), I 228–9, 400; N. M. Penzer, ed., *The Ocean of Story* III (1925), 163 f.; VIII (1927), 59 nt. 3; F. Boas, *Tsimshiam Texts* (Smithsonian Institute, Bureau of American Ethnology, Bulletin 27; 1902), 190.

G

hagiography.[1] He agrees that the author of this Life of Job 'n'a pas inventé ce détail de la transmutation en or des croûtes et ulcères du malheureux affligé. Sans aucun doute, on retrouverait cela dans un texte latin si malheureusement ce genre de littérature n'avait souvent péri.'

Although it is not stated explicitly in our poem, it is clear that Satan must be held responsible for the act of magic by which he subtly subjects Job's patience to its final trial in the cruel abuse of his shrewish wife. It is clear from the Job commentaries[2] that she was early regarded as Satan's trump card.

---

[1] *inter alia* W. Stokes, 'Life of S. Féchín of Fore', *Revue Celtique* XII (1891), 318–53; *Silva Gaedelica* (ed. and transl. by S. H. O'Grady, 1892), II 234; S. Baring-Gould, *The Lives of the Saints* (1914), I 310–11; J. Colgan, *Acta Sanctorum Hiberniae* (1948), 130–3; *Vita S. Mochuae Laegsiensis* (*Acta Sanctorum*, January I (1643), 46, c. III); *Annals of Ulster* (ed. W. M. Hennessy, 1887), I 197; *Vitae Sanctorum Hiberniae* (ed. C. Plummer 1910), I xliv, clxxviii, clxxxv; *Bethada Náem Nérenn* (Lives of Irish Saints, ed. C. Plummer, 1922), II 172–3; *The Passions and the Homilies from Leabhar Breac* (Text, Translation and Glossary by Robert Atkinson, Todd Lecture Series, vol. II 1887), 240–4; 477; R. T. Christiansen, *The Vikings and the Viking Wars in Irish and Gaelic Tradition* (1931), 81; *Annala Rioghachta Eireann* (Annals of the Kingdom of Ireland by the Four Masters, ed. John O'Donovan, 1851), I 337; *Lives of Saints from the Book of Lismore* (ed. Whitley Stokes, Anecdota Oxoniensia, Medieval and Modern Series, Pt V, 1890), 274.

[2] e.g. *inter alia:*

(a) *Expositio Interlinearis Libri Job*, Migne, *P.L.* XXIII, col. 1411 (App. to Jerome's works). Exp. to c. II: Dixit autem illi uxor sua etc.

Linguam mulieris diabolus instigavit, sed hac arte nihil praevaluit. Hic dictis simplicitatem deserere decuit . . . Ergo qui blasphemant Dominum, inter stultos deputandi sunt . . . Qui flagellanti patri gratias reddidit et malesuadenti conjugi doctrinam ministravit.

(b) Peter of Blois, *Compendium in Job.* Migne, *P.L.* CCVII, col. 818–19. Dixit autem illi uxor sua etc.

Adversarius, qui beato Job, et filios, et possessiones abstulerat universas, suam ei reliquit uxorem, non ad solatium viri, sed ad suae consummationem malitiae, ut per feminam vinceret, quem persecutione non vicerat, et quod verberibus non poterat, verbis mulieris efficeret. Non videbatur ei liberior, et opportunior nocendi occasio, quam per familiarem inimicum et domesticum proditorem. Scriptum est enim: Ab ea quae dormit in sinu tuo, custodi claustra oris tui. Sciebat quod natura mulieris, quanto fragilior est, tanto flexibilior ad culpam, ex quadam depravatione innata proclivior ad nocendum. Hujus autem rei fidem ei faciebat plenissimam frequens rerum experientia, et multiplicitas exemplorum. Per feminam Joseph incarceratus est, Naboth occisus, Samson vinculatur . . .

Cf. also *L'Hystore Job* (Adaptation en vers francais du *Compendium in Job* de Pierre de Blois; *Yale Romanic Studies* XIV, 1937), 99–102, ll. 2605–88. [*continued opposite.*]

Clearly the later author or authors took note of this and expanded her nefarious role accordingly. The contemporary anti-feminine satiric tradition no doubt helped in part. It is interesting that she plays a more important role as seducer in the Mohammedan tradition of Jobiana than in the Bible or the *Testament*.[1] We suspect that Mrs Job is the former Mrs Noah, and we are grateful to Francis Lee Utley[2] for his opinion in a letter in which he writes, 'whether you can tie up Noah's wife with Job's wife I don't know. I have a general memory that they are both related to each other in various places, as shrews and creatures of the Devil who bothered their respective spouses.' [3]

At line 124, the author of the English poem, speaking of the incident of the scabs turning into gold, adds 'as sayth the story' as a reference to authority. No immediate source for this incident however has been found, but the author, like the writer of the *Testament*, is perhaps using the trick of referring to other books which are quite imaginary. As M. R. James[4] says of the

---

(c) *Speculum Humanae Salvationis* (ed. J. Lutz and P. Perdrizet), I (1907), 43, cap. XX, ll. 69–74.

> Beatus Job fuit flagellatus duobus modis
> Quia Satan flagellavit eum verberibus, et uxor verbis;
> De flagello Satanae sustenuit dolorem in carne,
> De flagello linguae habuit turbationem in corde;
> Non suffecit diabolo quod flagellabat carnem exterius,
> Nisi etiam instigaret uxorem, quae irritaret cor interius.

This passage probably explains the revised role of Job's wife as her husband's last and worst trial, and is probably the source for this incident. L. Réau, op. cit. 316–17, thinks the passage may have been responsible for the increase of anti-feminism in the Job literature.

[1] Kohut, op. cit. 292–3; M. R. James, op. cit. lxxx.

[2] Cf. his 'The 103 Names of Noah's wife', *Speculum* XVI (1941), 426. 'Like Eve and Delilah and Lot's wife she [Noah's wife] betrayed her husband to the devil or to his instruments on earth.' See also his *The Crooked Rib* (1944), and R. R. Raymo's notes on *Speculum Stultorum* 2371 ff., (ed. cit. 171–2).

[3] This notion is surely behind *Piers Plowman* B XII 43:

> *Iob the Iewe his ioye dere he it abouȝte*

Cf. M. W. Bloomfield, 'Piers Plowman and the Three Grades of Chastity', *Anglia* LXXVI (1958), 234–5.

[4] op. cit. xcvii.

Testament, 'the trick – for it is no more – may be intended to give verisimilitude to the narrative, or to leave the author a loop-hole for future composition of a poetical kind, to which he was evidently addicted'. It is indeed likely that our author had a text before him containing l. 124, or something similar, and merely copied it. Could there have been a French or Latin *Testament of Job* behind the English poem and the French play? At all events it is clear that the fifteenth century was particularly interested in Job: Pierre de Nesson's paraphrase of the verses from the Book of Job in the Office of the Dead was written about 1425, and St Gregory's *Moralia in Job,* so influential in the Middle Ages, was reprinted in Venice in 1480 and again in 1494, and probably known[1] to Carpaccio whose 'Meditation on the Passion' shows Job seated in front of the dead Christ opposite to St Jerome. In England the popularity of Richard Rolle's *Commentary in Job* is clearly attested by the numerous manuscripts; Miss H. E. Allen (pp. 130–44) lists 42 MSS, nearly all of them fifteenth century, and one printed edition of the fifteenth century, and in addition to this there is the East Midland poem in twelve-line stanzas known as *Pety Job.*

It cannot be claimed that *The Life of Job* has much, if any, literary merit. It resembles the cycle plays in its rapid succession of scenes, enlivened by sensational incident and high-flown language. Its aureate diction with its occasional use of Latin words undoubtedly impedes the flow of the verse, but without it the poem would lose much of its superficial brilliance. If the rhyme royal is an apt vehicle for narrative poetry of this kind, it is also unfortunately true that, here and there, the verse creaks under a weight of embellishment, and the rhymes,

---

[1] Cf. F. Harth, op. cit. 28: 'By the Renaissance a quite different idea of the significance of Job emerges along with the rise of the bourgeois class in N. Europe. The intricate, symmetrical symbolic systems of the XIII and XIV centuries have begun to give way, and Job represents not so much the prefiguration of the Passion of Christ as an example of patience under suffering and continued faith in God after the loss of all one's possessions. The representations of him in art and in mystery plays relate these sufferings, but omit any reference to the symbolic and prophetic aspects so dear to the Middle Ages.'

though ingenious, often prove false and bathetic. With all its limitations, *The Life of Job* commands attention, and in an individual way successfully conveys its simple religious message.

THE LIFE OF JOB[1]

F. 93b   1   Most mercifull Lorde, by Thyne habundant good-
               nesse,
              This rightfull man Iob, with grete hospitalite
              Of men and women, ever kepte in perfite holynesse,
              Multiplied with richesse, indued with liberalite.
     5   Thre thousand camelis, vii thousand shepe had he,
              A thousand oxen in his habitacion,
              An hundred assis, as the bible makyth mension.

              VII sonnes and thre dowghters by his wyfe also
              Trewly begoten had this holy man,
   10   Whiche sonnes of custume used to do
              Sereatim to festen othir cotidian
              With myrthis most melodius plesantly than
              To in-yoye in other and with theire sustryn all
              In augmentacion of perfite love naturall.

   15   Here, lo, holy Iob his children doth sanctifie,
              And techith his sonnes with-oute presumpcion
              To kepe theire festes, and ever God to magnifie,
              And wysely to lyve with-oute any detraccion.
              And to his doughtres, with-outen pryde or ellacion
   20   Of their native beaute, he bad them have respect
              Hough bryght Lucyfer for his pryde from heven
                  was deiect.

---

[1] The *Life* is reproduced by the kind permission of The Henry E. Huntington Library, San Marino, California. The punctuation and the use of capitals is modern, and abbreviations are expanded. There is no title in the manuscript.

And by cause in grete festynges is ofte tymes sayn
Voluptuose fraylte and ydell loquacite,
This holy Iob for all his children, certeyn,
25   Lest they therin shuld synn or offende of sym-
plicite,
Here offreth to God and prayth unto his deyte
That his oblacio and holocaust myght habond
Ayenst theire synnes, if any in them were fownd.

F. 94a   Lo, here, the envy of this serpent and devyll
Sathan,
30   Whan he in erthe had ron in his perambulacion,
God axed of hym or he had considered His man
And servant Iob rightfull in lyveyng by demon-
stracion.
He aunswerd and desired power of persecucion
Of Iob, his possession, and godes, that God did
hym sende.
35   And so He did, but not in Iob his handes to
extende.

Here immediat begynnyth Iob his persecucion:
His asses and oxen, as they were in pasturyng,
By robbers of Sabe were take by grete oppression.
There hostes of peple, from Calda than commyng,
40   His royall cameles all with theym a-way ledyng,
All his servauntes there slewe with-oute compas-
sion,
Save one that brought to his maister relacion.

This tortuose serpent, oure auncient enemy of hell,
To bryng holy Iob owte of his pacience,
45   Rigouresly his bestys kylde with rancor so fell
Goyng in his plowgh, and wit irefull violence,
His servauntes slewe sodenly with-oute resistence.

The terrible fire with thunder clappes from hevyn
   did fall,
Consumed and devored his shepe and shepardes
   all,

50   Excepte tho that to Iob tydynges browgh[t]
Of all this trouble and grete mesaventure.
But the losse of his godes he settith at nought,
And ever thankith God with pacience puere,
For of Hym and from Hym procedeth all gode
   ure;
55   Unto Whos godenesse Iob here prayeth hertely
Apon the sowles of His servauntes ever to have
   mercy.

F. 94b   The myrthes in instrumentes with armony at the
   fest
Where Iob his children were gadred to-geder
So merely was toched that both most and leste
60   Ioyed in God in the house of the eldist brother.
And as thei ete and dranke, Sathan, wit wynde
   and wedyr
From the region of deserte, the house downe
   dressid,
And all the children of Iob their were oppressid.

Than cam a mesanger and tolde this fatal desteny
65   Of the pytevouse distruccion of his children all.
But ever Iob, with pacience and hole memory,
Lokyng upp to hevyn to the high Fader celes-
   tiall,
And said, "God gave, God takyth. Yt is His
   naturall.
Sicut Domino placuit factum est ita.
70   Sit nomen Domini benedictum in secula."

The scerge of sorowe this pacient Iob then felyng
Up rose, and his clothes a-sonder rentid,
Fill to the erthe, prayd, and this saying,
'Nakyd owte of the wombe of my moder I entrid,
75   Nakyd unto the erthe I shall be revertid.'
In all this sorofull troble Iob sennyd never,
But with hert and mowth he blessid God ever.

This crokyd Sathan to God ageyn did revert,
Seyng he cowde not torne this man from his
     pacience.
80   To toche his body axid he Iob to pervert,
Unto whom God of His myght and magnificence
Power of the body hym gafe with-oute resistence.
But the soule not to moleste, in no maner wyse,
So commaundid hym to observe, as He did devyse.

F. 95a   85   Whan Sathan this power had of God, full of
     myght,
And was departed from Goddes face omnipotente,
To this rightfull man Iob he cam full right,
Lyke a furiouse tyger and wode serpente,
And smote hym with plages and wondys right
     vervent.
90   From the fote unto the hede he no yonte spared,
But Iob for all this his pacience ever observed.

Syttyng on the dongehill, this gode and blessid
     man
Cam his wyf and to hym seid, 'Yet in thi simplicite
Thou here arte permanent? Corse thi God and
     dye than!
95   Thou beste, what is thi pacience nowe in thyn
     adversite?
This shalt thou never recover, trust verely me.'

Iob said, 'Folysshe woman, I counsell the, be styll,
For he that takyth gode thyng sumtyme must take
 ill.'

      The leches and visiscions cam then to hele
100 The sore body of Iob by crafte artificiall,
      But with theym in no wyse wold he then dele,
      For He that rayneth a-bove in the courte celestiall,
      That suffered hym to be made sore in his body all
      Cowde as lyghtly hym hele, he said, yf His wyll be.
105 'Wherefore the cure I remytte unto His deite.'

      The frendes of Iob, of grete generosite,
      Heryng of his troble and fatall aventure,
      Cam unto hym to comforth, councell, and se,
      Rentid theire vestures for doloure and love pure,
110 Sore sorowed and wepte for his perverture,
      VII dayes and nyghtes by hym, then downe sit-
        tyng,
      With many dyverse argumentes unto hym reher-
        syng.

F. 95b   Here the blessid Lorde of hevyn, God omnipotent,
      Unto his holy man Iob than He apperid,
115 And sore rebuked hym for that intente
      That he to-fore tym had his wyfe cursed,
      For whiche of God mercy than mercy he axid
      And of forgevenesse of grete offence
      Of his hasty spekyng and wilfull insolence.

120 This sore syk man syttyng on this foule dongehill,
      There cam mynstrelles be-fore hym, pleying
        meryly.
      Mony had he none to reward aftyr his will,
      But gave theym the brode scabbes of his sore body,
      Whiche turned unto pure golde, as sayth the story.

125 The mynstrelles than shewid and tolde to Iob
his wyfe
That he so reward them; where-fore she gan to
stryfe.

Than saying unto Iob in angre this woman,
'To mynstrelles and players thow [g]evyst golde
largely,
But thou hidest thi gode from me, lyke a false
man,'
130 And with many seducious wordes openly
There hym rebuked with langage most sharply.
Iob all suffered and thout yt for the best
To observe pacience and so to leve in rest.

Lyke as the filth from fyne golde tryed ys by fyre,
135 So nowe Iob is tryed from all corrupcion,
From the bondes of false Sathan and his desyre,
And with pacience overcom hath his temptacion
An angell of heven from God bryngeth revelacion,
Clotheth hym newe, makyth hym hole from al-
maner sore,
140 And hom ageyn resorte to lyve, as he dyd be-fore.

F. 96a   This blessid man Iob thankyd God of His excel-
lence
That yt pleasid His incomprehensible deite
So to indwe hym with the spyrite of recistence
In pacience to withstonde the devell his iniquyte.
145 And of his restoracion proude was never he,
But ever thankyd God in well and in sorowe,
For to-day a man may be and none in the morowe.

Than spake God, full of myght, unto Iob his
frendys,
And sore rebuked them for theire unrightfull
speche,

150 Whiche thei to Iob spake by many dyvers argu-
        mentis
    Contrarye to Goddes will, as Iob did theym teche.
    Wherefore God charged them His servaunte to
        seche
    And offer for theym-selfe holocaust, without de-
        laye,
    That His servaunte for theire offence specially
        may pray.

155 After Goddes commaundement, these persons thre
    Unto Iob cam with oblacion and offerynge,
    For whom unto God Iob of his benyngnyte
    Specially for theym prayed to God a-bove lyveyng.
    God, then, of His godenesse, of all maner thynge
160 That longed to Iob be-fore, both best gode and
        lond,
    Dobyll was restoryd by His gloryous sond.

    Nowe blessid Iob here makyth a ryall feest
    To his bredren and sustren and to his frendis all.
    And everyche of theym ioyed in God, bothe most
        and leste,
165 And to Iob grete yftes gafe that weren aureall.
    And by the plesaunce of God most celestiall
    Gretter hospytalite than ever he did to-fore
    All his lyfe after kepte he ever-more.

F. 96b   And, by processe of yeres and succession,
170 X children he had by his wyfe agayne,
    VII sonnes and thre doughters, as ys made men-
        sion;
    None so fayre as the doughters in the worlde were
        sayne.
    Iob hy[m]-self here lyveyng to Goddes plesaunce,
        certayne,

An c and xl^{ti} yeres aftyr his flagellacion,
175 And sawe the fourthe degree of his generacion.

Lo! thus by processe naturall every thyng draweth
   to ende:
Dethe sparith no creature of high nor lowe degre.
Iob, in his senectute, owte of the worlde ded
   wende,
His soule with oure fore-faders there to rest and be
180 Tyll after the passion of Criste that yt plesid His
   deyte
Hym to convey with patriarkes and prophetes all
Onto the perpetuall ioy and glory eternall. Amen.

Notes to the Text

2-3] A paraphrase of *Iob* I, 1: Vir erat in terra Hus, nomine Iob, et erat vir ille simplex, et rectus, ac timens Deum, et recedens a malo; XXXI, 32: Foris non mansit peregrinus, ostium meum viatori patuit.

4] *Iob* I, 3: Eratque vir ille magnus inter omnes orientales; I, 10: Et possessio eius crevit in terra.

5-7] *Iob* I, 3: Et fuit possessio eius septem millia ovium, et tria millia camelorum, quingenta quoque igua bovum, et quingentae asinae. Note the discrepancy in the number of asses.

8-9] *Iob* I, 2: Natique sunt ei septem filii, et tres filiae.

10-14] *Iob* I, 4: Et ibant filii eius, et faciebant convivium per domos, unusquisque in die suo. Et mittentes vocabant tres sorores suas ut comederent et biberent cum eis.

15] *Iob* I, 5: Mittebat ad eos Iob, et sanctificabat illos.

21] *Hough*, 'how' (*NED*).

24-28] *Iob* I, 5: (Iob) consurgensque diluculo offerebat holocausta pro singulis. Dicebat enim: Ne forte peccaverint filii mei, et benedixerint Deo in cordibus suis.

30] *Iob* I, 7: Circuivi terram, et perambulavi eam.

31] *Or*, 'whether' (*NED*, s.v. *or* (conj.) 3b).

31-32] *Iob* I, 8: Dixitque Dominus ad eum: Numquid considerasti servum meum Iob, quod non sit ei similis in terra, homo simplex, et rectus ac timens Deum, et recedens a malo?

33-34] An abstract of *Iob* I, 10-11: Nonne tu vallasti eum, ac domum eius, universamque substantiam per circuitum, operibus manuum eius benedixisti, et possessio eius crevit in terra? Sed extende paululum manum tuam, et tange cuncta quae possidet nisi in faciem benedixerit tibi.

35] *Iob* I, 12: Dixit ergo Dominus ad Satan: Ecce, universa quae habet, in manu tua sunt: tantum in eum ne extendas manum tuam.

37-38] *Iob* I, 14-15: Boves arabant, et asinae pascebantur iuxta eos, et irruerunt Sabaei, tuleruntque omnia.

39–42] *Iob* I, 17: Chaldaei fecerunt tres turmas, et invaserunt camelos, et tulerunt eos, necnon et pueros percusserunt gladio, et ego fugi solus ut nuntiarem tibi.

40] *Ryall* written above the line.

43–47] A reference to the ravages of the Sabeans and the Chaldeans at the instigation of Satan into whose hands God had placed Job's property (*Iob* I, 12: Ecce, universa quae habet, in manu tua sunt).

48–49] *Iob* I, 16: Ignis Dei cecidit e caelo, et tactas oves puerosque consumpsit.

50] *Browght*: MS *browgh*.

50–51] The messengers are the sole survivors of the foregoing and following incidents.

51] *Mesaventure*: the form not in *NED*.

58–63] *Iob* I, 18–19: Filiis tuis et filiabus vescentibus et bibentibus vinum in domo fratris sui primogeniti, repente ventus vehemens irruit a regione deserti, et concussit quatuor angulos domus, quae corruens oppressit liberos tuos et mortui sunt.

59] *Merely*, 'perfectly' (*NED*, s.v. *mere* (a.) 4).

68–70] *Iob* I, 21: Dominus dedit, Dominus abstulit: sicut Domino placuit, ita factum est: sit nomen Domini benedictum.

71–76] *Iob* I, 20–22: Tunc surrexit Iob, et scidit vestimenta sua, et tonso capite corruens in terram, adoravit, et dixit: Nudus egressus sum de utero matris meae, et nudus revertar illuc . . . In omnibus his non peccavit Iob labiis suis.

78–84] An abstract of *Iob* II, 1–6.

85–91] An expansion of *Iob* II, 7: Egressus igitur Satan a facie Domini, percussit Iob ulcere pessimo, a planta pedis usque ad verticem eius.

90] *Yonte*, 'joint' (*NED*).

92] *Iob* II, 8: sedens in sterquilinio.

93–94] *Iob* II, 9: Dixit autem illi uxor tua: Adhuc tu permanes in simplicitate tua? Benedic Deo et morere.

97–98] *Iob* II, 10: Qui ait ad illam: Quasi una de stultis mulieribus locuta es. Si bona suscepimus de manu Dei, mala quare non suscipiamus?

106–11] *Iob* II, 11–13: Igitur audientes tres amici Iob . . . venerunt singuli de loco suo . . . Condixerant enim, ut pariter venientes visitarent eum, et consolarentur . . . et exclamantes ploraverunt scissisque vestibus sparserunt pulverem super caput suum in caelum. Et sederunt cum eo in terrra septem diebus et septem noctibus.

110] *Perverture*, 'misfortune' (not in *NED*).

112] A reference to the dialogue between Job and his three friends (*Iob* III–XXXI).

128] *Geoyst*: MS *evyst*.

130] *Seducious*, 'caused by misleading influences' (*NED*, s.v. *seducive*: earliest reference given is 1602).

133] *and so to leve*: MS *and to so to leve*.

134–40] Omnino alcior est diaboli in natura. Maior est vincenci homini gloria *etc*. (Not in Vulgate.)

134–5] Cf. *Mankind* (ed. F. J. Furnivall and A. W. Pollard, *Macro Plays*, *EETS*, e. s., XCI, 1904) ll. 280–1: Lyke as þe smyth trieth ern in þe feer, / So was he (Job) triede by Godis vysytacyon.

141–7] De nulla dona dei superbio qui sumptus ex pulvere in pulverem me reddere cognosco. (Not in Vulgate.)

148–51] *Iob* XLII, 7: Postquam autem locutus est Dominus verba haec ad Iob, dixit ad Eliphaz Themanitem: Iratus est furor meus in te, et in duos amicos tuos, quoniam, non estis locuti coram me rectum, sicut servus meus Iob. Note that in the poem God addresses Himself to all three of Job's friends together.

152–4] *Iob* XLII, 8: Sumite ergo vobis septem tauros, et septem arietes, et ite ad servum meum Iob, et offerte holocaustum pro vobis; Iob autem servus meus orabit pro vobis.

155–61] *Iob* XLII, 9–10: Abierunt . . . et fecerunt sicut locutus fuerat Dominus ad eos, et suscepit Dominus faciem Iob. Dominus quoque conversus est ad poenitentiam Iob, cum oraret ille pro amicis suis. Et addidit Dominus omnia quaecumque fuerant Iob, duplicia.

162–8] *Iob* XLII, 11: Venerunt autem ad eum omnes fratres sui, et universae sorores suae, et cuncti qui noverant eum prius, et comederunt cum eo panem in domo eius. . . . Et dederunt ei unusquisque ovem unam, et inaurem auream unam.

161] *Sond*, 'mandate, ordinance' (*NED*, s.v. *sand* (sb.) 1).

165] *Aureall*, 'made of gold' (*NED*, s.v. *aureal*: earliest reference given is 1587).

169–71] *Iob* XLII, 13: Et fuerunt ei septem filii, et tres filiae.

172] *Iob* XLII, 15: Non sunt autem inventae mulieres speciosae sicut filiae Iob in universa terra.

173] *Hym-self:* MS *hy-self*.

173–5] *Iob* XLII, 16: Vixit autem Iob post haec, centum quadraginta annis, et vidit filios suos, et filios filiorum suorum usque ad quartam generationem.

178] *Iob* XLII, 16: et mortuus est senex, et plenus dierum.

G. N. GARMONSWAY and R. R. RAYMO

8 · The Cult of Odin in Danish Place-names

In comparison with Norway and Sweden, the place-names of Denmark contain only a few reminiscences of heathen cult-centres. According to Magnus Olsen, place-names in Norway attest the existence there of no fewer than six hundred such cult-places, and Elias Wessén has given a list of well over a hundred Swedish compounds in which the names of heathen divinities are combined with words for cult-centres.[1]

In Denmark, if we restrict ourselves to material preserved from the medieval period, there are not many more than thirty certain examples containing names of heathen gods. Even so, these place-names have had far from adequate consideration from philologists, and still less have they been put to full use by historians of religion.

The most striking fact in the Danish material is that compound elements of the -*vi* type – indicating, that is, a real cult-centre with a temple-building of some sort – are not only rare, but when they do occur, they are found practically only in combination with the name of a single god – Odin.

Among the compounds of Odin and *vi* there is only one recorded with the second element in its original form. This is the name of the town on Fyn, *Odense*, written *Othenesuuigensem* in Otto III's conferment of privileges in 988,[2] *ODSVI* on coins from the reign of Knud the Great (1018–35),[3] *Odansue* in Adam of Bremen towards the end of the eleventh century,[4] and

[1] See his 'Schwedische Ortsnamen und altnordische Mythologie', *APhS* IV (1929–30), 97 ff.

[2] *Hamburgisches Urkundenbuch* I (1842), 56.

[3] P. Hauberg, *Myntforhold og Udmyntninger i Danmark indtil 1146* (1900), 196.

[4] B. Schmeidler, *Magistri Adam Bremensis Gesta Hammaburgensis Ecclesiae Pontificum* (1917), 232.

Othenswi in Ailnoth soon after 1100.[1] In contrast to these forms, however, we find already in the twelfth century spellings showing loss of *w*, a loss due to the weakening of the stress on the second element.[2] *Othensi* appears in two documents from 1104–17 and 1104–34, both preserved in transcript in the Odense-book,[3] and *othense, othensø* are found in twelfth-century entries in the *Necrologium Lundense*.[4] The form with *-ø*, which also appears in younger Danish sources,[5] shows that the ending was reinterpreted as *ø* (= island), and this is the basis for the Icelandic form, *Óðinsey*, found e.g. in *Knýtlinga saga* as an alternative to *Óðinsvé*.[6] In the *Annales Ryenses* from the end of the thirteenth century the form *Othens, Othæns* appears, with apocope of the reduced vowel of the second element.[7]

Another compound with Odin attested in very early sources is the present-day *Onsved* in Horns Herred, Sjælland. In St Knud's donation charter of 1085 it was written *Othense* – the original is not extant, but this is the form both in the copy in the *Necrologium Lundense*, made about 1123, and in the independent copy in the Lund-book from 1494.[8] In the oldest source extant in the original, a document from 1320, the name is written *Othænsweth*, and in *Danmarks Stednavne* (written DS hereafter) II 139 the name has been interpreted on the basis of this spelling and its form in the charter of 1085 ignored. In DS it is suggested: 'the final element is possibly ODan *with*, "wood(land)" '.

We must however undoubtedly interpret the name on the

---

[1] M. Cl. Gertz, *Vitae Sanctorvm Danorvm* (1908–12), 113.

[2] Cf. the woman's name, *Thyri* in the twelfth century, with the forms in Runic Danish, *þurui, þqurui*, and WN *þorvé*; see J. Brøndum-Nielsen, *Gammeldansk Grammatik* II (1932), § 388.

[3] *Diplomatarium Arna-Magnæanum* (1786), I 243.

[4] L. Weibull, *Necrologium Lundense* (1923), 70, 94.

[5] See K. Hald in *APhS* XXI (1952), 116.

[6] Carl af Petersens and Emil Olson, *Sǫgur Danakonunga* (1919–25), 80, 129, 148, 185, 233, 236.

[7] Ellen Jørgensen, *Annales Danici* (1920), 67, 70.

[8] *Necrologium Lundense*, 5. In the index to this edition this name is given as a form of the name of the town, Odense, but the context clearly shows that Onsved is meant.

basis of the form found in the oldest source, the document from 1085. The form there, Othense, can be connected with ODan -wi (or the bi-form -wæ, corresponding to WN vé)[1] but not with ODan -with. There is no need to wonder at the loss of w as early as 1085 since, as we saw above, examples of the loss of w in the town-name Odense are only a few decades younger. The replacement of the original second element -wi by -with in younger sources must depend on the analogy of other names, especially Hornswith, which in the Middle Ages and later was the name for the great tracts of forest in the district where Onsved is situated.[2] It was all the easier to make the substitution because the w in -with names also tended to disappear early. Originally, it might very well have been used only as a scribal form, even though -ved has now prevailed in pronunciation. Another point to show that there was probably confusion over the correct form of the name in the fourteenth century is the spelling Othensthweth in an original document from 1334. Here the second element has evidently been connected with names in -tved, ODan -thwet (WN þveit).

The place-names in Jutland that have been interpreted as from original Odins-vi are unfortunately first recorded only in much younger sources. There are three of them: (1) Vojens, Gram Herred, S. Jutland; 1421 Wodens. (2) Oens, Hatting Herred, N. Jutland; 1464 Odhens. (3) Oddense, Hindborg Herred, N. Jutland; 1479 Otthensæ. There can be no doubt at all that the first element in these names is the name of the god. The form in Vo- in no. 1 depends on a medieval diphthongization of ODan ō. On the other hand, however, the late recordings make it impossible to assert with complete confidence that the second element is -vi. It might represent the reduced form of some other word, and this possibility is mentioned, along with that of derivation from -vi, in the articles in DS where these names are treated.[3] There is a lake at Vojens, and the possibility

---

[1] On the relationship between wæ and wi, see J. Brøndum-Nielsen, Gammeldansk Grammatik I (2 udg., 1950), § 101.
[2] DS II 151.   [3] DS IV 390, VIII 42, IX 19.

H

of -sø, ODan *siō* (= lake), as the second element is proposed in DS. But the same explanation would not fit the terrain at *Oens* and *Oddense*, and as long as it is wished to keep the three names under one head, this suggestion must then also be rejected for *Vojens*. In DS ODan *-with* is also mentioned as a possible second element in *Oens* and *Oddense*, but in other Jutland names this word has become [-ə]|or, more often, [-ət], and since *Oens* is pronounced [u'ns] and *Oddense* [wåj'ns] there is little likelihood that they are derived from original * *Othinswith*. The same conclusion must apply in the case of *-høgh* (= (burial-) mound; WN *haugr*) as a hypothetical second element, for although this has been reduced to [-ə] or [-i] in many Jutland names, it has rarely disappeared without trace.[1] There remains only *-vi*, against which no such objections can be raised, seeing that already in the thirteenth century we find *Odense* on Fyn appearing as a two-syllable word (in *Annales Ryenses*, cf. above). Thus, all things considered, it may be said that probability favours the interpretation of all three Jutland names as compounds of *Odin* and *vi*. If this is so, we then have five original *Odins-vi* names, five cult-places of Odin, distributed among the chief districts of the ancient realm of the Danes with the exception of Skaane.

Otherwise, as I mentioned earlier, the word *vi* is hardly to be found in Denmark compounded with the names of gods. The only possible exception is *Taars* in Vendsyssel, N. Jutland, 1408 *Thorssæ, Thorssoghen, Thoorssæ, Thoorssoghen*[2] – but it is by no means certain that the name is really compounded with *-vi*.[3] The theory has also been advanced that the name of the god *Tī*, Wn *Týr*, is compounded with *-vi* in two Jutland names, *Tise, Thise* in Vendsyssel and Salling. In an original document from 1375,[4] however, the former is written *Thisæ*, a spelling

---

[1] Cf. however the district-name *Revs, Refshøgheret* in the thirteenth-century *Valdemars Jordebog.*

[2] *Gammeldanske Diplomer duplikeret til Brug for Ordbog til det ældre danske Sprog*, 1 Rk., IV 36.

[3] One might perhaps think of *-sø* as the second element here. Sørup Sø, now drained, lies at Sørup farm about 2 km. from Taars and within the same parish.

[4] *Repertorium Diplomaticum*, 1 Rk., no. 3048.

which rules out the possibility of the god's name as the first element. And the latter name is written *Tüswed* in 1503 and must consequently be an original * *Tiswith*, like *Tiset* in E. and S. Jutland.[1]

Another element combined with the name of Odin is found in Jutland names, *Onsild* and *Vonsild* (*Vognsild*). The material is as follows: (1) The district name *Onsild* with the villages (and parishes) of *Nørre-Onsild* and *Sønder-Onsild*. In Svend Aggesen at the end of the twelfth century the name is written *Othenshylle*, the form found in both the extant redactions of his work, from the sixteenth and seventeenth century respectively.[2] A document from 1215–24 (in transcript in the Aarhus-book) has *Othenshillæ*,[3] and later spellings are 1241 *Othænshyllæheret* (main list in *Valdemars Jordebog*[4]), 1255–61 *Othenshul* (papal letter, Vidimus 1403[5]), 1334 *Othenshylhæræt* (document extant in original[6]). (2) *Vognsild* (*Vonsild*), Gislum Herred, N. Jutland; 1467 *odhenshyld*.[7] (3) *Vonsild*, Nørre-Tyrstrup Herred, (previously) S. Jutland; 1462 *Odenschulde* (*Jordebog* of the Bishop of Slesvig), 1475 *Odensskyld*.[8]

The forms with *k* and *ch* in no. 3 are difficult to explain. La Cour thinks that the second element is perhaps the world *kilde* (spring, well).[9] If the second element began with *k*, however, we should expect the sound to have remained, and, since this is not the case, there is hardly sufficient cause to reject the name's association with nos. 1 and 2. The oldest forms of *Onsild* show that the second element must have been an ODan *hyllæ* or *hillæ*. A step towards the solution of the problem of this word's etymology was taken by Oluf Nielsen, when he compared it with Norw. dialectal *hilla* (= shelf).[10] It is difficult however to accept his further interpretation of the word as

[1] DS IX 30.
[2] M. Cl. Gertz, *En ny Text af Sven Aggesøns Værker* (1915), 99 f.
[3] *Diplomatarium Danicum*, 1 Rk., V no. 66.
[4] Svend Aakjær, *Valdemars Jordebog* (1927), 4.
[5] *Bullarium Danicum*, no. 505.   [6] *Diplomatarium Danicum*, 2 Rk., XI no. 132.
[7] E. Tang Kristensen, *Herregaarden Lerchenfeldt* (1889), 6.
[8] DS VIII 163.   [9] *Festskrift Johs. Steenstrup* (1915), 21.
[10] *Blandinger udg. af Universitets-Jubilæets danske Samfund* I (1881–7), 258.

'height, hill', which he arrived at by comparison with English *hill*, since the latter is Gmc. **hulni-* and thus only remotely related to the Norwegian word. Svend Aakjær, on the other hand, thinks that in combination with a god's name the word *hillæ* can have the same meaning as the related WN *hjallr*,[1] which i.a. is used of the platform or stage on which the image of a god stood (see Fritzner, s.v.), and this interpretation has been accepted by other writers, including A. Bjerrum in his article on the name in DS VIII 163 f.

It is hardly possible to decide with complete certainty whether the second element was originally *-hilla* (< PN **helþiōn*) or *hylla* (< PN **hulþiōn*). The form in Svend Aggesen suggests original *-y-*, that in the Aarhus-book an original *-i-*, while the spelling *-y-* in *Valdemars Jordebog* may indicate either *y* or *i*.[2] Assuming *hilla* to be the original form, then in accordance with the function of the *iōn*-suffix, the word can mean 'something provided with or having the appearance of a *hjallr*'.[3] It is also possible that the substantives, Norw. *hilla* and Sw. *hylla*, Dan. *hylde*, are in fact originally the same word, with *y* resulting from labialization. This explanation has been offered by Manne Eriksson[4] and supported by Valter Jansson.[5] This variation between *hilla* and *hylla* would then be paralleled by the variations between *i* and *y* in the old spellings of *Onsild*.

There are no other certain instances of *-hillæ*, *-hyllæ* in Danish place-names, whether of sacral origin or no,[6] and at all events the word as a compounding element must be counted extremely rare.[7] Because of this it would seem extremely improbable that

---

[1] *Festskrift Verner Dahlerup* (1934), 52 ff.

[2] A. Bjerrum in *Ti Afhandlinger udg. af Stednavneudvalget* (1960), 178.

[3] Cf. Valter Jansson in *Svenska Landsmål* (1942-3), 274.

[4] *Hjäll och tarre* (1943), 256.   [5] loc. cit. 277.

[6] Aakjær, *Festskrift Verner Dahlerup*, 52 f., assumes that the names *Nærild* and *Torrild* are compounds of *hilla* with the names of the gods, Njörd and Thor, derived thus from original **Niartharhilla* and **Thorhilla* respectively. The absence of the genitive ending in the latter name however, excludes the god's name as a possible first element, and the origin of *Nærild*, of which we have no record before the sixteenth century, must remain uncertain.

[7] The comparatively numerous place-names which now end in *-ild* have extremely varied origins. In some cases we have compounds with words like

the element in the place-name *Othinshillæ*, attested several times as it is, should be regarded merely as a topographical term. It must rather have had some significance in the terminology of the cult, and it is this which lies behind its comparatively frequent connexion with the name of a particular god. In other words it must, as Svend Aakjær has assumed, mean a holy place, a sanctuary of some kind.

Within the ancient realm of the Danes there is one other place-name that indicates a sacred place of Odin. This is *Onsala* in what is now the Swedish province of Halland. In *Valdemars Jordebog* it is written (*de*) *othænsale*, probably an old dat. sg. form,[1] and the latter element is best regarded as the word *sal*, which must here be used of some kind of building connected with the cult.[2] The name is thus the same as ONorw *Óðinssalr* in Trøndelag and as *Odensala* in Jämtland.[3] The Swedish *Odensala* in Uppland, on the other hand, was originally *Othinshargh*.[4] The element -*hargh* (WN *hǫrgr*) does not appear in place-names in Danish territory in combination with Odin or any other god's name.

The district name *Onsjö* in Skaane also bears witness to a public cult of Odin.[5] It was written *Othænsheret* in *Valdemars Jordebog*. The name of the well-known lake, *Odensjön*, which is situated in the district, is undoubtedly secondary and derived

---

ODan *wæl(l)* (= spring) or *wæthil* (= ford), and in others -*ild* represents an original -*ald*, either a suffix or a substantive of uncertain origin and sense. On this reference may be made e.g. to the paper by K. G. Ljunggren, 'Studier över sydsvenska ortnamn', *SSON* (1946–8), 3 ff. Ljunggren also mentions -*hillæ*, -*hyllæ* in Onsild and other names, and thinks that the same second element might be found in *Gylle* in Skaane, *Gyyllæ* in *Valdemars Jordebog*, and he is not willing to exclude the possibility that the word could be used 'more or less figuratively' of hills and slopes (loc. cit. 40). – If we regard **hylla* as a descriptive topographical term, we should doubtless bear in mind the possibility of its derivation from adj. *huld*, WN *hollr*, which like *hallr* (with different vowel-grade), might have spatial sense, 'leaning in a certain direction, sloping' (see K. Hald in *APhS* XXI (1952), 109 note 2); *hylla* would then be a variant form to ODan *hælla* (= incline, slope).

[1] Cf. J. Sahlgren in *NoB* (1937), 185.
[2] K. G. Ljunggren in *Hallands Historia* II (1959), 1060.
[3] *Norske Gaardnavne* XIV 286.
[4] J. Sahlgren in *NoB* (1947), 118.
[5] idem in *NoB* (1918), 39.

from the district name. J. Sahlgren, it is true, has suggested that *Odense Herred* on Fyn might also have been named directly after the god and not after the town *Odense*, because the spelling for it in *Valdemars Jordebog* is the same as the spelling there for *Onsjö* (*Othænsheret*, see above[1]). But, as we have seen, the town-name could be written *Othæns* in the thirteenth century, so there is no compelling reason to accept such a suggestion.

The name of the god is also to be found in a number of what were originally nature-names. A noteworthy difference between these names and names compounded with *Thor-* and *Ti-*, for example, is that Odin appears only once in combination with a word for woodland, in *Onslunda*, 1401 *Othænslundæ*, in Skaane.[2]

Other original nature-names with Odin as the first element are e.g. *Vonsbæk*, a parish-name in S. Jutland, 1413 *Odensbek*;[3] *Onsbjerg*, a parish-name on Samsø, 1424 *Othensberg*;[4] and *Vonsmose*, a farm-name in S. Jutland, 1417 *Odhensmose*.[5] Compounds such as *Vojenshøj*,[6] *Onskilde* and others occur among Danish field-names, but the association of some of them with Odin is uncertain because early evidence of their form is lacking.

The relationship between Odinic cult and nature-names such as these is far from clear. A name like *Onslunda* is most likely to be the memorial of an ancient and primitive cult-place, as is the case with corresponding names compounded with *Frø-*, *Thor-*, and *Ti-*. It is more doubtful if this is also true of names in *-høj* and *-bjerg*. A legend recorded from Småland in Sweden in 1690 shows that people believed that Odin lived in a certain mountain,[7] and Ellekilde holds that people in Denmark similarly believed that Odin lived in Møns Klint.[8] Beliefs of this kind could obviously have given rise to names like *Odinsbjerg* and *Odinshøj*, and, strictly speaking, such nature-

---

[1] *NoB* (1920), 57.
[2] A. Falkman, *Ortnamnen i Skåne* (1877), 70.
[3] DS IV 167.   [4] DS I 48.   [5] DS IV 84.   [6] DS III 188.
[7] Quoted by H. Ellekilde in *Nordens Gudeverden* I (1926), 463 f.
[8] H. Ellekilde, *Odinsjægeren paa Møn* (Danske Folkeminder, Udvalgte Afhandlinger, 1961), 55 ff.

names need not belong to a real heathen period at all, any more than the other nature-names in which the name of the god figures. A possible instance of a post-heathen place-name compounded with OE Wōden is *Wansdyke*, the famous earthwork in SW. England. The name is first recorded, as *Wodnes dic*, in 903,[1] so there can be no doubt about the derivation, but it need not go back to pagan times. The earthwork could have been called 'Woden's dyke' simply because it was a venerable and impressive relic of antiquity which might fittingly be attributed to the chief heathen god. A similar example is doubtless to be found in *Torsburgen*, Old Gutnish *þorsborg*, on Gotland, the name of Scandinavia's biggest defensive work, probably built in the Migration Age.

More striking than the nature-names compounded with Odin are the comparatively many Danish names which directly refer to the sacred places of the god. As we saw above, there are probably five instances of *Odinsvi*, as against only one (uncertain) **Thorsvi* and no other cases at all of -*vi* compounded with other gods' names. There are three examples – or four if *Nørre Onsild* and *Sønder Onsild* are counted separately – of Odin compounded with -*hillæ*, -*hyllæ*, an element not otherwise found with divine names. There is probably one instance of -*sal* connected with Odin's name, but otherwise no example of a god's name with this as the second element. Finally, there is one district-name with Odin as the first element. The only other Danish district-name compounded with the name of a god is *Frøs Herred* in S. Jutland.[2]

The Danish place-name material of sacral significance is in itself comparatively small, but the summary just given shows that we can at any rate draw one important conclusion for the history of religion from it. It is that a single god, Odin, played a completely dominant role in the public cult. It was Odin who was worshipped in the *vi* and the temples, while the old

---

[1] A. Philippson, *Germanisches Heidentum bei den Angelsachsen* (1929), 156 f. Cf. also A. H. Smith, *EPNE*, II 272.

[2] K. Hald, *Vore Stednavne* (1950), 219; differently e.g. DS IV 498.

divinities of fertility, worshipped by the ordinary farming population, had to be content with primitive cult-places out in woods and groves.[1] Such concentration on the cult of a single god is unparalleled in the other Scandinavian countries. This predominance must be closely related to the social structure of Denmark in the Migration Age and succeeding centuries, a period in which we may conceive a concentration of political power and intellectual culture amongst the aristocratic families of the chieftains. In this connexion it is worth noting that amongst the West Germanic peoples who lived nearest the Danes in the Migration Age, i.e. the Angles and the Saxons, the Odinic faith was also dominant, at least amongst the aristocracy. Woden figures as the progenitor of all the Anglo-Saxon royal houses, with the sole exception of the dynasty of Essex.[2]

It is difficult to be sure what importance this concentration in Danish paganism may have had for religious developments in the following period. It seems by no means unlikely, for example, that the complete dominance of a single god in the public cult was of great significance in bringing about the relatively painless transition to the new monotheistic religion, Christianity. A factor that was perhaps of still greater importance was the close association between the cult of Odin and the royal power in the last pagan centuries. In connexion with this I may mention a piece of evidence which has not, I think, so far been adduced. The only villages in Sjælland whose names ended in -vi are Onsved in Horns Herred, mentioned above, and a place Winnincgawe (the name now lost) in Vindinge parish, Tune Herred.[3] Like Onsved, the latter name also occurs in St Knud's charter of 1085, so that we may be certain that in the eleventh century these two vi-places, both lying close to the ancient royal seat of Lejre, were wholly or partly the property of the king. And it is reasonable to think that this

[1] Cf. Hald, Vore Stednavne, 223. In this book I have given in brief and popular form some of the same ideas as are developed in the present paper.

[2] E. A. Philippson, op. cit. 147 f.

[3] K. Hald in APhS XXI (1952), 111.

royal ownership goes back to pagan times, not much more than a century away.

It is generally agreed that in the conversion of the Scandinavian peoples to Christianity an essential part was played by the royal power.[1] If all other evidence of the truth of this were lacking, we could still in the case of Denmark point to the words of King Harald Blue-tooth inscribed on the great Jelling stone, where he describes himself as *sa haraltr ias saʀ uan tanmaurk ala auk nuruiak auk tani karpi kristna* – that Harald who won for himself the whole of Denmark, and Norway, and made the Danes Christian. There can be no doubt but that in pre-Christian times the kings had played an equally essential part in the cult of Odin, which, as the place-names show, was the 'official' and 'higher' religion of the Danes.

KR. HALD

[1] See especially Helge Ljungberg, *Den nordiska religionen och kristendomen* (1938), 60 ff.

9 · A newly discovered rune-stone in Törnevalla church, Östergötland

One day early in September 1960 the report reached me that the caretaker of the church at Törnevalla in Östergötland had noticed some incised lines on one of the foundation stones of the church-tower. The stone was at the base of the west wall of the tower and part of it had just been uncovered when work was begun on repairing the steps at the tower-door. It was essential to see if this was a rune-stone that had been discovered and I set out at once for Törnevalla. The place lies in the middle of the Östergötland plain, 125 miles southwest of Stockholm, 7 miles eastnortheast of Linköping, the province's ancient centre for cult and commerce.

If I dared entertain the hope that the incised lines might turn out to be runes, it was because three rune-stones had already come to light in this church. The biggest of the three had been dug out seventy years ago from the south wall of the tower, where it had been placed as a foundation stone when the handsome tower was built some time in the twelfth century. Now I was to see whether the builders had selected another rune-stone from the neighbourhood to do duty in the foundations of the west wall as well.

The foundation stone under the west wall proved to be a good deal bigger than I had imagined. The stone was nearly 15 feet long and reached right from the southwest corner of the tower to underneath the entrance steps, now partly removed (Plate IV). And it was on this stone that the massive wall rested – a wall which seemed to me as I stood at its base to reach a dizzy height up towards the clouds. For a moment I hoped – may

God forgive me this blasphemous thought – that I should find that the lines noticed by the eagle-eyed caretaker were not runes at all. True enough, I had in the course of years removed a good many stones from church walls and house foundations, but this job looked altogether more menacing – and would certainly be expensive for the Central Office of National Antiquities.

After cleaning the parts of the stone that projected from the wall and were now available for inspection, it could be said at once that here was a completely unknown rune-stone (Plate IV). But all that was visible on the uncovered part was a short section of the rune ribbon, with some carved lines above it towards the top of the stone. Practically the whole of the inscription was thus still hidden under the wall. It was also possible to see that the pressure of the wall had broken the stone into five larger pieces.

What could possibly be said in favour of trying to get the stone out? The inscribed surface faced upwards – it might well be crushed and the inscription completely destroyed. (The use of the stone with the inscribed face upwards was doubtless because this side presented a more even surface.) Would it not be better to leave it where it was and let posterity do the work – if posterity was interested?

What happened was, of course, what usually happens. After a spell of unusually hard labour the stone stood repaired and raised by the southwest corner of the tower, just by the place where it had first been found (Plate V).

Grey granite with an uneven surface. Height 425 cm. Once it was clearly still higher because a projecting part at the bottom end has been split off while it lay at the base of the tower (see Plate IV). Height above ground 342 cm., width in the middle 130 cm. The runes themselves are 10–11 cm. high. The inscribed surface has partly flaked away with the sad loss of the beginning of the inscription, now not to be restored. A large piece at the top left shoulder of the stone has been struck off. This must have been done when it was put into use as a foundation stone for the tower. This damage done eight centuries ago has caused the loss of part of the picture inscribed on the stone's upper surface.

Since the rune-stone was removed so soon, already in the twelfth century, from its original site and has lain ever since more or less completely hidden under the wall, it might be thought likely that some trace of its original painting would be preserved. Traces of colour have been found in recent years on numerous stones in similar positions. But not a single sign of colour was visible on the Törnevalla stone. It must have stood long enough on its original site to lose all its original paint through the action of wind and weather.

Parts of the inscription are difficult to read. Runes that are so damaged as to be indecipherable are marked in the following by short dashes:

> **. . . - - -a : oliʀ : ristu : stin : þins- : iftiʀ · trik · aukis :**
>   5   10   15   20   25   30   35
>
> **sun : kilta : sin :**
> 40   45

As I said earlier, flaking of the surface has damaged the beginning of the inscription. There is however no need to think that much has been lost. In all probability the rune-carver wished his rune-ribbon to start and end at the same level on the stone. In that case, only an introductory division mark (like a colon) and a single rune have disappeared before the first extant symbol.

Although the total loss is thus small, it is still much to be regretted, for it means that the immediately following runes, much damaged as they are, cannot be reconstructed with any certainty. If we had a clearly defined rune at the beginning of the inscription, there would be some chance of puzzling out what was meant by the half-destroyed symbols (1–4 in the sequence).

The meaning of symbols 5–8 in the sequence, **oliʀ**, is also obscure. It may be that the rune-writer intended it to stand for the personal name *Ølvi*ʀ, *Alvi*ʀ, a name found on six Swedish rune-stones of the Viking Age and known elsewhere as well.

But it must be noted on the one hand that the 'spelling' is peculiar, and on the other hand that it is by no means certain that the inscription began with personal names (the verb is in the plural). Indeed, in this particular case there is good reason to consider the possibility that the men who caused the stone to be raised referred to themselves at the outset by a collective term. I shall return to this below.

The name given to the men who commissioned the stone thus remains a mystery, but fortunately we have full information about the man in whose memory this imposing monument was set up: **iftiʀ · trik · aukis : sun : kilta : sin :** *æftiʀ Dræng, Øygæiʀs(?) sun, gilda sinn.* There are three words in this part of the inscription which merit discussion.

The name of the dead man was *Drængʀ*. It is noteworthy that this word is otherwise unknown as a man's name in the whole of the extensive personal name material available in the Viking Age runic inscriptions of Sweden.[1] In the medieval period too the name was very rare in the East Norse area. In medieval Norway, on the other hand, it was quite common, and it is also found in Old English sources.

Some elucidation of the name is given by the context in which it occurs in the eddaic poem, *Rígsþula*. As is known, this poem, full of interest for the history of Norse culture, gives an allegorical description of the origin of the different classes of society: of the thralls, the free landowning yeomen and the chieftains. In his wanderings Rígr visits three families and the poet gives us lively glimpses of their very different living conditions; he also gives lists of personal names appropriate for members of the different social groups. (It is undoubtedly because of these lists of names that the poem is called a *þula.*)

After Rígr has visited the poor and wretched home of the thralls, he comes to a comfortable and well-appointed house –

---

[1] The personal name **treke** appeared on a rune-stone from Gräsgård, Öland, now unfortunately lost (S. Söderberg and E. Brate, *Ölands runinskrifter* (1900–6), no. 16). This is best interpreted as *Drængi*, a biform to *DrængR*. Four instances of the name *Drænge* are known from Östergötland in the fourteenth century, all of them referring to the same man.

kom hann at hǫllu. The son born to the housewife nine months after Rígr has stayed there is given the significant name of Karl. He was 'red and ruddy with flashing eyes'. Karl tames oxen, builds houses and barns, ploughs his fields. He marries a woman of his own class and their sons receive names fitting for free men and landowning yeomen:

> Bǫrn ólu þau,
> biuggu ok unðu,
> hét Halr ok Drengr,
> Haulðr, þegn ok Smiðr,
> Breiðr, Bóndi,
> Bundinskeggi,
> Búi ok Boddi,
> Brattskeggr ok Seggr.

It is of course the appearance of the name *Drengr* amongst these that interests us most here. Of the others we have certain instances of *þegn*, *Bóndi*, *Búi* and *Smiðr* in eleventh-century Swedish runic inscriptions. Like *DrængR*, all these names must of course originally have been nicknames, signifying that their owners belonged to an influential social group.

DrængR is identical with the appellative *drængR*, well known in inscriptions from the Rök stone onwards. The word especially appears as a term of honour applied to the dead man (**trik kuþan; kuþa + treka; harþa + kuþon : trok**, etc.). The appellative is also found in English place-names.[1]

The Törnevalla stone also tells us whose son *DrængR* was: he was **aukis : sun.**

It is unfortunately not altogether easy to be sure what name the rune-carver intended to reproduce in this instance, and the spelling evidently gave him some trouble. Of the various interpretations that may be offered, however, that which has most to commend it is that he wished to give the genitive of the name *ØygæiRR*. If this is so, he has then omitted an R-rune, carving

---

[1] A. H. Smith, *EPNE* I 136.

aukis instead of **aukiʀs**. A parallel to such a spelling of -*gæiʀs* is offered by a name-form on a rune-stone at Bro church, Uppland, where the inscription begins: **kinluk x hulmkis x tutiʀ** (*Ginnlaug Holmgæiʀs dottiʀ*).[1] Here, then, we find -*gæiʀs* reproduced as **-kis,** and we can consequently by no means exclude the possibility that the carver of the Törnevalla stone spelt the second element of *Øygæiʀs* in the same way. This assimilation of *ʀs* also occurs in an eleventh-century Gotland inscription: gen. *Roþgais* for *Roþgaiʀs*.[2]

The personal name *ØygæiʀR* is otherwise known on only three rune-stones, all from Uppland. Two of the instances refer to the same man.[3] The name was evidently a rare one in the Viking Age. On the Uppland stones the name is written **aykaiʀ,** with **ai** for *æi* in the second element. On the Törnevalla stone the writer uses **i** for *æi*: **ristu** (*ræistu*), **stin** (*stæin*, acc.) and presumably **-kis** (-*gæiʀs*) where the Uppland stones show **-ai-.**

But the most interesting item in the Törnevalla inscription is found in its last two words, runes 40–47: **kilta : sin :**

Here we undoubtedly have the substantive *gildi*, m. 'guild-brother'. The phrase implies not only that *DrængR* had been a member of a guild but also that it was the guild-brethren who caused his impressive monument to be inscribed and set up. This scrap of information is a valuable contribution to our knowledge of ancient Swedish culture. The country's internal conditions in this period are little known: the sources are defective, terse, their meaning often obscure. We may rejoice over any word that can cast a ray of light through the gloom.

We know then who commissioned the stone. It was the members of the guild-fraternity who *ræistu stæin þennsa æftiʀ Dræng, Øygæiʀs*(?) *sun, gilda sinn* ('. . . raised this stone in memory of Dräng, Öger's son, their guild-brother').

The Törnevalla stone can now be seen against another

---

[1] E. Wessén and Sven B. F. Jansson, *Upplands runinskrifter* III (1949–51), no. 617.

[2] Sven B. F. Jansson and E. Wessén, *Gotlands runinskrifter* I (1962), no. 111.

[3] E. Wessén and Sven B. F. Jansson, *Upplands runinskrifter* III (1949–51), nos. 723, 724.

background. There are three other stones on which the word *gildi* occurs, two from Uppland, one from Östergötland. The sites of these stones are not without significance: both the Uppland inscriptions are from Sigtuna, the Östergötland one is from Bjälbo.

Sigtuna, situated on a sheltered inlet of Mälaren, was founded *c.* 1000 by Olov Skötkonung, and it succeeded the once so rich and powerful Birka as the commercial centre of the Swedes. Over thirty rune-stones have been found there – the number a telling witness in itself of the town's importance in the eleventh century.

Bjälbo, well known in Swedish history as the dynastic home of Birger Jarl, lies near Skänninge, one of Sweden's oldest townships and from prehistoric times a trading centre for the western districts of Östergötland. Bjälbo lies about 30 miles westsouthwest of Törnevalla

The oldest parts of Bjälbo church are undoubtedly from the eleventh century. For the foundations of its vestry a huge rune-stone was employed. This was dug out twenty-five years ago and is nearly as tall as the Törnevalla stone (Plate VI). It too is a memorial raised by men who called the dead man **kilta + sin** – 'their guild-brother'. The part of the inscription that interests us here reads: **trikiaR + risþu + stin + þisi + aft + krib kilta + sin** . . . *DrængiaR ræispu stæin þennsi aft Græip, gilda sinn* (' "Comrades" raised this stone to the memory of Grep, their guild-brother.')

The Bjälbo stone was thus raised by the guild-brethren, who refer to themselves by the collective term **trikiaR,** *drængiaR*. This makes an interesting link with the Törnevalla stone, where the name of the dead man was itself *DrængR*. It seems not unlikely that the men who raised the stone in his memory would also have described themselves by a collective term with the sense of guild-brethren. But, as was said earlier, the problem cannot be solved because of the damage at the beginning of the inscription.

Neither do the two inscriptions from Sigtuna begin with per-

The Törnevalla stone in position as a foundation stone under
the west wall of the tower

First investigation of the partly uncovered stone

PLATE IV

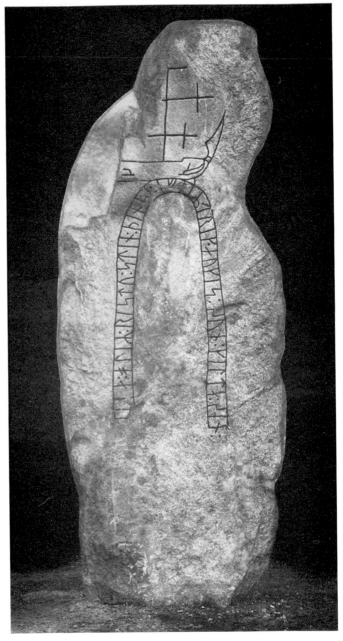

PLATE V   The Törnevalla stone, repaired and raised

PLATE VI   The Bjälbo stone

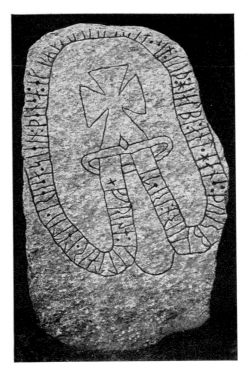

Rune-stone from Sigtuna

Inscription on a natural block of stone, Sigtuna

PLATE VII

sonal names. These stones, both carved by the same man, were commissioned by men who called themselves **frisa : kiltar**, *frisa gildaʀ*. One of them reads thus:[1] *Frisa gildaʀ letu ræisa stæin þennsa æftiʀ Þorkil, gilda sinn. Guð hialpi and hans. Þorbiorn risti.* ('The guild-brethren of the Frisians had this stone raised to the memory of Torkel, their guild-brother. God help his soul. Torbjörn cut [the runes].') This rune-stone (Plate VII) was discovered eighty years ago in the foundations of a thirteenth-century monastery building.

The other runic inscription commissioned by the guild-brethren of the Frisians is still on its original site. The runes are cut on a natural block near the middle of the town, and it may be plausibly conjectured that it stands on or near the site used by the guild of the Frisians itself. The inscription reads: *Frisa gildaʀ letu rista runaʀ þessaʀ æftiʀ Alboð, felaga Sloða. Kristr hinn hælgi hialpi and hans. Þorbiorn risti.* ('The guild-brethren of the Frisians had these runes cut to the memory of Albod, Slode's partner. Holy Christ help his soul. Torbjörn cut [the runes].') See Plate VII.

These three inscriptions, discovered and deciphered long since, prove the existence of guilds in Sigtuna and Bjälbo. The newly discovered Törnevalla stone makes a most welcome addition to their number.

It is perhaps not going too far to suggest that a personal name on another rune-stone from Törnevalla is also relevant in this connexion. This stone was raised in memory of a man named **farþakn**, *Farþegn*. This name was evidently rare in the Viking Age. I know it from only two other rune-stones, one at Jättendal church in Hälsingland, one from Njurunda parish in Medelpad. Both examples thus belong to the north country.[2] The meaning of the name is obvious: it was applied to a wayfarer, a traveller. *Farþegn* must have signified much the same as Icelandic

---

[1] E. Wessén and Sven B. F. Jansson, *Upplands runinskrifter* III (1949–51), no. 379.

[2] Other instances are known from medieval sources, most of them also from the northern provinces. (The names *Farði, Fale*, best explained as hypocoristic forms of *Farþegn*, are also predominantly northern.) *Farþegn* is also known from medieval Norway and Denmark.

I

fardrengr, farmaðr,[1] words designating a widely travelled man. In *Skáldskaparmál* Snorri says:[2]

Drengir heita ungir menn búlausir, meðan þeir afla sér fiár eða orðstír,[3] *þeir fardrengir, er milli landa fara.*

It is at least possible that the name *Farþegn*, meaning a traveller, a merchant, borne by a man from Törnevalla, has some association with the activity of the 'Törnevalla guild'.

This brings us to the question of what function was exercised by the guilds whose existence is thus demonstrated by the stones at Bjälbo, Sigtuna and Törnevalla.

The guild of the Frisians in Sigtuna must clearly have been a merchants' guild, *gilda mercatoria*. It is reasonable to assume that the 'Bjälbo guild' and the 'Törnevalla guild' were of a similar kind. Both the Östergötland guilds were probably composed of well-to-do yeomen who engaged in trade as well as farming.

The oldest evidence we have of the existence of a guild anywhere in Scandinavia is found in the Bjälbo inscription, probably carved at the beginning of the eleventh century. The Törnevalla stone appears to be somewhat younger than this, and the Sigtuna stones belong to the second half of the eleventh century. The new-found inscription at Törnevalla now enables us to say that already in this last period of the Viking Age at least two guilds were active in Östergötland, one in a central district of the province (near Linköping), the other in its western part (near Skänninge).

In conclusion I must mention the picture that appears on the upper part of the Törnevalla stone. Despite the damage done to it centuries ago (see p. 112), it is clear that it represents a ship. The mast and sail have been given the form of a so-called

---

[1] The name *Farmaðr* is found on a rune-stone from Södermanland (E. Brate and E. Wessén, *Södermanlands runinskrifter* (1924–36), no. 229).

[2] *SnE* 186.

[3] In Runic Swedish the use of the word *drængR* is not confined to 'young men without estates'.

'crossed cross'. There can be no doubt but that *Drængʀ* and his guild-brethren were Christian.

The ship and its rigging appear in almost heraldic guise. It is perhaps not too bold a conjecture to suggest that in this ship we have the badge of the Törnevalla guild.

A picture of a ship also figures on the Stratomta rune-stone, erected in the same parish immediately to the southwest of Törnevalla church. We may wonder whether it is pure coincidence that two rune-stones of about the same date and from the same locality are both decorated with pictures of a ship. Dare we see in the Stratomta ship – as we did in the personal name *Farþegn* – an association with the trading voyages of the guild we now know to have existed at Törnevalla?

SVEN B. F. JANSSON

10 · The Anglo-Saxon Unicorn

In the British Museum manuscript Cotton Julius A.II, Latin *unicornis* is glossed *anhyrned deor*, with this added comment taken from Isidore of Seville (*Etymologiarum* XII, 2, 12):

> Þæt deor hæfþ ænne horn bufan þam twam eagum, swa strangne and swa scearpne þæt he fiht wið þone myclan ylp, and hine bewundaþ on ðære wambe oþ deað. He hatte eac *rinoceron* and *monoceron*.[1]

From this description we learn that to the unknown glossator the unicorn was identical with the large quadruped today called the Indian rhinoceros (*Rhinoceros unicornis*). Nowhere in Anglo-Saxon literature do we find any reference to the fabulous beast of Pliny which was later to become not only a heraldic device but oddly enough also a symbol of virginity. The unicorn is mentioned only in the few extant interlinear Anglo-Saxon psalters, in the metrical Paris Psalter[2] and in four contemporary

[1] T. Wright, *Anglo-Saxon and Old English Vocabularies* (ed. R. P. Wülker, 1884), col. 319 f.

[2] The following printed Psalter editions have been used: G. Oess, *Der altenglische Arundelpsalter* (1909); K. Wildhagen, *Der Cambridge-Psalter* (1910); F. Harsley, *Eadwine's Canterbury Psalter* (1889); E. Brenner, *Der altenglische Junius-Psalter* (1908); U. Lindelöf, *Der Lambeth-Psalter* (1909); J. Wright and R. L. Ramsay, *Liber Psalmorum* (1907) – for the Paris Psalter; G. P. Krapp, *The Paris Psalter and the Meters of Boethius* (1932); F. Roeder, *Der altenglische Regius-Psalter* (1904); C. and K. Sisam, *The Salisbury Psalter* (1959); John Spelman, *Psalterium Davidis Latino-Saxonicum vetus* (1640), checked against manuscript Stowe 2, now in the British Museum; J. Stevenson, *Anglo-Saxon and Early English Psalters* (1843, 1847) – for the Surtees Psalter, of which G. K. Anderson, *The Literature of the Anglo-Saxons* (1949), 366, makes two OE Psalters, 'Lindisfarne' and 'Sarum'; H. Sweet, *The Oldest English Texts* (1885) – for the Vespasian Psalter. In addition, through the good offices of G. I. Bonner, Assistant Keeper of Manuscripts, British Museum, I have been able to obtain the corresponding glosses in manuscripts Cotton Tiberius C. VI and Cotton Vitellius E. XVIII, both utilized by Wildhagen for his edition of the Cambridge Psalter.

glosses. But these do not all render the Latin term in the same way. Indeed, the resulting loan-translations illustrate in an interesting way, the ease with which Old English was able to create adequate terms for new concepts out of the native linguistic material.

The glosses reprinted in Thomas Wright, *Anglo-Saxon and Old English Vocabularies*, include the above quotation as well as these two entries: 'Unicornis, vel monoceros, vel rinoceros, *anhyrne deor*' (Bishop Ælfric's Vocabulary), which appears as *anhurne deo[r]* in a twelfth-century redaction, and 'Monoceros, *anhyrne*' (MS Cotton Cleopatra A.III).[1] Among the Blickling Glosses, which have actually been excerpted from the unpublished Blickling Psalter, we find 'unicornis, *anhyrnede*' (Psalm 91, 11).[2] The metrical Paris Psalter has *anhornan* (MS *on hornan*) *ealra gelicast* 77, 68 and *anhorna ealra gelicost* 91, 9, whose *anhorna* obviously stands for *anhornan* as in the earlier verse; Eadwine, which copies Paris 90, 15–95, 2, has instead *ænhornæ eælræ gelicæst* 91, 10. The interlinear glosses to the four psalms of the Vulgate which mention the unicorn are as follows:

Psalm 21, 22 (a cornibus unicornium/unicornuorum):

Arundel	fram anhyrne deora
Cambridge	fram hornum anhyrnera
Eadwine	from horne þes anhornede
Junius	from hornum anhyrnera
Lambeth	fram hornum anhyrnendra
Paris	of þam hornum þara anhyrna
Regius	fram hornum anhyrnendra
Salisbury	fram anhyrnan
Spelman	fram hornum anhyrnendra
Surtees	fram hornum an-hyrnera
Vespasian	fram hornum anhyrnera
Tiberius	fram hornum anhyrnedra
Vitellius	fram hornum anhyrnedra deora

[1] op. cit. cols. 118, 543, 447.
[2] R. Morris, *The Blickling Homilies of the Tenth Century* (1874–80), I 254.

Psalm 28, 6 (filius unicornium/unicornuorum):

Arundel	sunu anhyrnra
Cambridge	bearn anhyrneráá (MS anhyrne ráá)
Eadwine	beærn ænhyrnedes diores
Junius	sunu anhyrnra
Lambeth	sunu anhyrnedra
Paris	þæs deores bearn, þe unicornus hatte
Regius	sunu anhyrnede
Salisbury	sunu anhyrne
Spelman	bearn anhyrnendra
Surtees	sunu an-hyrnra
Vespasian	sunu anhyrnra
Tiberius	sunu anhyrnra
Vitellius	sunu anhyrnede vel[1] anhyrnra[1]

Psalm 77, 69 (unicornis sanctificium/sanctificationem):

Arundel	anhyrnedra halignesse
Cambridge	anhyrnera gehalgunge
Eadwine	anhornæ halignesse
Junius	anhyrnra gehalgunge
Lambeth	anhyrned deor his haligdom
Regius	anhyrnedra halignesse
Salisbury	anhyrnede halira
Spelman	anhyrnendra halignysse
Surtees	an-hyrnra gehalgunge
Vespasian	anhyrnra gehalgunge
Tiberius	anhyrnede
Vitellius	anhyrnede anhyrna gehalg[ ][2]

Psalm 91, 10 (unicornis cornu meum):

Arundel	onhirnede horn min
Cambridge	anhyrnys horn min
Junius	anhornes horn min
Lambeth	anhyrnedes deores min horn
Regius	anhyrnede horn min

[1] In a different hand.

[2] *Anhyrna* may be a correction of *anhyrnede*; the final syllable of *gehalg*[ ] is missing.

Salisbury	anhyrne hor min
Spelman	anhyrnende horn min
Surtees	an-hornes horn min
Vespasian	anhornes horn min
Tiberius	anhyrnede horn
Vitellius	anhyrnede horn

Only one of the above glossators appears to have been at a loss how to render *unicornuorum*, namely the monk who paraphrased Paris 28, 6 as *þæs deores bearn þe unicornus hatte*, in which the genitive *þæs deores* is the antecedent of the relative clause containing *unicornus*. All the others have etymologized the two elements of *unicornis* correctly and come up with acceptable English coinages even though at times the syntax of a phrase may be problematical. Some have contented themselves with merely transliterating the Latin term into *ānhorn(a)* as in *anhornes* (Junius, Surtees, Vesp. 91) or *anhorna(n)* (Paris 77, 91) and *ænhornæ* (Eadwine 91), as did the Old High German monk who in the same situation coined *einhurno* (MHG *einhorn, einhurne, einhürne*, ModG *Einhorn, Einhörner*). Eadwine alone uses the syntactically ambiguous *þes anhornede* 21, which like *hornede* in *hornede nædran*[1] is an *-ede* (< WGmc *-ōdi*) extension of *horn*, otherwise not recorded until 1300 (*NED*, which however lists neither OE form); *hornede* occurs also as the first element of the Essex place-name *Hornchurch*, which is *Hornedechirche* 1291.[2] More common is the past participle *hyrned*, corresponding to *hurnid* in OS *hōh-hurnid* 'with large horns' and ON *hyrndr* 'horned'; its infinitive *hyrnan* 'provide with horns' < WGmc *hurnjan* (OHG *hurnen*) is unrecorded in OE but an eleventh-century charter has the present tense form *hyrnð* in the specialized sense 'juts out like a horn'.[3] It occurs in the compound *hyrned-nebba* 'horny-billed' (Brunanburh 61–62: *ðone sweartan hræfn,*

---

[1] S. Rypin, *Three Old English Prose Texts* (1924), 19.
[2] P. H. Reaney, *The Place-names of Essex* (EPNS XII, 1935), 112 f.; A. H. Smith, *EPNE* I 262.
[3] J. M. Kemble, *Codex diplomaticus ævi saxonici* (1839–48), IV 92: Ærest andlang ðæs streames on ðone mædham ðe hyrnð into Scylftune.

hyrnednebban – *hyrnet nebban* D, and Judith 212: *earn . . . hyrned-nebba*),[1] which may be either a weak noun or a weak form of the unrecorded strong adj. *hyrned-neb* (so Zupitza and Grein); further in *ofer-hyrned* (Rune Poem 4: [*ur*] *byþ . . . oferhyrned*),[2] which Bosworth-Toller and Hall translate 'having horns above' but Dickins interprets as 'having great horns', with *ofer-* as an intensifying prefix (cf. OS *hōh-hurnid* above), and in *gehyrnedræ* (Junius 97, 6: *stefne beman gehyrnedræ* – voce tubæ corneæ). It is combined with *ān* in the above *anhyrned deor* 'one-horned animal' and in the Lambeth gloss (77, 69) *anhyrned deor his*, a periphrastic genitive translating *unicornis*; further in *ænhyrnedes diores* (Eadwine 28), *anhyrnedes deores* (Lambeth 91), *sunu anhyrnede* (Regius, Vitellius 28), *anhyrnede horn* (Regius, Tiberius, Vitellius 91), *onhirnede horn* (Arundel 91), *anhyrnede halira* (Salisbury 77), *anhyrnede* (Tiberius 77), *anhyrnede anhyrna gehalg*[   ] (Vitellius 77), and in the gen. pl. *anhyrnedra* (Lambeth, Tiberius 28, Arundel, Regius 77), *anhyrnedra deora* (Vitellius 21). *Anhyrned* survived into ME as *an-hurnde* and *an-ihurnde* (Seinte Marherete, pp. 16 f.: *þe anhurnde hornes*, Royal MS, *þe an-ihurnde hornes*, Bodleian MS).[3] Other compounds with *hyrned* are *þryhyrnede* 'triangular', *sixhernede* 'sexangular', and *eahtahyrnede* 'octagonal'. We may compare OHG *gahurnit*, MHG *gehürnt*, *gehurnet* 'horned', and ON *einhyrndr* 'one-horned' (ModI *einhyrndur*) as well as the ON noun *einhyrningr*, ModI *einhyrningur*, ModSw *enhörning*.

The two glosses *anhyrne* and *anhyrne deor* cited above are interesting, though somewhat ambiguous, in terms of word-formation. According to Bosworth-Toller the first *anhyrne* is a noun, the second an adjective, but Hall recognizes only the noun, apparently taking the adjective to be a variant of *anhyrned* with which he equates it; this can hardly be correct in view of the other examples of the adjective in the Psalters. A noun *anhyrne* would parallel the above *anhorn(a)* as a compound

---

[1] E. v. K. Dobbie, *The Anglo-Saxon Minor Poems* (1942), 19.
[2] ibid., 28, 153 f.
[3] F. M. Mack, *Seinte Marherete* (1934).

of *ān* and the weak feminine *hyrne* 'horn, corner, angle', of which there are several instances in Bosworth-Toller;[1] it corresponds to ON *hyrne* < PGmc **hurnjōn*, ModSw *hörna* by the side of *hörn* < Osw (and ONorw) *hyrne* < PGmc **hurnja-* (Hellquist). In Paris (21) and Vitellius (77) *anhyrna* appears to be this noun in the strong gen. pl., unless it developed from *anhyrnena* through haplology (see below). All other Psalter forms of *anhyrne* show unmistakable adjectival inflexion: *anhyrnra* (gen. pl., Arundel, Surtees, Vesp., Tiberius, Vitellius 28, Junius, Surtees 77) and *anhyrnan* (Salisbury 21); only *fram anhyrne deora* (Arundel 21) is ambiguous – it looks like an uninflected adjective. Like *þreohyrne* 'triangular' (Leechdoms l. 316: *Ðæt sæd byþ þreohyrne*), *anhyrne* is a bahuvrīhi compound. Some of these formations have as their second element a noun, e.g. *mildheort* 'gentle', but others are adjectival *-ja* stems like *ānfēte* 'one-footed', *twibēte* (also *twibōte*) 'subject to double compensation', *fēowersciete* 'four-cornered', *fīfflēre* 'five-storied', *twispræce* 'double-tongued', *fægerwyrde* 'smooth-speaking', etc.[2] Since OE possesses such noun doublets as *scēat–*sciete*,[3] *word–wyrde*, and *horn–hyrne*, the second elements of these particular compounds may, at least theoretically, be the *i*-mutated nouns rather than the corresponding adjectives. Yet we seem to have three instances of an independent OE adjective *hyrne*, namely in Psalm 97, 6, whose 'uoce tubæ corneæ' is glossed *stefne hornes hyrnes* (Surtees, Vesp.) and *stefne hornys hyrnys* (Cambridge). Sweet and Wildhagen interpret these as syncopated variants of *hyrnenes*, which I think is both questionable and unnecessary. It is true that we have such conclusive but rare cases of haplology (the handbooks do not even report them) as *stænan* and *stēnan* for *stænenan* in two Anglo-Saxon charters,[4] but in view of the large number of analogous *-ja* stems in OE, an adjective *hyrne* 'of horn' would be a normal formation. It would of course be synonymous with *hyrnen* (like

---

[1] It is also a place-name element, see A. H. Smith, *EPNE* I 276.

[2] F. Kluge, *Nominale Stammbildungslehre* (1926), 88 f.; J. Wright, *Old English Grammar* (1925), §§ 434, 641.

[3] A. H. Smith, *EPNE* II 102 f., 108 f.

[4] J. M. Kemble, op. cit. III 418; H. Sweet, op. cit. 436.

OHG *hurnin* < PGmc *hurnīnaz), which is also used to translate 'corneæ' in Psalm 97, 6: *hyrnenre* (Lambeth, Regius, perhaps Tiberius), and *hyrnene* (Arundel), probably a scribal error for *hyrnenre*. As we shall see, it is found besides in the compound *anhyrnen* as a variant of *anhyrne* and *anhyrned*.

It is uncertain whether the five cases of *anhyrnera* (Cambridge, Junius, Surtees, Vesp. 21, Cambridge 77) should be analysed as the gen. pl. of the adjective *anhyrne* with an excrescent medial *e*, as is common in late WS, or rather as illustrating the loss of *n* before *r* in *anhyrnenra* (cf. late WS *mīre*, *mīra* < *mīnre*, *mīnra*, etc.), perhaps or probably furthered by dissimilation. This latter explanation presupposes of course the existence of an adjective *ānhyrnen* 'one-horned', which I am convinced is the source of *anhyrnendra* (Lambeth, Regius 21, Spelman 21, 28, 77) and of *anhyrnende* (Spelman 91), apparently a conflation of *anhyrnen* and *anhyrnede*. Bosworth-Toller interprets *anhyrnendra* as a present participle 'having one horn', which is morphologically and semantically unlikely, since such a participle, if it ever existed, would have to mean 'providing with one horn'. In my opinion we have here – as in *byman hyrnendre* (Spelman 97), corresponding to Tiberius *hyrne*[ ]*re*, probably with a missing *n*, and Vitellius corrupt *hyrnenred* – six instances of an excrescent *d* between *n* and *r* in *anhyrnenra*, *hyrnenre* as in late WS *gandra* 'gander', earlier *ganra* (Girvan § 256, 3). And finally we come to the strange Cambridge form *anhyrne ráá* (28), which Wildhagen prints *anhyrneráá* with an appended note posing the question whether the glossator is indulging in an etymologizing pun on -*ra* and *rā* 'roe(buck)' or is actually translating the Latin term as *anhyrne ráá*. This is a rhetorical question to which no answer seems necessary or even possible.

HELGE KÖKERITZ

11 · *Béowulf B*: a Folk-Poem on Béowulf's Death

Foreword

Some time ago I published a paper[1] in which I advanced the view that *Béowulf* ll. 2009b–2176 might well be regarded as a variant, a genuine folk-variant, of the matter preceding it (*Béowulf A*) and that this was at some time inserted in its present position by some scribe for the very reason that it was a variant with its own special features and points of interest. From many points of view the act of including material not available in *Béowulf A* may indeed be looked upon as something fortunate, certainly in no sense detrimental to the all-over effect of the text so produced. In the same paper (p. 101 *ad fin.*) I remarked that I should at some time like to present reasons for viewing *Béowulf B* (ll. 2200–3182) as originally an independent work, like *A'* soldered on to what precedes. In the following pages I discuss certain features of the total work which persuade me to this view, though before going further I should like to point out that to view the Béowulf material in manuscript Cotton Vitellius A. XV as made up of originally independent songs by different singers can in no way alter for better or worse the final effect achieved in the manuscript; such a view can in fact do no more than remove from the literary scene the conception of an unknown and unknowable poet or singer who composed the *Béowulf* of the editions in a single and continuous artistic effort.

[1] '*Béowulf A'*: a Folk-Variant', *Arv* XIV (1958), 95–101. Passages quoted here from *Béowulf* follow the text of my *Béowulf and Judith* (Department of English, Harvard University, 1959).

1. The Non-Cyclic Character of Oral Songs

Seldom if ever does a folk-singer, composing extemporaneously without benefit of writing materials,[1] compose a cyclic poem, that is, sing in a single session or series of sessions a story which he or she feels is a unit dealing with several consecutive events in a character's life. Oral singers normally sing episodically, treating of some discrete body of material, be it the ten months of the Trojan War in the *Iliad* or Völundr's kidnapping and escape in the Eddic *Völundarkviða*; oral singers' songs are often in response to an audience request for a song about some subject or other. This habit of singers to sing episodically was in fact a matter of real concern to Dr Elias Lönnrot when as a medical student he was first engaged in trying to put together a Finnish 'national epic'. In his Foreword to the first or 1835 version of the *Kalevala*,[2] now known as the *Old Kalevala* (*Vanha Kalevala*) he quite frankly remarks after discussing his effort to achieve a pleasing concatenation: 'You, reader, may ask whether our ancestors ever sang these songs in any ordered

[1] There is some basic bibliography on the subject of oral poetry in my paper 'The Oral-Formulaic Character of Anglo-Saxon Poetry', *Speculum* XXVIII (1953), 446, n. 2; for valuable discussion of Anglo-Saxon music and the singing of songs see Jess B. Bessinger Jr, 'Béowulf and the Harp at Sutton Hoo', *University of Toronto Quarterly: a Canadian Journal of the Humanities* XXVII (1958), 148–68. As for Milman Parry's pioneer work it may be noted that his collected writings will be issued under the title *The Structure of Homeric Verse*, edited with an introduction by Adam M. Parry, Oxford University Press, in the course of 1962. Among other studies of Homeric verse see Frederick M. Combellack, 'Milman Parry and Homeric Artistry', *Comparative Literature* XI (1959), 193–208, also Cedric H. Whitman, *Homer and the Heroic Tradition* (1958), especially ch. VI ('Image, Symbol and Formula'). On the Serbo-Croatian singing tradition see now Albert B. Lord, *The Singer of Tales* (1960). The study of oral poetry is an expanding field of investigation and before long will require a classified bibliography. Merely to suggest the extension of this field of study I mention somewhat at random Jean Rychner, *La Chanson de Geste*, etc. (1955), R. A. Waldron, 'Oral-formulaic Technique and Middle English Alliterative Poetry', *Speculum* XXXII (1957), 792–801, Albert C. Baugh, 'Improvisation in the Middle English Romance', *Proceedings of the American Philosophical Society* CIII (1959), 418–54, James Ross, 'Formulaic Composition in Gaelic Oral Literature', *Modern Philology* LVII (1959), 1–12, and, yet to appear, a study of modern Greek oral poetry by Professor James A. Notopoulos, announced as forthcoming in *The Year Book of the American Philosophical Society* for 1953, pp. 249–53.

[2] Reprinted in *Suomen Kansalliskirjallisuus* ('Finnish National Literature') II (1935), 241–478.

sequence or sang them singly? It seems to me that in this regard these songs, as things happen, turn up singly,' [1] In the second or 1849 version, Lönnrot's *New Kalevala* (*Uusi Kalevala*), now the *Kalevala par excellence*, he does a great deal of rearranging without any help from the singers themselves. This general lack of cyclic poems among oral singers does not, however, preclude the existence of story cycles, that is, of the coexistence of two or more songs about different events in a character's career. In Old Icelandic, for example, one finds no cyclic poem but *Fáfnismál* and *Reginsmál* are two songs making up a little cycle and were likely enough concatenated by the scribe of Gl. kgl. sml. 2365 4to, the *Codex Regius* of the *Poetic Edda*; one may altogether reasonably doubt if in the living singing tradition these two songs were ever viewed as constituting any sort of indivisible whole. In the much studied area of Serbo-Croatian oral poetry Professor Albert B. Lord tells us that anything like a cyclic song exists or occurs only more or less accidentally and perhaps only and very occasionally in connexion with a feud and the ensuing vengeance. Often a singer who knows how to sing of the feud may not even know the revenge story!

In view of a general lack of cyclic composition in oral singing the apparent cyclic character of the Béowulf material in Brit. Mus. MS Cotton Vitellius A. XV is *a priori* immediately suspect and a close examination of the material strengthens the suspicion that this is not a single poem, no continuum produced by a single singer singing on a single occasion. What we actually have are two stories about the Gautish hero Béowulf. The first is about a youthful adventure with a couple of trolls at the Scielding court on the site of the present hamlet of Gamle Lejre on Sjælland in Denmark and is told twice, once at some length by a narrator (*Béowulf A*, or Béowulf at Gamle Lejre), once much more briefly (cp. ll. 1999–2176) by Béowulf himself

---

[1] ibid., 244: 'Kysynet lukia jos esivanhempammeki näitä runoja missään järjestyksessä laulovat taikka yksitellen? Minusta näyttää näien runojen sitä myöten, kun asiatki tapahtuvat, yksitellen ilmautuneen.'

to his uncle Hyʒelác,[1] king of the Gauts (*Béowulf A'*). *Béowulf A'* ends up with a somewhat curious miscellany of remarks (ll. 2177–99) that seem only casually to concern what precedes or follows. The second Béowulf story starting at l. 2200 tells of Béowulf's death at the hands of a sort of flying dragon and begins in an almost jolting fashion, considering that some odd sixty-five years separate this part of Béowulf's life history from what precedes:

> Eft þæt ʒe-éode   uferrum dógrum
> hilde-hlemmum,   siþþan Hyʒe-lác læʒ
> and Heard-ræde   hilde mécas
> under bord-hréoðan   to banan wurdon,
> þá hine ʒesóhton   on siʒe-þéode
> hearde hild-frecan,   Heaðu-Scielfingas,
> níðe ʒenæʒdon   nefan Here-ríces:
> siþþan Bío-wulfe   bráde ríce
> on hand ʒehwearf.   Hé ʒe héold tela
> fíftiʒ wintra . . .   (ll. 2200–09a)

('Afterward it happened in later days in the clashes of battle after Hygelác lay dead and battle-blades were fatal to [his son] Heardréd though protected by a shield, when bold battle-warriors sought him out among the glorious [Gautish] people, when Battle-Scielfings violently attacked Hereríc's nephew [Heardréd] –: afterward the vast [Gautish] kingdom passed into Béowulf's hands; he ruled well for fifty years.')

The lapse of time involved between Béowulf's return from Sjælland and his death cannot of course be figured exactly but it would be the fifty years of his reign plus Heardréd's reign plus the period of Béowulf's regency before Heardréd actually ascended to the throne plus the time between Hygelác's death on the Lower Rhine and Béowulf's return from Denmark. One might guess that sixty to sixty-five years in all might have been involved and, if Béowulf was in Denmark when he was between twenty and twenty-five, that he might be supposed to be

[1] *Arv* XIV 95–9.

between eighty and eighty-five at the time of his death. In any event there is a very large time-gap between the Denmark episode and the events immediately leading to Béowulf's death.

If *Béowulf B* is an independent song, only more or less accidentally in its present position in the manuscript where it follows directly on material that chronologically precedes, the opening words 'Then it happened in later days' can hardly have been the original beginning but would represent a transition verse substituted by some anthologizing scribe, not necessarily the scribe of the surviving manuscript, for some original verses more appropriate for starting a brand new song. That there were Anglo-Saxon scribes who knew enough about oral singing to manage such a bit of original composition is clear from material discussed elsewhere.[1] But apart from verse 2200 the rest of the opening passage may well be original; it has an orienting function not unlike, though on a much smaller scale, that of ll. 1–63 of *Béowulf A*. In both cases the purpose of the verses is to let the audience know more or less how it was that matters had reached the state in which they are when the song opens. Professor Lord tells me that such gambits are not uncommon in the Serbo-Croatian tradition. On a more extensive scale ll. 1–193 of the *Elene* serve a similar purpose.

Taking into account the general lack of cyclic songs in the oral singing tradition anywhere, the extraordinarily large time-gap between *Béowulf A–A'* and *Béowulf B* and the so very mechanical l. 2200, it is, as suggested, *a priori* reasonable to assume that in the case of *Béowulf B* we have to deal with an independent song. An additional feature likewise pointing in

---

[1] ibid., 100–1. This in a sense raises the general question of the existence of lettered singers. Whereas the overwhelming majority of Anglo-Saxon singers must have been unlettered, it is a matter of record that at least some highly educated members of the clergy were singers, an art no doubt learned in their youth. One conspicuous example is Aldhelm of Malmesbury, discussed in *Speculum* XXVIII (1953), 454–5 (l. 4 for 'Aidan's' read 'Aldhelm's') and n. 16; it is also clear there were monks at Lindisfarne in the year 797 who sang traditional songs, including songs centring on Ingeld; see Eleanor S. Duckett, *Alcuin, Friend of Charlemagne* (1951), further ibid., 10 (middle). Such lettered singers would have had no difficulty in composing soldering verses where the occasion might arise, as in concatenating bits of verse.

this direction is that *Béowulf A'* seems itself to be a song independent of what precedes and what follows. Furthermore if we had to do with a singer who had set out to compose a cyclic song about Béowulf's career, it might strike one as odd that he did not include between *Béowulf A–A'* and *B* the story of Hygelác's death in the Rhineland, a story – and with the story of course a song – with which the *B*-singer in particular shows himself so familiar.[1] Much indeed of a general nature speaks for the independence of *Béowulf B*.

I would now turn to certain specific features which seem to me to confirm a view based on general grounds and which lead me to think of the *B*-singer as an altogether different person from the *A* or *A'*-singer.

2. *The Treatments of Genealogies*

Both *Béowulf A* and *Béowulf B* have occasion to give their audiences genealogical data, the *A*-singer to account for the rise to a dazzling prosperity of the Scielding dynasty from the apparently poor state in which Heremód had left the Danish kingdom. The *B*-singer works in his genealogies, first, to account for Béowulf's succession to the Gautish throne, from which as a youth he was far removed, then to account for Hygelác's succession earlier to the same throne. The methods of these two singers are strikingly different. The *A*-singer works deftly and in 60 lines (not counting the initial flourish of ll. 1–3) takes us through four generations. Here the *pièce de résistance* is, of course, Scield Scéafing's ship burial which is quite generously presented, otherwise just enough is told of the persons concerned to carry the narrative along. In fact, after line 63 he quite omits any statement about King Heorugár's reign – referred to passingly by Hróthgár in ll. 467b–69 – so eager does he seem to be to get on with the business. (The *A'*-singer is the person who has any real interest in this older brother; cp. ll. 2158–62a).[2]

---

[1] See my paper 'Béowulf and King Hygelác in the Netherlands', *English Studies* XXXV (1954), 1–12.

[2] *Arv* XIV 99.

Nothing could be more different than the *B*-singer's handling of genealogical material. He clearly felt the need of telling his audience how Béowulf came to reach the Gautish throne and he furnishes the essential information right at the outset (ll. 2207–09a). But this alone does not satisfy him and in ll. 2354–79a we are again given an account of Hygelác's death in the Rhineland, the circumstances of Béowulf's regency and a mention of Heardréd's reign of unstated length. In ll. 2379b–90 there is a circumstantial account of Heardréd's death at the hands of the Uppland Swede Angantýr (Angenthéow) and a restatement of Béowulf's ascent to the throne. After a few lines (2397–2424) concerning the dragon the genealogizing starts up again (ll. 2426–43), this time to explain how Hygelác attained the Gautish throne, since at birth with two older brothers he was as far from the line of succession as is Princess Anne of England today. All through this run accounts of earlier wars between the Gauts and the Swedes which have their own relevance with regard to the impending fall of the Gautish kingdom at the hands of the Swedes, but these disorderly and almost randomly presented backflashes fed to the audience are, like the backhanded presentation of the genealogies themselves, truly confusing to a person not saturated with the material and are quite unlike anything I can imagine the *A*-singer's doing. In effect, I find it more than difficult to associate two such different approaches to genealogical problems with a single personality.

3. *Hygelác's Death in the Rhineland*

It is all but certain that Hygelác's death in the Rhineland *c.* A.D. 525 was the subject of songs,[1] also that this material was known to both the *A*- and *B*-singer, though no version of this, if ever taken down, has survived. In this adventure Béowulf performed prodigies and, at least according to the *B*-singer, he considered it important in his whole life's picture. Our knowledge of it comes from various sources, including the Béowulf

---

[1] See n. 1, opposite.

K

songs. The *A*-singer refers to this event, and in a sense casually, only once (ll. 1204–13a) in order to indicate the ultimate fate of a great neck-ring given Béowulf at Lejre.[1] For the *B*-singer it seems to be of far greater interest, for he refers to the event five times and though the visit to Heorot is mentioned twice and without much emphasis both the singer and Béowulf, as presented by the singer, evidently regarded it as *the* great adventure of his youth. One might well say that this proves nothing concerning a difference of taste or personality in that in the *A*-singer's song there could only be some casual reason to look thus into the future, but it seems to me that the point is that the *B*-singer is obviously far more interested in the Rhineland episode than in the Heorot adventure to which he refers only twice (ll. 2351b–54a, 2521). When, for instance, Béowulf reminisces about the former strength of his grip, he thinks of the time he crushed the Frank Dæʒhræfn to death (ll. 2501–8a), not of Grendel. So marked a difference in interest in Béowulf's own past does not strike me as compatible with the attitude of a single person composing a continuous song.

4. *Certain Short A-Verses Peculiar to* Béowulf A' *and* B

In the *Béowulf* there are a number of A-verses with a very short second measure,[2] of which *wan-scæft wera* (l. 120) may be taken as an example; these verses tend to be used as off-verses. Particularly striking are six in which the second measure is filled out with the masc. acc. sing. *þone* of the demonstrative *sé,* giving in effect an unusual postpositive use of the article, though with no suggestion of enclisis as in Scandinavian. As on-verses are:

grund-wang þone (l. 2588a)

friðu-wang þone (l. 2959a)

---

[1] See my paper 'The Old-Germanic Altar- or Oath-Ring (*Stallahringr*)', *APhS* XX (1949), 277–93.

[2] See John Collins Pope, *The Rhythm of Béowulf* (1942), 272–3, 333 (type A2a), idem, *Old English Versification with Particular Reference to the Normal Verses of Béowulf* (trial mimeographed ed., Department of English, Yale University, 1957), 62–3 (type A4).

and as off-verses

> úht-hlemm þone (l. 2007b)
> eorþ-weard þone (l. 2334b)
> wæl-hlemm þone (l. 2969b)
> gold-weard þone (l. 3081b)

As far as I know these are the only instances of this particular type of A-verse, i.e. with a second measure *þone*, in the surviving corpus, though this is not to say that the type was so relatively infrequent in the actual singing tradition. But as things are, it is striking that five of these six examples occur in *Béowulf B*, only one (l. 2007b) in the far shorter *Béowulf A'* and none at all in the quite long *Béowulf A*. In a word, these formulaic systems[1] – for so such verses may be described – would seem to be somehow characteristic of the *B*-singer's versemaking habits and thus set him off from the *A*-singer and the singers of other recorded Anglo-Saxon songs.

5. *Béowulf's Promising and Unpromising Childhood*

The *B*-singer knows quite definitely about Béowulf's childhood and according to his ll. 2428–34 the hero declares that he was brought up from the age of seven in fosterage at his grandfather Hrœthel's, where the latter is said to have favoured him as one of his own children, Béowulf's uncles:

> Héold meć and hæfde   Hrœðel cyning,
> ȝeaf mé sinc and symbel, sibbe ȝemunde;
> næs ić him to lífe   láðra áwihte
> beorn [*for* bearn?] on burgum   þanne his bearna hwelć
>   (ll. 2430–34)

(King Hrœthel kept me and protected me, gave me treasure and sustenance, was mindful of our kinship; I was never less liked by him as a warrior (child?) there than any one of his own sons . . .)

There is nothing about these verses and Béowulf's remarks to

---

[1] On formulaic systems see *Speculum* XXVIII (1953), 450.

give one an instant's pause, and for the B-singer they are surely
intended as a sincere statement of fact by Béowulf as the singer
was accustomed to sing about this. But there was another tradition concerning Béowulf's childhood years – a variant tradition
– that is quite the opposite, where Béowulf appears in the role
of the 'unpromising hero' or 'male Cinderella'. This is recorded in ll. 2183b–89 in the course of some, to me, puzzling
miscellaneous remarks found between *Béowulf A'* and *B* which
run as follows:

> Héan wæs lange
> swá hine ʒéata bearn   gódne ne tealdon
> né hine on medu-benće   mićeles wierðne
> dryhten Wedera   ʒedón wolde;
> swíðe wćéndon   þæt hé sléac wǽre,
> æðeling unfram.   Edwenden cóm
> tír-éadigum menn   torna ʒehwelćes.

(He was long looked down upon to the extent that the sons of
the Gauts considered him no good nor was the lord [Hrœthel]
of the Storm-Gauts willing to bestow much on him on the
mead-bench; they very much thought that he was a sluggard,
a lazy prince. An end [lit. change] came to these troubles for
the man destined for glory.)

   It seems to me hard to assign these verses, to decide whether
they form part of *Béowulf A* (with *A'* wedged in between) or to
Béowulf A' or whether they are altogether separate, but the
main point is that they can hardly be associated with *Béowulf B*
which knows this matter so differently. Accordingly, it is only
natural to feel that this small but telling difference in the
knowledge in the Béowulf tradition points to two different
singers. Were all this body of material a play by T. S. Eliot or
the American poet-dramatist Archibald McLeish with their
studied subtleties one might well imagine that the unpromising
child was the reality and that the highly regarded child represented wishful thinking on the part of the ageing king. But we
do not have to do with T. S. Eliot nor apparently with a

lettered work at all and accordingly should probably not indulge in such psychologizing.

It is also possible that the *A*-singer knew the tradition of the unpromising childhood and assumed a similar familiarity on the part of Unferth and his audience when he introduced Unferth's insulting and apparently unmotivated outburst against Béowulf, coupled with Unferth's doubts as to Béowulf's general competence to cope with Grendel (cp. ll. 506 ff.) In this case it would be a question of Unferth's having heard about what the boy Béowulf was like but had not been brought up to date about the change (*edwenden*) in his personality and fortunes. In l. 408b–9a Béowulf says to Hróthgar

'. . . hæbbe ić mǽrða fela
ongunnen on ȝeoguðe . . .'

(in the course of my youth I have undertaken many glorious deeds), but this 'youth' presumably has nothing to do with his actual childhood and thus refers to what he did in, say, his late teens.

6. *The Consistency of Béowulf's Character*

Whatever may be the mutual relationship of the preserved *Béowulf* there is one great unity, namely, the consistency of the hero's character. Everywhere his nobility, courage, gentleness, youthful strength and eagerness to leave behind a fair name (*dóm*) emerges. In a lettered work such consistency would ordinarily point to the consistent conception on the part of a single poet and, if applied to the Béowulf material, would strongly suggest unity of authorship. In an oral, folk tradition, however, such an offhand conclusion can scarcely be drawn, for in such a tradition the basic conception of an important or even relatively unimportant but familiar character will normally be the same everywhere and among all singers. In the Karelo-Finnish the 'Big Three' of the *Kalevala*-type songs and of course in the *Kalevala* itself, Väinämöinen, Ilmarinen and Lemminkäinen, not to mention lesser lights, are characterized with striking consistency by singers all over the singing area, from Archangel down to Ingria, and have what Parry calls 'fixed epithets'. To quote from Väinö Salminen's competent article 'Kalevala' in the Finnish *Great Encyclopaedia* where he is speaking specifically of Lönnrot's work, conflated and concatenated out of many songs by many singers: 'But the consistency of the personal characterizations which continue unchanged through the whole work . . . gives coherence to its poetic story.' [1] In the case of Serbo-Croatian singing Professor Lord tells me that more or less the same situation prevails, though he adds that sometimes an historical or semi-historical figure who is treated by Christian singers as a great hero will be treated as an equally great villain by Moslems. Apparently, however, such conflicting points rarely if ever come into direct conflict with one another. More or less the same situation prevails in the case of the thoroughly contradictory treatment of the character of the great Gothic king Ermanaric in different widely separated parts of the Old Germanic world. In Scandinavia he is a great king while German singers and later poets knew him as an avaricious tyrant. [2] Consequently, the consistency of Béowulf's character throughout the preserved material is in itself no argument for unity of authorship, no more, in fact, than is the high degree of consistency in the style, diction, and syntax of the poetic corpus in general.

7. Hróthgár's Prophecy of Béowulf's Future Kingship

In ll. 1845b–53a Hróthgár in his farewell address to the departing Gauts in effect prophesies that Béowulf will be king of the Gauts in the event of Hygelác's death and possibly, too, refers specifically to Béowulf's refusing the throne of the boy king Heardréd (cp. ll. 2373–6):

> ȝief þæt ȝegangeþ   þæt-þe gár nimeþ,
> hild heoru-grimme,   Hréðles eaforan,
> ádl oþþe íren   ealdor þinne,

---

[1] *Iso Tietosanakirja* V (2nd ed., 1933), col. 1153.
[2] See Caroline Brady, *The Legends of Ermanaric* (1943), *passim*.

folces hierde,   and þú þín feorh hafast,
þæt þé Sǽ-ʒéatas   sélran næbben
to ʒecéosenne   cyning ǽniʒne,
hord-weald hæleða,   ʒief þú healdan wilt
mága ríce.

(I count it likely, if it so happens that a spear, sword-fierce battle takes off Hróðel's heir [Hygelác], disease or a sword your lord, guardian of the people, and you are still alive, that the Maritime Gauts will not have a better king than you to elect, better guardian of the national treasure, if you will be willing to rule the kingdom of your kinsmen.)

The same seems to be hinted at in ll. 1707b–9a where Hróthgár says:

þú scealt to frófre weorðan
eall lang-twídiʒ   léodum þínum,
hæleðum to helpe.

(You are bound to become a consolation, long be granted to be a help to your people, to the warriors.)

In view of what is told about Béowulf's gradual advance in the Gautish line of royal succession and his final accession to the throne, these passages in *Béowulf A* take on the air of a prophecy, as indeed they are, but again they can point in no special way to a single poet anticipating an event which he plans to deal with a bit later. To me it only points to the fact that almost any singer who knew any part of the Béowulf material was likely, though not perhaps inevitably, to know all parts. Hence, given a situation such as Hróthgár's in the present context, namely, the need of making an appreciative and flattering farewell speech, the singer could look into the future in a general way without in the least committing himself to sing about it in the immediate future or perhaps ever. In a word this prophecy has no bearing one way or another on the question of unity of authorship.

Summary

In the preceding pages I have been arguing for a multiple authorship of the surviving Béowulf material. In § 1 I tried to show that a cyclic poem is *a priori* an unlikely creation in an oral tradition. In §§ 2–5 I called attention to three details where a difference of treatment suggests the work of two singers rather than one. In §§ 6–7 I have remarked on two features which might be taken as signs of a single authorship but which in reality are presumably dependent on the general conditions of oral singing. It is impossible to anticipate whether these arguments will strike other students of oral singing as cogent or whether others will find substantial explanations permitting a different interpretation of the phenomena at issue.

FRANCIS P. MAGOUN JR

12 · *Fjallið Mikla, Áin í Dal, Millum Fjarða* and *Urð Mans*

For anyone concerned with the vocabulary and idiom of the wholly or partly Norse-speaking areas of the west – I am thinking especially of those stretching from the Isle of Man to Iceland – it is natural to argue that the external form of place-names in these areas cannot be entirely without significance. But when a comparative study of external formal elements is begun, grave difficulties are soon encountered. In the first place, there is still too little known about the Norwegian material, and in the second place, the Icelandic material, despite the great quantity and variety of Iceland's medieval literary sources, can only make a partial contribution towards a more precise definition of the formal types met with in the place-names of Shetland, Orkney, and the Faeroes. In nature-names, which are my chief concern in this paper, there appear to be quite close correspondences between these three island-groups. This may be seen by a comparison of the material collected by Jakobsen for Shetland, Marwick for Orkney, and myself for the northern isles of the Faeroes.[1] In this essay I should like to present some further information on certain formal types of Faeroese place-names which have parallels elsewhere.

---

[1] Jakob Jakobsen, 'Shetlandsøernes Stednavne', *Aarbøger for nordisk Oldkyndighed og Historie* (1901), 55–258; English edn, *The Place-Names of Shetland* (1936); idem, *Etymologisk Ordbog over det norrøne Sprog på Shetland* (1908–21); English edn, *An Etymological Dictionary of the Norn Language in Shetland* (1928–32). Hugh Marwick, *The Place-Names of Rousay* (1947); idem, *Orkney Farm-Names* (1952); idem, *Orkney* (1951). See also his contributions to the *Proceedings* of the Orkney Antiquarian Society. Chr. Matras, 'Stednavne paa de færøske Norðuroyar', *Aarbøger* (1932), 1–322.

I

An important name in Orkney, that of the island *Eynhallow*, contains postpositional adjective, just as in the identical old Norwegian island-name, *Eyin helga* (now *Helgøy*). In Shetland we find *Papa Stour* (and *Papa Little*). The only instance where one might expect to find an island-name of this type in the Faeroes is for the pair of islands called *Dímun in meiri* (or *in bygða*) and *Dímun in minni* (or *in litla*) in the Icelandic *Færeyinga saga*. Although we find that, in fact, the modern Faeroese names for these are *Stóra Dímun* and *Lítla Dímun*, there remain nevertheless numerous examples of this type of construction in minor names. When the Faeroese material[1] is set beside that from Shetland and Orkney one is tempted to conclude that the Norwegian colonial settlements offered a particularly fruitful soil for the development of this type of place-name formation.

The appellatives found in the Faeroese place-names of this formation are, e.g.: *á* f., *berg* n. (usually = rock-wall, cliff, but here = boulder, rock), *bládýpi* n. (deep water, where the bottom cannot be seen), *brekka* f., *fjall* n. (cf. *-felli* n., in *Tungufelli* below), *fles* f., *fløta* (< *flata) f., *gil* n., *gjógv* (< *gjó* < *gjǿ*; gen. sg. *gjáar* < *gjár*; pl. *gjáir* < *gjár*) f., *hálsur* (< *háls* < *hals*) m. (projection – usually sloping gently – from rock-face), *hamar* m., *hella* f., *heyggjur* (< *haugr*) m., *horn* n. (small projection, usually pointed), *jørð* f. (land, enclosed fields around farm or village), *kelda* f., *lið* (< *hlíð*) f. (grass-grown mountainside), *mýri* (now generally *mýra*; < *mýrr*) f. (bogland), *møl* f., *mørk* (and *hálvmørk*) f. (a unit of measurement, a piece of enclosed land with a corresponding share in the common pasture), *nakkur* (< *hnakkr*) m. (high headland with sharp edge), *nev* n. (low pointed foreland), *oyggj* (< *ey*) f. (usually = island, but in the name in question = cliff-ledge), *reyn* (< *hraun*) n., *rók* (< *rǿk; gen. sg.

---

[1] The Faeroese material is partly derived from collections made by V. U. Hammershaimb *c.* 1850 and by Jakob Jakobsen chiefly in the 1890's (Landsbókasavnið, Tórshavn) and from the collections of others (found both in Landsbókasavnið and in the Institut for Navneforskning, Copenhagen).

rákar or usually *rókar*; pl. *røkur*) f. (cliff-ledge, sloping shelf between two steep rises), *ryggur* (< *hryggr*) m. (part of grass-
grown mountainside – between two streams or gullies), *rætt*
(< *rétt*) f. (sheep-pen), *skarð* n., *skriða* f., *steinur* (< *steinn*) m.,
stíggjur (<*stígr*) m. (way, up or down, over a crag), *tá* (= *tógv*
< *tó*) f. (grass-patch in a cliff), *tjørn* (pl. *tjarnir*) f., *torva* f., *urð* f.
Finally, the mountain-names *Hestur* and *Tungufelli* may be
included.

The adjectives used in this type of compound name may be
arranged as follows: (1) indicating position – *ein* (alone, soli-
tary): *Heyggjurin Eini* (cf. Icel. *Fjallið eina, Hóllinn eini*); *heimari*
(nearer): *Gjógvin Heimara*; *ytri* (further): *Gjógvin Ytra*; *norðari*
(more northerly): *Gjógvin Norðara*; (2) indicating age – *fornur*
or *gamal* (old): *Gjógvin Forna, Mølin Gamla*; *nýggjur* (new): *Rættin*
Nýggja; (3) indicating size – *mikil* or *stórur* (big): *Áin (Fjallið,*
Jørðin, Mørkin, Skarðið, Urðin) Mikla, Hamarin (Heyggjurin) Mikli,
Áin (Bergið, Brekkan, Gjógvin, Skriðan) Stóra, Heyggjurin Stóri; *lítil*
(little): *Áin (Bládýpið, Fjallið, Gjógvin, Hálvmørkin, Tungufellið)*
Lítla, Tjarnirnar Lítlu; *langur* (long): *Flesin (Hellan, Oyggin, Rókin,*
Rættin, Táin, Torvan) Langa, Nakkurin Langi; *háur* or *høgur* (high):
Hesturin Há(v)i, Hornið Háa, Hálvmørkin Høga; (4) indicating
shape: *brattur* (steep): *Táin Bratta*; *breiður* (broad): *Stíggjurin*
Breiði; *mjáur* (narrow, thin): *Rókin Mjáa, Mørkin Mjá(v)a*;
hvassur (sharp): *Heyggjurin Hvassi*; *bøllutur* (round): *Regnið* (i.e.
Reynið) Bølluta; *bogin* (curved, bent): *Steinurin Bogni*; *rættur*
(straight): *Áin Rætta*; (5) indicating colour: *bláur* (dark, black):
Hellan Bláa; *gráur* (grey): *Steinurin Grái*;[1] *reyður* (red): *Kletturin*
Reyði; *svartur* (black): *Áin (Jørðin, Mýrin) Svarta*; (6) indicating
temperature: *kaldur* (cold): *Gilið Kalda*; *ófrosin* (unfrozen): *Áin*
Ófrosna; (7) indicating taste: *søtur* (sweet): *Áin Søta*.

Some of the adjectives used indicate qualitative appreciation.
Favourable ones, doubtless given for reasons such as the ground's
fertility or the good catches made at a place, are e.g.: *fríður*
(fine, beautiful): *Fløtan Fríða, Gilið Fríða* (the adj. in this name

---

[1] As with the name *Grásteinur*, the colour 'grey' indicates that this is a home of
the supernatural folk (*huldufólk*).

is pronounced [frø:a]); *góður* (good): *Gilið Góða*; *loðin* (shaggy, rich in grass): *Liðin Lodna*; *ríkur* (rich): *Ryggurin Ríki*. Two others that possibly belong to this group are: *dýrur* (precious, splendid): *Mørkin Dýra* (also known from a medieval source); and *feitur* (fat): *Fløtan Feita*. (In *Hellan Feita*, on the other hand, as in the synonymous *Feitahella*, the name of a rock on the coast, the adj. may refer to its smoothness or slipperiness.) Unfavourable terms are: *illur* (bad): *Stíggjurin Illi*; *beiskur* (harsh, bitter): *Hálsurin Beiski*; *óður* (mad, furious, wrong) occurs in the point-name *Nevið Óða*, cf. a skerry-name such as *Óðafles*; *ógongdur* (impassable – on foot) appears in *Rókin Ógongda*.

The frequent spring-name *Keldan Vigda* (from *vígdur*, con-secrated) is undoubtedly of medieval origin.

It is frequently so with names of this type that, because the declension appears a little troublesome, the nominative form is not used, and the principal forms are thus the acc. and dat., e.g. *Tánna Longu* and *Tánni Longu*. (In such cases regular nom. forms have been constructed to figure in the lists given above.) In Shetland and Orkney the acc. form is commonest. It should be noted that the stress always falls on the adj. in these name-formations.

Many of the names of this type – substantive (with definite article) + (weak) adjective – are comparatively young, but others may be from the Viking Age. The Orkney island-name *Eynhallow*, for example, shows that the type was fully developed in that early period. Per Thorson has recently shown that an old name in Caithness, *Landhallow*, must be from an ancient *Landit helga*.[1] Otherwise in Orkney, as in Shetland and the Faeroes, the type is especially common in names for coastal places and features, such as those, for example, containing the word *geo* (i.e. *gjá*, *gjó*): *Geo Na Gui* (North Ronaldsay), *Doonagua* (Birsay), where the final element in each case is from the adj. *góðr* (good). Other Orkney examples are *Breckan-swarta* (the dark slope), *Hinegreenie* (< *Haginn græni*, the green pasture), etc. From Shetland may be mentioned: *Gjona stura* (the big 'geo'),

[1] *Fram daa, Frendar* (1959), 35.

Heljena gro or *grø* (< *Helluna grá,* the grey rock), *Hulen brenda* (from *hóll* m., height, hill, and *brendr* adj., burnt), etc.

From Iceland we have *Fjallið eina* and *Hóllinn eini,* quoted above, and one can add a name like *Heiðin há,* but in general the type is uncommon there. The same seems more or less true of Norway also, although there is the ancient *Eyin helga,* and Per Hovda has told me in conversation that the type is represented in minor names in some places. Two important names of indubitable antiquity found on the Norwegian coast must also be included: *Landet gode,* known in three places, and *Holmengrå,* of which several instances are known. On these names and their connexion with popular beliefs (amongst seafaring folk) reference may be made to Svale Solheim, *Nemningsfordomar ved Fiske* (1940), 133, 136.

II

Names of the type *Fjallið Mikla* occur by the hundred in the Faeroes, but there is another type that is found by the thousand. This type contains a substantive in the form of a common appellative (usually with the definite article) followed by a prepositional phrase which defines the locality, e.g. *Tangin á Barmi, Gjógvin á Oyggj, Áin í Rók.* The stress in these names also falls on the final element (*Barmi, Oyggj, Rók*). As with the group considered above, many of the names of this type occur in ordinary speech only in the acc. and dat. The type is well known in Orkney and Shetland, but while in these islands the prepositional element is restricted to *-o'-* (< *of*), the Faeroese names show *í, á,* (and *við, undir, yvir,* etc.). It may be noted in passing that prep. *á* in Faeroese place-names may be derived from old *á* as well as old *at.*

The first element in such names consists of a descriptive appellative: *á* (stream), *boði* (underwater skerry), *brekka* (slope), *bugur* (bight), *drangur* (pointed rock-pillar, usually of some height and in the sea), *egg* (edge – of rock or cliff), *enni* (sharp projection in a steep mountain-slope), *eyga* (round hollow in cliff-face, where guillemots and razorbills lay or sit), *fjall* (hill, mountain; *Fjallið millum Botna(r)*), *flatur* (flat ground), *fles* (flat skerry, low rock islet – in the sea), *fløta* (plain), *fløttur* (grass-patch in rock-face), *gil* (gully, water-course), *gjógv* (cleft in rock, ravine, sea-cave), *gjóta* (smaller, long-shaped cleft), *glyvur* (cleft, fissure; *Glyvrið á Tjørnini*, in enclosed land), *grógv* (hollow, depression), *hamar* (projecting rock in face of hill or slope), *hella* (shore with flat rocks), *herða* (a rise, ridge), *heyggjur* (hill), *høvdi* (high projection or point), *kelda* (well, spring), *ketil* (round-shaped hollow; without art. in *Ketil í Skor*), *klettur* (perpendicular rock-face, not high), *knøttur* (knob, knoll; without art. in *Knøttur í Egg*), *koppur* (round top? – *Koppurin í Fjalli*), *lág* (depression, hollow), *land* (grass-grown ledge in cliff-face), *møl* (pebble beach; *Mølin við Hús*), *nasi* (rock projection), *petti* (properly means a piece; *Pettið í Skor*), *reyn* (stony ground, stony ridge), *rók* (terrace, cliff-shelf), *rust* (projecting ridge in steep mountain-side), *røð* (sharp edge, level or rounded), *sandur* (sandy shore), *skarð* (cut, pass), *sker* (rock, skerry), *skriða* (landslip), *steinur* (stone, both on land and in the sea), *tangi* (point), *tjørn* (pool, small lake), *torva* (grass-patch in cliff-face, especially in the fowling-cliffs), *túva* or *túgva* (hillock, mound – usually grass-grown), *urð* (scree, especially at the foot of fowling-cliffs), *vatn* (lake). – This list, which is far from exhaustive, contains only terms that are purely descriptive of natural features. Other elements which refer more or less directly to human activity have been intentionally omitted.

How old are names of this type? From written sources we learn only that the construction was common two centuries ago. I am prepared to assume that the oldest of such names now in use come from the Middle Ages, but in the case of a stream-name such as *Áin í Dal*, there is no reason why it should not go back to the Viking Age. Some names of this kind were evidently given by fishermen who used the topographical features for fixes. There are even examples which show as their last element the name of a *strát* (fishing ground), e.g. *Gilið* (and *Steinurin*) *á Heygastráti.*

As was mentioned above, this type of name corresponds to the very common formations found in Orkney and Shetland, e.g. *The Cup o' Whurligar* (Orkney) and *De Gil o' Skörd* (Shetland). A thorough study of this Shetland-Orkney type has been made by W. F. H. Nicolaisen, who shows that the names accord with Scottish forms based on Gaelic prototypes.[1] Whatever the final answer may be, it is hardly possible to dissociate the Faeroese names – *Áin í Dal* and the others – from the similar forms in Orkney and Shetland. It is the same *Sprachgefühl* that has found expression in all three groups of islands.

III

In Faeroese place-names the situation of a place or feature between (two) others is indicated by the use of *Mið-* (*Miðberg, Miðrók*, etc.), or, less often, *Miðal-* (< *Meðal-*; e.g. *Miðalberg*). Not infrequently however the situation of an area between two places or topographical features is indicated by the use of the prep. *millum* + gen. pl., so that place-names of the following type result: *Millum Fjarða* (the name of the district between Skálafjørður and Funningsfjørður), *Millum Fjalla* (= *Mellen Fjella* in Shetland), *Millum Vatna* (cf. a Norwegian name such as *á Vatnamillum*[2]), etc. As far as I know, such names as these are not found in Iceland, but they are fairly common in Shetland. The type is also known in England where *Twin(e)ham*, for example, is derived from *betwēon ēam* (between (the) rivers).[3] In Gaelic parts the formation is especially frequent, but in Irish names it appears that *da* (*dha*), i.e. two, always stands before the substantive,[4] and the same is probably to be regarded as the general rule in Gaelic names in Scotland, although an exception such as *Edirdovar* (< *eadar dobhair*, between the brooks[5]) may occur. I know only one instance in Faeroese nomenclature where a word for 'two' occurs in place-names of

[1] *Scottish Studies* III (1959), 92–101; IV (1960), 194–205.
[2] O. Rygh, *Norske Gaardnavne: Indledning* (1898), 16, and I 113.
[3] See A. H. Smith, *EPNE* I 32.
[4] P. W. Joyce, *Irish Names of Places* I (1901), 251 ff.
[5] W. J. Watson, *The History of the Celtic Place-Names of Scotland* (1926), 454.

this type: *Millum Báða Fjalla,* and here *báða* is a young gen. form (older *beggja*) of *báðir,* both.

A point to be noted in these Faeroese names is that in younger instances the acc. form has replaced the gen., e.g. *Millum Skørðini* (between the passes), and that an *-r* is often added to the original gen. ending, e.g. *Millum Gjánar* (older *Millum Gjána;* between (the) geos). Both these changes accord with the general development in the colloquial language.

This type of formation must be regarded as old, both in Shetland and the Faeroes. Even though the type is not completely unknown in Norway, one is tempted to assume that some connexion exists between the Shetland–Faeroese name-giving habit and the similar Gaelic type. But any such assumption must remain extremely uncertain.

IV

A document written 4 April 1329 in Kirkwall (*j Kirkiuwaghe i Orknæyium*) refers to property (*i*) *Kuikobba* and (*i*) *Þordar eckru* (now Thurrigar, South Ronaldsay). The latter name has a normal Norse form, the former shows influence from Gaelic. It must represent an original *Kví Kobba* (with stress on *Kobba*), sheep-pen of Kobbi (the personal name doubtless from Kolbeinn or Kolbjǫrn). The second element is thus a personal name in the gen., such as we find in *Quybernardis* (1492) and many other *quoy*-names and names formed with other appellatives in Orkney. Ekwall has shown that the same type of name is known in Norse settlements in northwest England, and that such 'inversion-compounds' can serve as a criterion for classifying a settlement as Norwegian (as distinct from Danish).[1] A similar touchstone in English names is the word *erg,* derived from the Norwegian of the western colonies (*ǣrgi* n., gen. pl. *ǣrgja,* dat. pl. *ǣrgjum;* the original long vowel is attested by

---

[1] See E. Ekwall, *Scandinavians and Celts in the North West of England* (1918); idem, 'Some further notes on inversion-compounds', *Studier tillägnade Axel Kock* (1929), 217–22; idem, in A. Mawer and F. M. Stenton, *Introduction to the Survey of English Place-Names* (EPNS I 1, 1933), 35.

Faeroese place-names, as well as the spelling *Asgrims ærgin*, *Flb.* II 511[25]).[1]

Place-names of this type are also known in the Faeroes, chiefly in the Norðuroyar area. As in the Orkney names, the second element consists of a personal name or other word designating a person, either in the gen. or, in accordance with ordinary colloquial development, in the acc. with gen. function. All the names are young, however, dating from the seventeenth to the nineteenth century. The oldest example is doubtless *Urð Mans* on Borðoy, which in all probability is named after a man who is referred to in 1619 as, in Danish form, Oluff Mand. As in most of the other instances, some special event must have given rise to the name, but here, as in general, we are ignorant of the circumstances. The name in the gen. seldom indicates possession.

What are we to think of the Faeroese type *Urð Mans*, regionally limited as it appears to be? Is it possible to trace its origin to the same linguistic instinct, the same name-giving habits, that produced the type *Kuikobba* in Orkney? It is hard to say. Even though many of the Orkney 'inversion-compounds' have long since disappeared, it would be rash to conclude that the type was also productive in the Faeroes, say in the fourteenth century, and that all the instances have since been lost. We must not forget, moreover, that *Urð Mans* does not mean that Ólavur Mann ever owned the scree in question – only that for some reason or other he was associated with it. The similarity between the Faeroese and Orkney types may thus be of a more incidental character, and be due for example to the general postpositional use of the appellative gen. in West Norse. But however this may be, names of the type *Urð Mans* (with the stress on *Mans*) are forceful and expressive, and rhythmically – if I may use the term – they harmonize with the other types considered above, both with stress on the last element: *Fjallið Mikla* and *Áin í Dal*.

CHR. MATRAS

---

[1] On *ærgi* see Chr. Matras, *NoB* (1956), 51 ff.; cf. A. H. Smith, *EPNE* I 157.

L

13 · Poetic Language and Old English Metre

I

Already in the nineteenth century, a good deal of interest was shown in the function of fixed expressions – 'die epischen Formeln', as Banning called them – in *Beowulf* and other early poems in the Germanic languages. More recently, several scholars have undertaken detailed comparative analyses to show the extent to which traditional formulas and themes alike constitute the basis of such poetry.[1] Thus, the *Metodes meahte* of Cædmon's Hymn is closely paralleled in a good many poems;[2] the widespread use is itself an indication that there is no question of specific borrowing, still less of plagiarism, but rather suggests that a premium is set on the traditionally determined expression, and, as Milman Parry said in discussing another literature, one poet is 'better than another not because he has by himself found a more striking way of expressing his own thought but because he has been better able to make use of the tradition'.[3] Although there are obvious dangers and limitations in such an approach, it is undoubtedly valuable for sharpening our perspective as we try to evaluate our early poetry.

The formula is a habitual collocation, metrically defined, and is thus a stylization of something which is fundamental to

---

[1] See especially Francis P. Magoun, Jr, in *Speculum* 28 (1953), 446 ff., and 30 (1955), 49 ff.

[2] To Professor Magoun's list (*Speculum* 30, 62), one might add 'meotud meahtum swið', *The Gifts of Men* 4 (Exeter Book, f. 78a).

[3] 'Studies in the Epic Technique of Oral Verse-making II: The Homeric Language as the Language of an Oral Poetry', *Harvard Studies in Classical Philology* 43 (1932), 13.

linguistic expression, namely the expectation that a sequence of words will show lexical congruity, together with (and as a condition of) lexical and grammatical complementarity. It may be said of 'wide' and 'way', for example, that in Old English they set up a reciprocal expectancy of each other, which may operate strictly within the 'half-line' structure (as in 'wegas ofer widland', *Andreas* 198), but equally across half-lines (as in 'Wærun wegas ðine · on widne sæ', Paris Psalter 76, 16), and also of course in prose: 'þæt geat ys swyðe wid, and se weg ys swyðe rum', Matt. 7. 13.[1] An example with a thematically more powerful connexion (and in consequence one still more widely exploited) is the pair *mod* and *mægen*, perhaps most familiarly contrasted in Byrhtwold's words, 'mod sceal þe mare, · þe ure mægen lytlað' (*Maldon* 313). Hroðgar tells Beowulf, 'þu eart mægenes strang · ond on mode frod' (l. 1844), which links with the treatment of 'sapientia et fortitudo' that R. E. Kaske has seen as being central to the theme of *Beowulf*, and in particular to the relationship of the hero with Hroðgar.[2] The collocation occurs frequently elsewhere: for instance, in *Gifts of Men* 98, *Elene* 408, the Paris Psalter 144, 5, 150, 2, and in prose, Bede's Eccl. Hist. Bk I Ch. 16 (p. 484, ll. 14–15 in the EETS edition).

It goes without saying, of course, that in discussing alliterative collocations in Old English, one must always remember that metrical demands may determine the connexion between words in a particular case; it is in fact easy to demonstrate that the connexion between words is frequently determined primarily by metrical demands. On the other hand, it is still more important to note that, given the natural phenomenon of collocation together with the existence in Old English (and

---

[1] On the formulas found in OE diplomatic and epistolary prose, such as 'swa full 7 swa forð swa', 'binnan porte (∼ byrig) 7 buton', 'on wudu 7 on felde', 'heora saca weorðe 7 heora socne', see F. E. Harmer, *Anglo-Saxon Writs* (1952), 61, 85 ff.

[2] See *Studies in Philology* 55 (1958), 423 ff. My quotations from *Beowulf* follow the text of C. L. Wrenn, from other OE poetry that of the Krapp and Dobbie, *Anglo-Saxon Poetic Records*.

kindred languages) of alliteration as a metrical device, the two work together so that alliteration becomes a regular mode of endorsing the linguistic connexion – whether complementary or contrastive – between collocated words. 'Hawk' and 'hand' are brought together in prose and verse from Old English times (as in 'heafoc on honda', *Fortunes of Men* 86) to our own times and the comic verse recited by Stanley Holloway: and it may perhaps (through popular etymology) be the basis of Hamlet's 'I know a hawk from a handsaw'.

Since alliteration in Old English verse serves not only to connect stressed forms within the half-line but also to connect two half-lines to form the next higher metrical unit, the poet is necessarily involved not only in the simple collocation of pairs like those already illustrated but also in extended collocations. Thus, for example,

> Wid is þes westen,   wræcsetla fela
>
> (*Guthlac* 296)

extends the association of *wid* and *westen* (found for instance in Paris Ps. 74, 6, Heptat. Deut. 32, 10); *wid* and *wræc-* (as in *Christ and Satan* 119 f.); *westen-* and *wræc-* (as in Ælfric, Cath. Hom. I. 560, 22). The device of 'variation' is important in this process, since by its nature variation encourages extended collocation and at the same time allows the collocation to proceed beyond the two alliteratively bound units (the half-line and the full line); thus in

> . . . mid hondum con   hearpan gretan;
> hafaþ him his gliwes giefe,   þe him God sealde
>
> (*Maxims I* 170 f.)

hand is collocated with *hearp* (as in *Genesis* 1079), *hearp* with *gretan* (as in *Beowulf* 2107 f. – also in an extended collocation), *hearp* with *gleo* or *gliw* (as in *Beowulf* 2262 f.); and all these connexions are manifested together in *Gifts of Men* 49 f. One might add that *giefu* and *God* are also closely collocated elsewhere (as in *Beowulf* 1271, 2182). The lines immediately following those quoted above from the Exeter Book *Maxims* provide a further example of the phenomenon:

Earm biþ se þe sceal   ana lifgan,
wineleas wunian   hafaþ him wyrd geteod (172 f.)

where we have the connexion between *earm* and *an-* (as in *Beowulf* 2368), and between *earm*, *an-*, and *wineleas* (as in *Resignation* 89 ff.).

II

It may therefore be fairly claimed that an expectation of the congruous and complementary, expressed through recurrent collocations, is built into the poetic system of Old English, and it may be supposed that this is close to the starting point in estimating the original audience's pleasurable experience, as it is close to our starting point in criticism of the poetry today. There is evidently a prime satisfaction in the propriety of like belonging with like, of traditional correspondences being observed. 'Ellen sceal on eorle' as surely as 'wulf sceal on bearwe' or as 'gim sceal on hringe · standan steap and geap', we gather from the Cotton Tiberius gnomic verses: each must be where each belongs. So it will happen (through the corresponding association of *eorl* and *æþeling*, witnessed for instance in the *Rune Poem*, 55, 84) that the right heroic tone can be established at the opening of *Beowulf* by the assurance that the Danish *æþelingas ellen fremedon*; indeed *wæs seo þeod tilu*, as we are told later (1250): the behaviour of their princes fits the heroic ideal, enshrined in the metrical and lexical system. The idea that the setting up of lexical expectations is basic in the composition and enjoyment of the early poetry would seem to be supported[1] by the description of Hroðgar's *scop*, 'se ðe eal-fela eald-gesegena worn gemunde, word oþer fand soðe gebunden' (896 ff.), the latter part recalling the quest for wisdom and expression in *Hávamál*:

þá nam ek frævaz
ok fróðr vera

[1] As has been suggested: see R. W. Chambers, *Beowulf* (1914), note to ll. 870–1.

ok vaxa ok vel hafaz;
orð mér af orði
orz leitaði,
verk mér af verki
verks leitaði.

(st. 141)[1]

If however one were to reduce Old English poetry to metrically endorsed habitual collocations, lexically and syntactically
complementary, this would be merely to agree with Milman
Parry's view quoted earlier that the best poet was the one who
knew and adhered most completely to the conventional diction.
And this – to put it at its highest – would be a misleading conclusion, failing to account for much of our experience of the
poetry. There are several ways in which the sophisticated poet,
well learned in the conventions, could 'shade and knit anew
the patch of words', as Dylan Thomas puts it. One of the most
widely used devices is to allow the conventional lexical connexions and the conventional grammatical connexions (normally in unison, as in 'Sum mid hondum mæg · hearpan
gretan' *Gifts of Men* 49) some degree of independence, with an
area of overlap. The phenomenon is easily illustrated from post-
Renaissance poetry also; in Shakespeare's thirty-third sonnet,
we have

Full many a glorious morning have I seen
Flatter the mountain-tops with sovereign eye

where the lexical congruity of *flatter* and *sovereign* effects one
valuable connexion (since there is some similarity with the
courtly situation in which sovereigns are flattered), but where
the grammatical connexion is necessarily independent of this,
since here it is the majestic sun itself that performs the flattery.
Again, in Shelley's 'The World's Wanderers',

Tell me, moon, thou pale and gray
Pilgrim of heaven's homeless way

[1] Ed. Jón Helgason, *Eddadigte* I (1951).

homeless works in a grammatical connexion ('space provides no homes') and in an independent lexical connexion (with *pilgrim*). One might further illustrate the point from the complementary but independent lexical and grammatical relations of *human* and *softly* in these lines by W. H. Auden:

> Lay your sleeping head, my love,
> Human on my faithless arm

and

> Let the winds of dawn that blow
> Softly round your dreaming head.[1]

It can be shown that in a good deal of Old English poetry, too, words 'interanimate' each other, to use Donne's admirable expression. The name *Grendel*, for instance, is alliteratively linked in more than half its two score occurrences with words congruently indicative of fierceness, especially *guð* and *gryre*: and it is surely unnecessary to point out that there is no question of the poet's being obliged to make such selections by reason of a scarcity of words which will alliterate. Frequently, the lexical connexion is in unison with the grammatical one; for instance: 'he hraðe wolde   Grendle forgyldan   guð-ræsa fela' (*Beowulf* 1576 f.; and similarly 483, 591, and elsewhere). But we find notable instances in which the lexical connexion is maintained without a grammatical one, an effect which can be achieved not only because the particular type of lexical connexion is already established in the poem, but also because the whole metrical tradition has, as we have seen, established

---

[1] The power of a collocation may, however, result from purely contextual developments and need not depend on previous experience of a particular lexical connexion. In *Richard II*, for example, when it has become painfully clear how feeble a substitute for kingship is the *name* of kingship, the king – who is almost alone in failing to see the gulf between the two – cries:

> Is not the king's name twenty thousand names?
> Arm, arm, my name! A puny subject strikes
> At thy great glory.   (III. ii. 85 ff.)

The lexical relationship between 'my name' and 'puny' effectively deflates the preceding line.

an expectation of lexical connexion. There is a good example in Unferð's flyting:

> Ðonne wene ic to þe   wyrsan geþingea,
> ðeah þu heaðo-ræsa   gehwær dohte,
> grimre guðe,   gif þu Grendles dearst
> niht-longne fyrst   nean bidan. (525 ff.)

The grammatical connexion of *grimre guðe* here is with Beowulf's skill in the past, but its equally potent lexical connexion is with Grendel and his present threat. Similar relationships appear in lines 819, 1538, and elsewhere.

When Beowulf's ten cowardly comrades rejoin Wiglaf after the fatal combat, it is said of them, 'hy scamiende · scyldas bæran' (2850). The lexical and metrical connexion between *scamiende* and *scyldas* points the irony of their external equipment and their internal inadequacy, which is made explicit in the context, especially by Wiglaf's words in ll. 2865-6. The syntactic connexions state that, feeling shame, the men approached with their shields; the metrically endorsed lexical connexion states that their shame actually lay in their shields, their own well-protected condition.[1]

The establishment of a lexical connexion 'by secretly evoking powerful associations', as Professor C. S. Lewis has put it,[2] is well demonstrated in the relationship of *death* and *doom*. The lexical and grammatical connexions are concurrent in *Beowulf* 1387 ff.:

> wyrce se þe mote
> domes ær deaþe;   þæt bið driht-guman
> unlifgendum   æfter selest

---

[1] The double relationship finds a parallel in the 'prosodic counterpoint' that J. W. Lever sees in Sidney and other poets, the one depending upon syntax, the other (which may reinforce it or be in contrast) depending upon rhyme-scheme; see *The Elizabethan Love Sonnet* (1956), for example, p. 62. One should also refer, of course, to the complexity of effects that W. Empson is able to see generated by polysemy and the concurrent operation of lexical and grammatical connexions: *Seven Types of Ambiguity* (second edn, 1947), 30 ff., 49 ff., for example.

[2] *Studies in Words* (1960), 218.

as they are also in *Hávamál*:

> ek veit einn,
> at aldri deyr:
> dómr of dauðan hvern.
>
> (st. 77)[1]

In the Tiberius gnomic verses, the lexical connexion is independent:

> and ealle þa gastas   þe for gode hweorfað
> æfter deaðdæge,   domes bidað
> on fæder fæðme
>
> (*Maxims II* 59 ff.)

with which we may compare *Beowulf* 885 'æfter deað-dæge · dom unlytel'; the connexion is also independent of grammar later in the poem, l. 1490 f.:

> ic me mid Hruntinge
> dom gewyrce,   oþðe mec deað nimeð

and in the Exeter Book maxims:

> holen sceal inæled,   yrfe gedæled
> deades monnes.   Dom biþ selast.
>
> (*Maxims I* 79 f.)

With differing degrees of grammatical independence, there is an identical lexical connexion between the root 'lie' and *lic* in

> þær his lichoma,   leger-bedde fæst,
> swefeþ æfter symle   (*Beowulf* 1007 f.)

and

> þæt he for mund-gripe   minum scolde
> licgean lif-bysig,   butan his lic swice.
>
> (ib. 965 f.)

The well-established connexion between *brucan* and *beag*, the very type and symbol of reward, is exemplified concurrently

---

[1] Ed. Helgason, op. cit.

with a grammatical connexion in *Beowulf* 894 ('he beah-hordes
· brucan moste'), but occurs independently with no less effectiveness, as when lexical collocation proclaims that bright
treasure may now be enjoyed again in Heorot:

> Heorot is gefælsod,
> beah-sele beorhta;   bruc, þenden þu mote,
> manigra medo . . .   (1176 ff.)

We have the same independent relationship a little later:

> . . . ic gum-cystum   godne funde
> beaga bryttan,   breac þonne moste.
>   (1486 f.)

It would take more space than is available here to explore this
phenomenon as it manifests itself in a poem as thematically
rich as *Beowulf*, but mention might be made of a passage in
the Finn episode where it occurs with particular density and
effectiveness, especially perhaps in lines 1103, 1113, 1121,
1122, 1123.

III

Most of the examples we have considered so far have been of
metrical two-stress units being complementary to each other.
But strong as is the expectation of this, it is important to note
that there is comparable power in the expectation of parity, of
equivalence, of grammatical apposition – the relationship which
has as its primary vehicle the metrical convention known as
'variation'. This is so common as to need little illustration. One
well-known type is seen in 'Beowulf maðelode, · bearn Ecg-
þeowes' or 'Eala Ioseph min, · Iacobes bearn' (*Christ* 164).
When Hroðgar says to Beowulf, 'gemyne mærþo, · mægen-ellen
cyð' (659), the lexical congruity of *mærþo* and *mægen-ellen* (well
attested in hymns and psalms, for instance), together with the
grammatical parallelism of the two metrical units (imperative
plus object), would prompt an audience used to the patterns of
Old English poetry to see a variation-equation here: bearing

glory in mind is one aspect of showing mighty valour. So too when we are told (of Byrhtnoð's avengers),

> þa hi forð eodon,   feores hi ne rohton
>
> (*Maldon* 260)

it is the expectations determined by the metrical conventions as much as by the context that make us aware that going forward *meant* not caring about their own lives. The plight of the pagan Danes in *Beowulf* is expressed by this means: their *hyht* is collocated – significantly – with *hell*:

> Swylc wæs þeaw hyra,
>
> hæþenra hyht;   helle gemundon
>
> in mod-sefan,   Metod hie ne cuþon . . .
>
> (178 ff.)

By contrast, it is said of the hero:

> Huru Geata leod   georne truwode
>
> modgan mægnes,   Metodes hyldo
>
> (669 f.)

and the metrical dependences thus directly attribute Beowulf's might to the Lord's favour. In the same way, the description of Grendel's *glof*, 'gegyrwed deofles cræftum ond dracan fellum' (2087 f.), is not to be read as sylleptic. One further illustration may be offered to show how close is this idea of an equation between metrical units in variation to the idea discussed earlier of congruity between such units when they are complementary:

> Ful oft gebeotedon   beore druncne
>
> ofer ealo-wæge   oret-mecgas . . .
>
> (*Beowulf* 480 f.)

In these transverse sets (*beot–beor*; *ealo–oret*), we have a witness to the dependence of challenge upon beer that would be difficult to parallel.

Now that we have seen to some extent how immensely powerful are the tendencies towards a relationship of at least lexical congruity between metrical units, and have observed some of the ways in which Old English poets exploited these tendencies to sharpen communication, we may turn to what would seem to be the most attractive potentiality for exploitation provided by the system of conventions. For the very reason that there was a high expectation of congruity at specific points in metrical structure, the impact of the incongruous at such points could be the greater.[1]

After *sæl* in the sense of 'happiness' has been used three times in *Beowulf* in a congruent context (the occurrence in line 643 collocates with *sige-folca sweg* as a variation), we have Hroðgar's reply to Beowulf's polite inquiry on the morning after the attack by Grendel's mother:

> Ne frin þu æfter sælum;   sorh is geniwod
> Denigea leodum.   Dead is Æschere . . .
>
> (1322 f.)

Later on in the same poem, it is said of Unferð that he did not dare 'drihtscipe dreogan; · þær he dome forleas' (1470). The turned tide of Beowulf's fortunes as he embarks on the dragon fight is symbolized by the contrast between *goldwine* (which invites exultant collocations) and *geomor sefa*, with which it is metrically linked (2419). In a similar way, the incongruity of youth and sadness, external gaiety and inward grief, is sharpened in the *Wife's Lament*:

> A scyle geong man   wesan geomormod,
> heard heortan geþoht,   swylce habban sceal
> bliþe gebæro,   eac þon breostceare . . .
>
> (42 ff.)

In *Beowulf*, line 281, *bealu* is contrasted with a redeeming *bot*, and the line which follows provides a good example of what could be done with lexical and metrical patterning:

> þa cear-wylmas   colran wurðaþ . . .

The collocation of *care* with *cool* would in itself be a congruous

---

[1] See the discussion of 'warranted' and 'frustrated expectations' by Roman Jakobson, 'Linguistics and Poetics', in *Style in Language*, ed. T. A. Sebeok (1960), 350–77.

commonplace (compare l. 2396 or – an illustration with greater morphological and semantic complexity – *Seafarer* 14). But here (as in l. 2066, equally effectively and in a far more pregnant passage) the semantic relationship is enriched by the presence of *wylm*, the lexical relations of which elsewhere are often the antithesis of cold:[1] compare *Genesis* 2586, *Juliana* 583, *Christ* 831, 965, *Phoenix* 283, *Daniel* 463, and *Beowulf* 2546. The collocation thus subtly implies the possibility of both a contrast and a paradox, parallel on the one hand to the change from *bealu* to *bot* (281) and on the other to the connexion between conjugal love and slaughterous enmity (2065).[2]

Metrical and lexical links which are incongruous may have a sharply poignant effect, as when Hildeburh is forced to commit her son to the funeral pyre ('hire selfre sunu · sweoloðe befæstan' 1115),[3] or when Hroðgar knows that his noble thane Æschere is lifeless, 'aldor-þegn · unlyfigendne, / þone deorestan · deadne' (1308 f.). There is a whole series of such incongruities in the description of the mourning father (*Beowulf* 2444 ff.), such as the link of *sunu* with *sarig sang* (2447) and with *sorh* (2455), of *hearp* with *hæleð in hoðman* (2458).

Again, incongruous links may be sinister, as when it is said of Heorot, at the triumphant moment of completion, that 'heah ond horn-geap, · heaðo-wylma bad' (82).[4] Or they may point an ironic antithesis. In *Beowulf* 1709, *hæleðum to helpe* (predicted of the hero) is collocated with *Heremod*, the symbol of evil kingship, and the passage which follows develops this antithesis between the good and evil types of king, with several pairs of alliterating units defying congruous complementarity:

ne geweox he him to willan,   ac to wæl-fealle
ond to deað-cwalum   Deniga leodum.

[1] In *Elene* 1257, the same compound *cearwylm* is in construction with the verb *cnyssan*, and the image in this instance relates emotion rather to a storm at sea.

[2] See p. 168 below.

[3] There is a poignant irony with similar exponence in *Hildebrandslied*: 'nû scal mih suâsat chind · suertu hauwan'; it is implicit earlier too: 'muotîn . . . untar heriun tuêm, / sunufatarungo; · iro saro rihtun, / garutun se iro gûðhamun'. Cf. also *Beowulf* 1261 f.: 'Cain wearð to ecg-banan angan breþer', perhaps used to emphasize – by the parallel – Unferð's baseness.   [4] See p. 167 below.

Breat bolgen-mod   beod-geneatas,
eaxl-gesteallan,   oþþæt he ana hwearf,
mære þeoden,   mon-dreamum from,
ðeah þe hine mihtig God   mægenes wynnum,
eafeþum stepte,   ofer ealle men
forð gefremede.   Hwæþere him on ferhþe greow
breost-hord blod-reow;   nallas beagas geaf
Denum æfter dome.   Dream-leas gebad . . .

(1711 ff.)

The ironical presentation of antitheses, 'not *this* (as might be expected) but *that*', is clearly of great appeal as a rhetorical device, and it is something for which the features of poetic style that we have been considering have an extraordinary potential, exploited in many poems. For instance:

Wa3ð hine wræclast,   nales wunden gold,
ferðloca freorig,   nalæs foldan blæd.

(*Wanderer* 32 f.)

Abraham sealde
wig to wedde,   nalles wunden gold,
for his suhtrigan,   sloh and fylde
feond on fitte.   (*Genesis* 2069 ff.)

þæt þam banan ne wearð
hleahtre behworfen,   ah in helle ceafl
sið asette   (*Andreas* 1702 ff.)

Hwilum ylfete song
dyde ic me to gomene,   ganetes hleoþor
ond huilpan sweg   fore hleahtor wera,
mæw singende   fore medodrince.

(*Seafarer* 19 ff.)

(Welund) hæfde him to gesiþþe   sorge ond longaþ,
wintercealde wræce . . .   (*Deor* 3 f.)

While the ironies here are achieved through the juxtaposition

of incompatibles like 'laughter' and 'hell' at points in the
metrical structure where lexical relationship is expected, one
may also find a comparable effect achieved by retaining complementary and normal collocations rendered contextually
ironical. In the flood which is brought about by Andreas's
prayer, his revelling and feasting tormenters find rather different *byrlas* serving up a great deal of unwelcome 'drink':

> Fæge swulton,
> geonge on geofene   guðræs fornam
> þurh sealtne weg.   þæt wæs sorgbyrþen,
> biter beorþegu.   Byrlas ne gældon,
> ombehtþegnas.   þær wæs ælcum genog
> fram dæges orde   drync sona gearu.
>
> (*Andreas* 1530 ff.)

The ironical tones can be dissipated into the almost wholly
commonplace in descriptions of retribution, for which this
rhetorical device (as we have already seen) is very commonly
used; words for 'payment' or 'repayment' all too readily con-
note 'punishment':

> Gyldað nu mid gyrne,   þæt heo goda ussa
> meaht forhogde,   ond mec swiþast
> geminsade,   þæt ic to meldan wearð.
> Lætað hy laþra   leana hleotan
> þurh wæpnes spor   (*Juliana* 619 ff.)

> þæs hi longe sculon
> ferðwerige onfon   in fyrbaðe,
> wælmum biwrecene,   wraþlic ondlean
> (*Christ* 829 ff.)

> sealde him wites clom,
> atole to æhte   (*Christ and Satan* 451 f.)[1]

At times, however, the conjunction of words, metre, and

---

[1] Compare such expressions as 'for recompense he will receive great torment' in
the OS *Heliand*, ll. 4585, 5424, 5563, etc.

situation have a very powerful effect, as in Byrhtnoð's reply to the Vikings' demand for tribute:

> Gehyrst þu, sælida,   hwæt þis folc segeð?
> Hi willað eow to gafole   garas syllan,
> ættrynne ord   and ealde swurd,
> þa heregeatu   þe eow æt hilde ne deah.
>   (*Maldon* 45 ff.)[1]

And similarly, Hadubrand's rejection of the gifts offered by the man whom he cannot believe to be his father:

> Mit gêru scal man   geba infâhan,
> ort widar orte.   (*Hildebrandslied*)

In the Edda, likewise:

> Kvǫddo síðan   Sigmundar bur
> auðs ok hringa   Hundings synir,
> þvíat þeir átto   iǫfri at gialda
> fiárnám mikit   ok fǫður dauða.

> Létat buðlungr   bótir uppi,
> né niðia in heldr   nefgiǫld fá;
> ván kvað hann mundo   veðrs ens mikla
> grára geira   ok gremi Óðins.
>   (*Helgakviða Hundingsbana I*, st. 11 and 12)[2]

[1] I am grateful to Professor I. L. Foster for discussing and expounding (in correspondence) a notable Welsh parallel. The poem *Armes Prydein* in the Book of Taliesin (ed. J. G. Evans, 1915) has 'tribute' and 'pay' used ironically several times in prophesying the lot of King Athelstan's stewards. For example, *anaeleu dretheu, dy · chynullant* (l. 72) – 'grief (will be) the tributes that they gather'.

[2] Ed. Jón Helgason, *Eddadigte* III (1952). The device is used with comic effect in *Þrymskviða*, st. 29, 32:

> Inn kom in arma   iǫtna systir,
> hin er brúðfiár   biðia þorði:
> 'Láttu þér af hǫndom   hringa rauða,
> ef þú ǫðlaz vill   ástir mínar,
> ástir mínar,   alla hylli' . . .

> Drap hann ina ǫldno   iǫtna systur,
> hin er brúðfiár   of beðit hafði;

When, in the *Nibelungenlied*, the sight of Hagen's gold arm-ring attracts the avaricious Danube ferryman, we are told:

> dô wold' er verdienen   daz Hagenen golt sô rôt:
> des leit er von dem degene   den swertgrimmigen tôt.

(st. 1554)

Among the many other occasions on which we find expressions of similar irony in medieval literature, one might mention the fourteenth-century German poem on the Battle of Sempach where the Swiss defensive resolution before the battle is expressed in terms of penance. A priest can certainly be found to hear confession:

> er kan wol büsse geben:
> mit scharpfen hallenbarten
> so gibt man inen den segen.
> Das ist ein scharpfe büsse . . .[1]

I V

It is with irony of this kind that the extreme bitterness is expressed towards the close of *Beowulf*; the dead hero is surrounded by incongruous wealth:

> þa sceall brond fretan,
> æled þeccean,   nalles eorl wegan

> hón skell um hlaut   fyr skillinga,
> en hǫgg hamars   fyr hringa fiǫlð.

(Ed. Helgason, *Eddadigte* II, 1952). It has a similar comic effect in the prose Edda too, as we find in the account of how Thor dealt with the smith from Jotunheim: 'Galt hann þá smíðarkaupit, ok eigi sól ok tungl [as had been agreed], heldr synjaði hann honum at byggva í Jǫtunheimum ok laust þat it fyrsta hǫgg, er haussinn brotnaði í smán mola, ok sendi hann niðr undir Niflheim' (*SnE* 47, normalized).

[1] Ludwig Tobler, *Schweizerische Volkslieder* II (1884), 10 f. We may compare our use of 'short shrift'. In Sir Walter Scott's version of the poem, we have:

> The Switzer priest has ta'en the field,
> He deals a penance drear.
> Right heavily upon your head
> He'll lay his hand of steel;
> And with his trusty partisan
> Your absolution deal.

M

maððum to gemyndum,   ne mægð scyne
habban on healse   hring-weorðunge,
ac sceal geomor-mod,   golde bereafod,
oft, nalles æne,   elland tredan,
nu se here-wisa   hleahtor alegde,
gamen ond gleo-dream.   Forðon sceall gar wesan
monig morgen-ceald   mundum bewunden,
hæfen on handa,   nalles hearpan sweg
wigend weccean,   ac se wonna hrefn
fus ofer fægum   fela reordian,
earne secgan,   hu him æt æte speow,
þenden he wið wulf   wæl reafode.

(3014 ff.)

This passage, however, is more than merely an additional
example of a recurrent theme, contrasting comfortable possibility with bitter fact through what can now be seen as a
characteristic departure from the basic metrical and lexical conditions: we see here the use of incongruous collocations to form
a critical undercurrent of a kind which notably enriches *Beowulf*
from time to time and which is prominent among the features
making it a great poem. Mention has already been made of
the predicted fate of Heorot (82): this is immediately followed
by a direct link between *ecg-hete* and *aþum-swerian* (84);[1] somewhat later, we see the sinister character of Unferð – particularly in relation to his past faithlessness towards kin (587) – and
his sinister proximity to Hroðgar (500). In Fitte XV, we have
an important passage as follows:

Ne gefrægen ic þa mægþe   maran weorode
ymb hyra sinc-gyfan   sel gebæran.
Bugon þa to bence   blæd-agande,
fylle gefægon;   fægere geþægon
medo-ful manig   magas þara,
swið-hicgende,   on sele þam hean,
Hroðgar ond Hroþulf.   Heorot innan wæs

---

[1] See the excellent note on this passage in C. L. Wrenn's edition.

freondum afylled;   nalles facen-stafas
þeod-Scyldingas   þenden fremedon.

(1011 ff.)

The passage begins by portraying *comitatus* solidarity and reflecting this in the stable, traditional and congruous heroic collocations: kinsmen united over mead, brave-minded in a brave hall; the metrical arrangement should also suggest the unity of Hroðgar and Hroþulf within Heorot (1017), but this has been made equivocal (84) and irony is explicit in 1018 with the link between *freondum* and *facen-stafas* – a link which however is metrical without being syntactic.[1] The sinister suggestions become more explicit a hundred and fifty lines later when what Jakobson calls a 'warranted' link (metrically and lexically) between 'suhtergefæderan' and 'sib' is broken by the foreboding *gyt*.[2] The metre gives a further hint of Unferð's place in the ultimate tragedy:

þær þa godan twegen
sæton suhtergefæderan;   þa gyt wæs hiera sib ætgædere,
æghwylc oðrum trywe.   Swylce þær Unferþ þyle
æt fotum sæt frean Scyldinga;   gehwylc hiora his ferhþe treowde,
þæt he hæfde mod micel,   þeah þe he his magum nære
ar-fæst æt ecga gelacum.   (1163 ff.)

By the time we come to Wealhþeow's speech beginning at line 1216, we are no longer disposed to take 'warranted' links at their face value; as for instance:

Her is æghwylc eorl   oþrum getrywe . . .
(1228)

The internal disharmonies of a subsequent *comitatus* scene are even more forcibly emphasized by lexical disharmonies pointed by the metre. After the description of the Queen's and

---

[1] As J. W. Lever says (op. cit. 6), the 'progressive logic of syntax' can be 'overborne by the emotional suggestions of rhyme'.
[2] See n. 1, p. 160, above.

Freawaru's relations with the court of Heorot (2016 ff., a passage characterized by congruence of vocabulary, syntax, and metre), mention is made of the marriage to Ingeld, and at once an undercurrent becomes noticeable, running independently of and at first in opposition to the syntax, with the lexical-metrical links of *wif* and *wæl-fæhð* (2028), *bon-gar* and *bryd* (2031). The tragedy moves to its climax with the goading of a young Heathobard by the 'eald æsc-wiga' (2042) who says of the Danish courtier that he 'morðres gylpeð · ond þone maðþum byreð' (2055). The metre here achieves the inciter's end by seeming (in terms of variation) to give equal authority to the *fact* (wearing the sword) and the *inference* (exulting in the earlier slaughter of Heathobards). The rhetorical equation – 'morðres gylpeð' *in that* 'maðþum byreð' – is given further point by the alliterative link and syntactic parallelism of *murder* and *sword*. So too, the absence of direct responsibility on the part of those who now suffer is emphasized in the metrical and grammatical parallelism of 'se fæmnan þegn · fore fæder dædum' (2059); and the bitterness of Ingeld's situation is summed up in the collocation (independent of grammar) of *wæl-niðas* and *wif-lufan* (2065).

With the dragon fight, and beginning in Fitte XXXII, we find all the devices of metre, word-relationship, and grammar so far discussed being used to mark what is surely the most important thematic undercurrent in the poem: an undermining of the heroic values attached to gold. The treatment of the lone survivor emphasizes the dubious and transient value of treasure by such metrically endorsed collocations as *deore maðmas* and *deað* (2236), *lytel fæc* and *long-gestreona* (2240), and syntactic connexions like *hæðen gold* (2276). The fitte ends with the metrical link of *sinc* and *sar*, confirming a connexion between the hero's death and a distorted valuation of treasure, and anticipating the same collocation in 2746, where it applies to the dragon, whose death (also brought about by the gold) is explicitly compared with Beowulf's in 2844. From the thirty-second fitte onwards, whatever the difficulties we have with the narrative account of the treasure's history,[1] *hord* is a suspect word (it is collocated with 'hate' in 2319), and *hord-weard* is identified with the dragon (2293, 2302, 2554). The damning collocations of treasure continue: *wrætta ond wira* is linked metrically to *weard unhiore* (the dragon) in 2413, *gold* to *guð* (2414, 2536), to *geomor* (2419, 3018), to *grim* (3012), to *bær* (3105), and to *greot* (3167); *feoh* to *fyren* (2441); *beah-hord* to *bealu* (2826). There is a metrical but not syntactic relation of *searu* with *sinc* at the very point where we have the explicit condemnation of treasure as such:

> . . . earm-beaga fela
> searwum gesæled.   Sinc eaðe mæg,
> gold on grunde,   gum-cynnes gehwone
> oferhigian . . .   (2763 ff.)

The devaluation is completed when we have the supreme irony of the lines describing the disposal of the gold for which Beowulf died:

> Hi on beorg dydon   beg ond siglu,
> eall swylce hyrsta,   swylce on horde ær
> nið-hedige men   genumen hæfdon;
> forleton eorla gestreon   eorðan healdan,
> gold on greote,   þær hit nu gen lifað
> eldum swa unnyt,   swa hit æror wæs.

> (3163 ff.)

And that it *is* the supreme irony, the poet's elaborately equivocal use of familiar formulas has made perfectly clear. Over the last seven hundred lines of the poem, the dragon fight is repeatedly referred to as a pitifully unequal bargain of Beowulf's life in exchange for gold, terms like *ceap* both enhancing the irony and probing the morality of worldly purchase and wealth:

> Weard unhiore,
> gearo guð-freca   gold-maðmas heold,

---

[1] See, for example, K. Sisam in *Review of English Studies* 9 (1958), 129 ff.; C. L. Wrenn, edition, notes to ll. 3051 ff., 3074 ff.; G. V. Smithers in *English and Germanic Studies* 4 (1951–2), 75 ff.

eald under eorðan;   næs þæt yðe ceap
to gegangenne   gumena ænigum.
                                    (2413 ff.)

Beowulf finds himself recalling another 'feoh-leas gefeoht'
(2441), which in turn leads to his parable of the mourning
father who is brought in grief to see the worthlessness of
material treasures (2455 ff., especially 2461 f.). Beowulf mentions life in terms of bargaining, 'ealdre gebohte, heardan
ceape' (2481 f.), and after the fight he uses the same expression
to describe the price he has paid:

Nu ic on maðma hord   mine bebohte
frode feorh-lege . . .   (2799 f.)

So too, a little later, we are told that

Biowulfe wearð
dryht-maðma dæl   deaðe forgolden
                                    (2842 f.)

and the immensity of the treasure that his death has secured,
the 'hord . . . grimme gegongen' (3084 f.), only emphasizes its
ultimate, comparative worthlessness:

þær is maðma hord,
gold unrime,   grimme geceapod;
ond nu æt siðestan   sylfes feore
beagas gebohte: þa sceall brond fretan,
æled þeccean,   nalles eorl wegan
maððum to gemyndum . . .   (3011 ff.)[1]

In view of this, it is worth recalling that, at the point where
Beowulf was represented as seeking out the dragon's hoard, the
poet has told us – in one of his most telling ironic uses of familiar
collocations – that *wyrd* would be seeking out the treasure-
hoard of the hero's soul and that the only dividing up that day
would be of life from body:

wyrd ungemete neah,
se ðone gomelan   gretan sceolde,

---

[1] Accepting the usual editorial readings in ll. 3012, 3014.

secean sawle hord,   sundur gedælan
lif wið lice . . .   (2420 ff.)

It should therefore be emphasized that, while formulaic utterances and habitual collocations are the necessary starting point in the study of the early alliterative poetry, they are *only* the starting point. The very fact that he could depend on his audience having a firm expectation of certain dependences and determined sequences involving metre, vocabulary, and grammar gave the poet his opportunity to stretch linguistic expression beyond the ordinary potentialities of prose, and to achieve a disturbing and richly suggestive poetry.

RANDOLPH QUIRK

14 · The name of the town Eslöv

Most of the town-names in Skåne are older than the towns themselves. Usually the place where a town was established already had a well-known name. The town *Skanör*, for example, got its name from the dangerous *ör* (ON *eyrr*), the sandspit now called Falsterbo-spit. The city of *Lund* took its name from a grove (ON *lundr*), probably a sacrificial grove. The name of *Malmö* came from the mounds of gravel (ON *malmhaugar*) found on the site. *Falsterbo* was originally the name for the huts used by the herring-fishers. An exception to the general rule that the towns were given the names already belonging to the sites on which they were built is, e.g., *Kristianstad*, named after its founder, King Christian IV.

Among the towns of Skåne *Eslöv* is one of the youngest. It did not get its charter until 1911. But its name is very ancient and was borrowed from the village of Eslöv, on whose land the town was built.

A deed of gift made by Archbishop Eskil of Lund in 1145 and preserved in a copy from 1494 refers to a place called *Haeslef*. The document has been published in SD I 50,[1] but the index of that volume does no more than localize the place to Skåne. There can however be no doubt but that *Haeslef* represents the village-name *Eslöv*.

It is by no means uncommon to find the writers of Latin documents inserting an initial *h-* in place-names beginning

---

[1] The following abbreviations are used: DD = *Diplomatarium Danicum*; LDLV = *Liber daticus Lundensis vetustior*; LÄUB = *Lunds ärkestifts urkundsbok*; NL = *Necrologium Lundense*; Rep = *Repertorium diplomaticum Regni danici*; Rep 2 = *Repertorium diplomaticum Regni danici. Series secunda*; SD = *Svenskt Diplomatarium (Diplomatarium Suecicum)*; SDns = *Svenskt Diplomatarium från år 1401*.

with a vowel. An original document from the end of the twelfth century writes *horebro* for *Örebro* (SD I 682), and another, written between 1167 and 1199, writes *heluacharlaby* for *Älvkarleby* (SD I 95). An original document from 1275 has *henecopiæ* for *Enköping* (SD I 718).

Uppåkra in Skåne is called *Huphackre* in a document from 1200–1201 (preserved in transcript, SD I 686), and *Örtofta*, also in Skåne, is written *hørtyftæ* in a document from 1283 (preserved in transcript, SD I 631). In a statement of the boundaries of Ballingslöv made in the first half of the thirteenth century appear the words *Hæschikærs wæthil*. This form conceals a place-name **Äskekärr*.[1] In 1221 the Danish monastery *Øm* is called *Høm* (DD I: 5, 197, from the original).

On this intrusive *h*- further reference may be made to Jöran Sahlgren, *Namn och Bygd* (1925), 187, Stig O:n Nordberg, *Fornsvenskan i våra latinska originaldiplom före 1300*, I (1926), 165, and J. Brøndum-Nielsen, *Gammeldansk Grammatik* II (1932), 282.

If we thus remove the initial in *Haeslef*, we are left with *Aeslef*. In an original document from 1424 the name is written in a more correct form, *Esløff*, and it occurs in another extant original source from 1426 as *Æsløff*.[2]

The second element in this name is clearly the old word *lev* (ON *leif*), 'inheritance', found, for example, in OSw *ättalef*, 'family property, patrimony'. It is related to the word *leva* in *kvarleva*, 'something allowed to remain, something remaining', and to English *leave*.

Place-names in *-lev*, *-löv* most probably originated in the Migration Age.[3] They are especially common in the ancient realm of the Danes, and in Skåne alone there are over sixty of them, including the well-known *Svalöv* and *Arlöv*. As far as one can see, the original *lev*-names are always compounded with personal names as the first element.[4]

[1] See M. P:n Nilsson in *NoB* (1926), 109.
[2] LÄUB III 37, 63.
[3] J. Sahlgren in *Hälsingborgs Historia* I (1925), 111 ff.
[4] On a number of unauthentic *lev*-names, see K. G. Ljunggren in *SSON* (1946–1948), 3 ff.

In *Eslöv*, therefore, we have to expect a personal name. I have previously assumed that it contained the genitive form, *Äsa*, of the man's name, *Äse* (*Ese*), known in ODan and undoubtedly a hypocoristic form for names such as *Äskil* (*Eskil*) and *Äsbjörn* (*Esbjörn*).[1] That such a man's name was known in Skåne may perhaps be inferred from the reference to a *Thord Æsesun*, i.e. Thord Äse's son, in the will of archdeacon Håkan of Lund, made in 1283 (extant in transcript, SD I 632). But see what follows below.

This explanation of mine has found favour in a number of reference books. All the same, I now believe it to be wrong.

The point is that in originally trisyllabic Scanian place-names in -*lev*, -*löv* the vowel of the second syllable usually remains in the older medieval period. Thus, for example, *Gödelöv* is written *Gøteleue* in the twelfth century (NL 9) and *Gødeleff* in 1478 (Rep 2, no. 4242; original); *Kvärlöv* appears as *Quædelöf* in 1245 (Rep, no. 169; transcript), *Ölöv* as *Øtheløf* c. 1250 (LDLV 132; original), *Fjärlöv* as *Fyærdeløff* in 1403 (SDns I 206; original), *Gnalöv* as *Gnaffueløff* in 1431 (LÄUB III 99; original), *Gualöv* as *guthælef* in 1347 (SD V 697; original), *Härlöv* as *Herthalef* in the fourteenth century (LDLV 305; original), and *Roalöv* as *Rothaleef* in 1363 (Rep, no. 2686).

The exceptions to this rule usually depend on the fact that an unstressed vowel was lost early between two consonants that were the same or similar. In the same way *åttatio* was reduced to *åttio* by the loss of *a* between identical consonants.

Already in the twelfth century an older *Svalalev (*Svalulev) was contracted to *Swalleue* (NL 7).[2] The first element is doubtless the genitive *Swala* of the masculine personal name, OSw *Swali*, ONorw *Svali*. According to E. H. Lind, *Norsk-isländska dopnamn* (1905–15), col. 983, and *Danmarks gamle personnavne*, I col. 1312, the *a* in the name was long. But evidence in favour of regarding the *a* as short may be found in the personal name *Svale*, still used in Norway, and in a number of Scandinavian

---

[1] See J. Sahlgren in *SSON* (1925).
[2] See J. Sahlgren in *Hälsingborgs Historia* I (1925), 115.

place-names. Thus, for example, *Svalered* in Västergötland is written *Swalarydh* in 1391 and is probably compounded with the personal name *Svali* (so in *Sveriges ortnamn, Älvsborgs län*, VI 8). Nevertheless, the possibility that the first element in the place-name is the genitive of the word *svala* (swallow, the bird), used as a nickname, cannot be completely dismissed.

Another example from Skåne of such haplological syncope is in the parish-name *Gislöv*, spelt *Gisløue* about the middle of the twelfth century (NL 9). The first element undoubtedly represents the genitive of the personal name *Gisle*.[1]

The Scanian place-names in *-lev* also show that the medial vowel was lost early when it occurred between a preceding liquid sound and the following *l* of *-lev*. About 1150 the parish-name *Arlöv* was still written *Areleue* (NL 9), but in 1200 or 1201 it appears as *Arleff* (SD I 686; transcript). The first element in the name is certainly the genitive of the masculine personal name *Ari*.[2] In a document from 1303, extant in the original, the parish-name *Burlöv* is written *burlef* (SD II 389). Its first element is undoubtedly, as Falkman long ago saw, the genitive of the man's name *Buri*.[3] Thus, through the early loss of the vowel between liquids, an **Aralef* and a **Buralef* appear to have become *Arlef* and *Burlef*.

Under such circumstances it is not likely that an old *Äsalev* should have been contracted to *Äslev* as early as the twelfth century. But it would, on the other hand, have been possible for the medial vowel in an ancient form *Äsislev* to be lost very early through haplological syncope. The first element in such a name would then be the genitive of a personal name or a word designating a person, nominative *Äsir*. The *Thord Æsesun* (1283) mentioned above might have been the son of a man called *Äsir*.

Äsir may be readily explained as dependent upon a substantive *äsir*, 'ridge-dweller', an *ia*-derivative from *ås* (ON *áss*), 'ridge'.

[1] Thus B. Ejder in *Svensk Uppslagsbok* 11 (1947).
[2] A. Falkman, *Ortnamnen i Skåne* (1877), 105.   [3] ibid., 116.

The word *äsir*, 'ridge-dweller', is known in other place-names. The parish of *Edsbro* in Uppland is called *hæsabro* in 1287 (SD II 22; original) and *Esabro* in 1291 (SD II 104; original). An explanation of this name, undoubtedly correct in all essentials, has been given by Otto von Friesen.[1] He wrote:

> In the middle ages the parish was called *Äsabro*. It was probably no single farm, on whose land the church was built, that had this name, but we may suppose that the church stands on land belonging to the village of Åsby. Åsby takes its name from a ridge, some 800 foot long, which runs northward from the church and is rich in relics of the past, *bauta*-stones and graves. *Äsir* is the Old Swedish term for the inhabitants of Åsby, and *Äsabro* thus means 'bridge of the ridge-village inhabitants'. There is in fact a bridge right by the church, over which the main road south to Rimbo now goes, crossing the little river that connects the lakes Såttern and Närdingen.

Äsir, the form given by von Friesen, must however be corrected to *äsar*.

Von Friesen has also explained the Uppland parish-name *Estuna* (*Äsetunum* 1289, SD II 73; original) as 'Tuna of the ridge-dwellers', but without any discussion of his reasons.[2] Estuna church stands on a ridge.

As the original for modern Eslöv, the name *Äsislev, 'ridge-dweller's inheritance', makes admirable sense. Eslöv lies about 9 miles south of the southernmost slopes of the great rock-ridge Söderåsen, which extends for some 18 miles in a NW–SE direction and reaches a maximum height of some 650 feet, the highest point in Skåne. It is from this ridge that the district-names, Norra and Södra Åsbo, are derived. *Åsbo härad* means 'the district of the ridge-dwellers'. The name shows that Söderåsen played an important part in the formation of Scanian place-names. The division of Skåne into *härader* is much

[1] In the Christmas Number 1915 of *Upsala Nya Tidning*.
[2] See *NoB* 18 (1930), 97.

younger than the name *Eslöv*. When the district was called Åsbo härad, the old word *äsir* had already been replaced by the younger, synonymous *åsbo*.

But ancient Eslöv itself lay on a little ridge. It is perhaps not utterly impossible that the name *äsir*, which in the genitive provides the place-name's first element, was applied to a dweller on this very site.[1]

JÖRAN SAHLGREN

[1] After I had published an article in *Sydsvenska Dagbladet* explaining the name Eslöv as derived from an older *Åsislev*, Professor P. Wieselgren pointed out to me in a letter that the ridge at Eslöv itself might have given rise to the name.

15 · Uppsala, Iceland, and the Orient

In the oldest literature of the Scandinavian North the name of Uppsala shines with a splendour all its own. Uppsala is the seat of the noblest royal dynasty and is always the scene of great events and extraordinary adventures.

Descent from the kings of Uppsala meant not only that the bluest blood in Scandinavia ran through your veins, but divine ancestry as well. It was believed that the dynasty sprang directly from the gods, Njörð and Frey. We owe our knowledge of the oldest Uppsala kings, from the fifth and sixth centuries and later, to the family pride of one member of this lineage. Towards the end of the ninth century, Rögnvald, a cousin of Harald the Fairhaired, proud of his dynastic origins in Uppsala, gave a Norwegian scald the task of making a poem on his pedigree. So, in the *Ynglingatal*, we now have a catalogue of his ancestors through twenty-six generations, going back to a mythical king in Uppsala, Fjölnir, who died by drowning in a butt of mead. According to the legend Fjölnir was a son of Uppsala-Frey.[1]

There grew up in oral tradition a body of tales and legends about these ancient kings of Uppsala, and Uppsala figures in many connexions in the Icelandic sagas and histories. The references to it are concerned with its ancient legal administration, with its religious practices derived from remote antiquity, with the persons of great kings and heroes, and with extra-

---

[1] On *Ynglingatal* see especially A. Noreen, *Ynglingatal* (Kungl. Vitterhets Historie och Antikvitets Akademiens Handlingar 28, 1925), and W. Åkerlund, *Studier över Ynglingatal* (Skrifter utg. av Vetenskaps-Societeten i Lund 23, 1939).

ordinary adventures at the courts of its rulers. In all these
stories it is an exciting and fascinating task – although not
always an easy one – to try to decide what is pure invention
and what contains a kernel of historical truth. Later in this
paper I shall show what conclusion may be drawn concerning
this question from a critical analysis of one such Uppsala
motive.

In these traditions Uppsala acquired a special repute as the
centre of a strange fertility cult, which is spoken of with
curiosity and embarrassment. Things almost unbelievable were
enacted there in the middle of the realm of the Swedes. According to one story, Harald the Fairhaired had a daughter Ingigerd
who was given in marriage to Erik, king in Uppsala. The super-
stitious men of *Svíaríki* put her on an island and worshipped her
as a goddess and made sacrifices to her. Horrified by this treatment of a queen in Uppsala, the Norwegians, her countrymen,
fetched her home.[1] In another story we are told of a Norwegian
subject who by strange chance became involved in the mysteries
of the fertility cult itself. In this case the man was a fugitive
from Norway who arrived in Sweden just as the festival in
honour of the god Frey was at its height. He followed the
procession which carried the god through the domain of
the Swedes. When opportunity offered, he got secretly into the
wagon, in which Frey and his priestess sat, then overcame the
god and took his place, travelling on through the country with
the priestess. He was venerated as the god, and he enjoyed the
ritual meals prepared in his honour, but let it be understood
that he preferred gold, silver, and other valuable offerings to
blood-sacrifices. Finally he married the priestess and escaped
with her to Norway, not forgetting to take with him a good
part of the treasure he had collected during his divine career
amongst the Swedes.[2]

Among the early events connected with Uppsala it is possible

[1] *Flb.* I 577. On this passage see also Dag Strömbäck in *Festskrift til Finnur
Jónsson* (1928), 290 f.
[2] *Flb.* I 337 ff. On this tale's motive see H. Reuschel, *ZDA* 71 (1934), 155 ff.

to discern, in the dim history of the early sixth century, a great
battle fought there between Swedish and Danish kings. The
site of the battle is *Fýrisvellir*, the wide plains of the river Fyris
to the south of Old Uppsala. This battle naturally made a welcome theme for Icelandic story-telling, and here we again meet
accounts of wonderful events at the royal court of Uppsala.
This time it is the great Danish hero of legend, Hrólf kraki, and
his men who are the protagonists. They meet treachery at the
hands of Adils, the Swedish king, and narrowly escape being
burnt in the hall to which they are shown. Then they make off
across Fýrisvellir, with Adils at the head of his host in hot pur-
suit after them. To delay the pursuers Hrólf strews from the
horn he carries golden ornaments and other precious things
over the plain. Adils's host is thrown into confusion and only
he continues the chase. Then Hrólf takes his own arm-ring and
throws it to the ground. The temptation is too much for Adils –
he halts his horse, bends down and takes up the ring on the
point of his spear. This is what Hrólf is waiting for, and he cries
out in scorn and triumph: 'Now I have made the mightiest of
the Swedes root like a swine!' [1]

Kennings for gold (e.g. *fræ Fýrisvalla*, *barr Kraka* – seed of
Fýrisvellir, barleycorn of Kraki) which occur in the Nor-
wegian-Icelandic poetry of the tenth and eleventh centuries
show that this traditional tale of adventure in its setting on the
plains of Fyris is of respectable age.

These plains are famous in other connexions too. There, near
the end of the tenth century, Erik the Victorious won a decisive
victory over invading vikings. According to the legend, it was
his own nephew, Styrbjörn the Mighty, who, with the help of
King Harald Bluetooth of Denmark, gathered a great army
and marched against Uppsala. Erik the Victorious is certainly
a historical figure, and the battle of Fýrisvellir is attested in no
less a reliable source than near-contemporary runic inscriptions, as well as in the verses of an Icelander who had witnessed
the fight himself. But here again the Icelandic narrative art

[1] *SnE* 139 ff. Cf. Finnur Jónsson, *Hrólfs saga kraka og Bjarkarímur* (1904), 90 ff.

of later centuries has overlaid and embellished the historical basis. In the *Styrbjarnar þáttr* in the late fourteenth-century *Flateyjarbók* we find a fascinating account of Styrbjörn's expedition and of the battle itself.[1] Now it is thanks to his wise counsellor, Thorgný, and to a vow and sacrifice to Odin, that Erik the Victorious inflicts a crushing defeat on his nephew.

King Erik's son was Olaf, usually called *inn sænski*, the Swede, in Icelandic sources, and *Skötkonung* in his homeland. He too makes a notable appearance in the Icelandic stories. In conservative Uppsala he figures as an authentic representative of the old autocracy, but beside him Snorri Sturluson has placed a popular character to show the other side of the coin. This is Thorgný Thorgnýsson who stands out as a significant representative of Swedish legal order and who is presented as an incarnation of wisdom, reason, and power. In Snorri's incomparable description, written about 1225, of the meeting of the Uppsala thing at the beginning of the eleventh century, Thorgný appears as the true leader of the yeomen and people, while in comparison the king appears rather like a wilful and badly brought-up boy.[2]

As I have already suggested, it was characters, events, and circumstances in Uppsala like these which busied the imaginations of Icelandic story-tellers round about 1300. Uppsala became a focus for exciting incidents and experiences, a magnet which drew to itself narrative material of completely remote origin. – And in this way we come to a remarkable little tale of a merchant in Uppsala in the reign of Erik the Victorious – at the end of the tenth century, that is. The story is found in the *Flateyjarbók*, and in all probability it was composed about 1300 or early in the fourteenth century. It is called the *Hróa þáttr heimska*, the tale of Hrói the Simple.[3] The story goes as follows.

[1] *Flb*. II 71 ff.

[2] Finnur Jónsson, *Heimskringla* (1893–1901), II 135 ff.

[3] *Flb*. II 73–80; a fragmentary text is also in AM 557 4to, see my edition of this manuscript in *Corpus codicum Islandicorum medii aevi XIII* (1940).

N

Hrói is an ordinary Danish merchant, enterprising, stubborn, bold. He is strongly built and has a peculiarity which distinguishes him from other men: his one eye is blue, the other brown. This energetic and industrious man succeeds in gaining the favour of Svein Forkbeard, king of Denmark. And no small gain it is, for, according to the Norse way of thinking, a man who undertook something with his king's agreement and protection also shared in the king's luck (*gæfa, gipta, hamingja*) and power and prospered in his affairs. Hrói's trading ventures are in fact extremely profitable as long as he is in partnership with the king, but one day he withdraws from their compact and starts off for Sweden on his own account.

He sails through Mälaren to Fýrisvellir, where he secures his ship and goes ashore to do business with the people of Uppsala. He soon meets a man called Helgi, a member of King Erik's retinue. They talk business at once and Hrói is astonished by the size of the deal, for Helgi wants to buy all his cargo at once. He takes Hrói to a storehouse full of goods and offers him everything inside it in return for the cargo. Hrói is impressed and delighted and they soon agree. The next day Helgi and his men come down and quickly begin to unload Hrói's ship, emptying it completely. Hrói takes things much more leisurely and it is not until some days later that he goes to Helgi's storehouse to move the goods down to his empty ship. But when he gets there he finds the doors wide open and the storehouse empty. There is nobody to be seen, but after some search he finds Helgi asleep. From him he hears to his great surprise that the merchandise has been taken away, because Helgi claims that in accordance with their agreement Hrói should have removed it on a prescribed day. On that day he had piled the goods outside the storehouse, but when Hrói had not come to fetch them, he had had them moved to safe keeping – 'for', he adds, 'it is the law of the land here [in Uppsala] that everyone must take care of his own property so that no thief can steal it. If he does not, the king can prosecute him, and now the king shall judge in this case of yours.' Thus far Helgi.

Hrói goes off, not best pleased, and wanders over the Fýris-vellir, until he is suddenly stopped by two men who have been following him for some time. One of these is Thorgils, Helgi's brother and one of King Erik's counsellors. He tries to snatch a valuable knife that hangs from Hrói's belt, claiming that both knife and belt really belong to him. He accuses him of stealing them on one occasion when they met in Valland (France). Hrói succeeds in retaining his property, but remarks that there seems to be small prospect of profit for him on this trip.

As he goes on his way over the Fýrisvellir he meets a big, powerful, evil-looking man with only one eye. This man accuses Hrói with harsh words of having stolen his other eye by magic. Hrói has, after all, one blue and one brown eye, and the big man says to him, 'Everybody can see that my eye and one of yours belonged once in the same head. The king shall decide this case tomorrow, as well as the case of my brother Thorgils whose knife and belt you stole.'

Hrói the Simple returns ruefully to his ship. You meet curious people in Uppsala!

Next day he goes to the 'town-gate' (borgarhlið), as it says in the text. There are a lot of small huts there and from one he hears voices. He listens and hears one say, 'Will Hrói the Simple come to the thing tomorrow?' Another answers, 'It looks bad for him, since the king always judges in accordance with what those brothers say, whether it is right or wrong.' Hrói passes on, pretending he has heard nothing.

He walks in another part of the town and then catches sight of a young and beautiful lady who is just going to fetch water. She comes up to him and asks if he is Hrói the Simple. He can-not deny it but adds that he has had better nicknames in the past. 'And what is your name?' he asks the girl. 'My name is Sigrbjörg,' she says, 'and I am the daughter of Thorgný the Lawman.' Now an idea hits Hrói – if anyone can help him, it is Thorgný the Lawman. He asks her if she can arrange for him to meet her father. She replies, 'My father is not very fond of Danes, but on the other hand he is no friend of Helgi and his brothers, who have far too much influence with the king.' So they arrange Hrói's opportunity – he is to station himself under the balcony of their loft-room and listen while she talks to her father about his affairs. All goes according to plan. Hrói hears Sigrbjörg's questions about his problems and the answers given her by Thorgný, who is presented as a blind man and, naturally, of the greatest wisdom and experience. She asks, amongst other things and after telling of Helgi's deceit, 'What would you do if you were in Hrói's difficult situation with no one to defend you?' 'I should match trick for trick,' says the old man, and he then describes what he would do, adding at the end, 'And in any case Hrói certainly knows already what he ought to do.' 'Hrói would not be the Simple, if he were as wise as you,' says she. She asks him again what he would do if someone claimed an eye from him, to which he says, 'Match marvel for marvel', and again tells her what ought to be done.

In this way Hrói is well prepared to defend himself in his suits before the thing at Uppsala. The beautiful girl advises him to join Thorgný the Lawman's following when he rides to the assembly. This works out as it should and Hrói arrives at the thing in good company. Now the cases are presented before the king, and the brothers Helgi, Thorgils, and Thórir think they have Hrói in a cleft stick. Helgi comes first and maintains that Hrói has forfeited the wares he should have had from his store-house, because he had not collected them when they were brought out for him. Now Hrói replies: 'When Helgi and I made our bargain, it was to the effect that I should have everything that was in the storehouse. Helgi had all the goods taken out, but I wanted to have all the little beasties that were inside as well, all the moths and the worms, and Helgi did not bring those out! Moreover, I lay claim to Helgi himself, for he was also in the storehouse when we made our bargain. And although he is a wicked man, he will do as my slave, or I can sell him as one. Now it is for you, king, to judge in this case.' The king says, 'Now Helgi, it is a crafty man and no fool you have to deal with –'. And Hrói gets a few encouraging words from Thorgný the Lawman, 'You have spoken well, Hrói, and it is hard to find any objections to your case –'.

The next suit concerns Hrói's knife and belt. Thorgils claimed them because, as we remember, he accused Hrói of stealing them once in Valland (France). Hrói has a cunning answer ready for him too. He does not deny that the knife had belonged to Thorgils, but he maintains that he himself had found the knife in Valland (France) – found it beside his brother who had been murdered and robbed. And now that it appears that the knife is Thorgils's, then it must have been Thorgils who had done the murder. Now the case takes quite a different turn, and again we hear Thorgný the Lawman express his approval, 'Rogues like these brothers indeed deserve to die –'.

Now they pass to the third and last suit. The one-eyed Thórir comes forward and addresses the king, claiming his other eye back from Hrói. 'That is a rare and strange demand,' says the king, 'but now you, Hrói, must defend yourself in some way in this suit.' Hrói in reply flatly denies that he has stolen an eye from Thórir. 'But,' he goes on, 'for your sake, king, I will make an offer. I propose that one eye is taken from us both. Both shall then be put on the scales. If they originally belonged in the same head, they ought to weigh the same. If they are exactly the same weight, then Thórir will receive whatever compensation the king awards, but if they are not the same weight, or if Thórir will not accept this offer, then it will be clear that this is not the only thing he is capable of lying about!'

Thórir declines Hrói's offer – naturally enough since his only eye is at stake – so Hrói is victorious in this suit as well. Now Thorgný forcefully intervenes and makes a speech in which he says, amongst other things, that the brothers had enjoyed long enough and undeservedly the confidence of the king. Now they must at last receive their punishment. And so it happens: Helgi is banished, and Thorgils and Thórir are hanged at once on the thing-place! Hrói now becomes a much honoured and respected man, and is called not Hrói the Simple but Hrói the Wise. He asks for the hand of the fair Sigrbjörg and becomes Thorgný's son-in-law. After the wedding he goes back to Denmark and meets there King Svein Forkbeard, his old protector, and then returns to Uppsala. Thorgný has died in his absence, and Hrói shares Thorgný's property with his brother-in-law, also named Thorgný. All say that Hrói is a mighty man, and the tale adds that many men of rank in Sweden are descended from him.

Inevitably, the following questions present themselves in connexion with this tale: Has the account any basis in truth? and can it be used in any way as a historical source? Scholars of earlier generations would probably have taken note of every detail and combined names and events in an attempt to establish connexions between the story and facts known in reliable sources. Many would perhaps have pointed to the place-name Rosta in Bälinge parish near Uppsala and claimed that this was *Hróastaðir* – the place where our Hrói had settled down with Sigrbjörg after his success at the Uppsala thing· And perhaps many too would have taken the story of Hrói as further proof that Thorgný the Lawman was a historical figure, a man who in all essentials was just as Snorri had depicted him.

But now our reply to such questions and assumptions must be that the story is invention from start to finish. It is a very cleverly constructed story which has been located in Uppsala and attached to some of that place's most famous characters. The origin of the tale lies far off in the East, and it appears both in the *Thousand and One Nights* and in Indian literature. In the *Hróa þáttr heimska* we have in reality a märchen which is known in the various collections of tales of the 'Seven Sages'.[1] This märchen tells essentially of a merchant who comes to the city of rogues and is thoroughly swindled there. In the end, however, he gets justice through the daring intervention of a woman

---

[1] On the various versions of the tale *Senex caecus*, the tale which is the ultimate foundation for *Hróa þáttr*, see my commentaries in *Donum Grapeanum* (1945), 410 ff.

or some other helper. In the *Thousand and One Nights* and in
other related märchen of the Near East, the tale runs on these
lines:

A merchant comes to a strange city in order to sell some
valuable wares. The city is full of rogues and swindlers, who lay
their snares for the merchant and use their cunning to get him
into their toils. On one occasion he falls in with some gamesters
at dice, and after winning at first, he then loses steadily until
finally he finds himself pledged to drink all the water in the sea
– down to the last drop. He leaves these cheats in dejection, but
he has not gone far before he is suddenly seized by a dangerous
one-eyed man who demands an eye from him – the eye he had
stolen from him long ago! This claim and the other are to be
heard before the city judge on the following day. The merchant
wanders downcast through the city until he meets an old
woman, in whom he confides his troubles. She helps him by
telling him that the rogues meet every evening at the house of a
blind old man, to tell him of their tricks and ask him for advice.
There the merchant must go and eavesdrop on the counsel he
gives them. This he does and learns right enough how he can
get out of his difficulties. When one of the rogues relates how
he has cheated the merchant into undertaking to drink all the
water in the sea, the old blind man says, 'That was stupid! For
the stranger can make the condition that all the rivers running
into the sea are first dammed up before he begins to drink.'
This is something none of the rogues could manage. The wise
old man also tells the one-eyed man that he had got himself
into an awkward and foolish position, because the merchant
could make a counter-proposal – namely, that he should take
out his only eye while the merchant took out one of his, so that
a comparison in weight and size might decide whether they
originally belonged in the same head. The merchant of course
makes use of these wily answers before the court on the following day, his causes are upheld and he leaves the city of rogues
as the victor.

An Indian version is closely similar to that found in the

Arabian and Near Eastern collections, but like the Scandinavian story it makes the helper a young and beautiful girl, who gives the merchant good advice and saves him from his perilous situation. The Indian variant also has the characteristic motive of the one-eyed man who demands his other eye back from the merchant.[1]

Thus we find in the far north and the far east concordant versions of one and the same märchen. How are we to discover and explain a connexion between these geographical extremes? Is there some European link which can bridge the gap between the Orient and Iceland? Such a link is indeed to be found – in the Middle English poem called *The Tale of Beryn*, written in the fifteenth century.[2] As we shall see, however, this is not the first literary treatment of the tale in west European sources.

Beryn is a seafarer who after an adventurous life finally becomes a merchant. He sails with a valuable cargo to an unknown land, moors his ship and goes to a strange city. There he meets a pack of rogues. Amongst others he meets a man who calls himself Hannibal and who owns a great warehouse full of merchandise. Hannibal swindles Beryn in exactly the same way as Helgi cheats Hrói. Later Beryn meets a blind man who lays claim to his eyes. Finally he falls in with a third scoundrel who tries to take away his knife, maintaining that Beryn had committed a murder with it. Beryn gets into other trouble, but he also finds help, not from a woman as Hrói did but from a cripple, who turns to an old man, wise and skilled in the law, named Lord Esope. This Lord Esope is the only ruler in this peculiar country. In the following lawsuits everything happens as it did before the thing at Uppsala. Lord Esope condemns the rogues, Beryn gets large compensation and in addition wins the hand of the wise Esope's daughter.

Behind this English poem lies a French prose romance from the fourteenth century, *L'histoire du chevalier Bérinus*, which

[1] J. Hertel in *Zeitschrift der deutschen morgenländischen Gesellschaft* 74 (1920), 458 ff. Cf. also *Donum Grapeanum* (1945), 413 f.
[2] *The Tale of Beryn*. Re-edited by F. J. Furnivall and W. G. Stone (Chaucer Society: Supplementary Canterbury Tales 1–2, 1876–1887).

contains very nearly the same story as in the English version.[1] We thus find a complete tale of the swindlers fully developed in France in the course of the fourteenth century. And we can go further back, for this fourteenth-century version is in turn based on a poem of Berinus which was composed in the thirteenth century. In the French version the land of scoundrels is called Blandie, the merchant Berinus, and the ruler Esope. Esope corresponds to Thorgný the Lawman in the *Hróa þáttr*: he is old and blind but in spite of this he still maintains his position as ruler of the country. And Esope helps the merchant Berinus just as Thorgný the Lawman helps Hrói. The end of the French version varies slightly but insignificantly from the Icelandic. The merchant marries Esope's niece, Kleopatra, while in the Icelandic he marries Thorgný's daughter, Sigrbjörg.

The agreements here are so obvious that there is hardly any room left for doubts as to the origin of the Icelandic tale of the merchant who visits Uppsala. It is based throughout on west European sources, i.e. on the French märchen-material. We know from other similar instances what an important part was played by France as the intermediary by which oriental märchen-motives found their way to Scandinavia in the Middle Ages. In thirteenth-century French literature many elements were borrowed from Eastern stories, transformed and given fresh artistic treatment. Later they are used again in new contexts and for new purposes. And it was either directly from this productive French literature or indirectly by way of England that the märchen-motives in a number of Icelandic stories were obtained.

Märchen-motives of European-Oriental origin might thus be borrowed in any part of the Scandinavian world, but it was the narrative art developed in Iceland in the thirteenth and fourteenth centuries that was able to stamp such material in a Norse mould. This is at once the astonishing and the misleading thing about the tale of Hrói the Simple. The old märchen was

[1] R. Bossuat, *Bérinus. Roman en prose du XIVᵉ siècle* (Société des Anciens Textes Français, 1931–3).

set in a Norse milieu, the characters were given Norse names, the whole was stamped with the hallmark of Icelandic narrative art. As I said in my introduction, Uppsala was recognized in Iceland as a place of wonderful things and strange adventures. There a stranger might easily be hard done by, if he did not take care of himself and 'match trick for trick', as it says in the *Hróa þáttr*. But at the same time Icelandic saga-tradition knew of Uppsala as a place with a firmly founded system of law and justice, developed and administered by the old law-skilled men of Tíundaland, i.e. by Thorgný the Lawman and his ancestors. This offered a point of contact with a vagrant tale – a tale in which just such a wise man of law was needed to keep the rogues of the city in check. In this way Thorgný the Lawman became an important figure in the story. His ride to the thing and his opposition to the king have dramatic force, and a tension is built up which reminds us of the masterly description which Snorri, writing perhaps some eighty years earlier, had given of the clash between Thorgný and Olaf Skötkonung at the same great assembly in Uppsala.

And now, my dear Hugh, it would be interesting to hear of your experiences when you first came to Uppsala in 1928!

DAG STRÖMBÄCK

16 · Whence the Semicolon?

THOUGHTS ON SIGN AND SIGNAL IN WESTERN SCRIPT

It would be interesting to know what kind of instruction William Caxton gave to a compositor when handing out copy. Caxton, we know, was interested in linguistic problems, as his prefaces (for example that to his *Eneydos*) show. But what was the attitude of his employees, Wynkyn de Worde, Pynson, Copland, to punctuation? When they set up their own presses, did their compositors point copy as they went along? Moxon's description of seventeenth-century practice would suggest that they would almost certainly have done so, but we cannot exclude the possibility that an occasional author, or a few early master printers, anticipated contemporary practice in pre-reading and 'marking-up' copy. Certainly a writer such as Petrarch was keenly interested not only in orthography but in punctuation, and some of his holograph manuscripts are carefully pointed and for a long time an *Ars punctandi* was ascribed to him.[1]

Punctuation had often been especially cared for in monastic scriptora. Alcuin of York (735–804), in one of his poems, refers to the care taken in pointing a text either during or after copying:

> Per cola distinguant proprios et commata sensus
> et punctos ponant ordine quosque suo,
> nel vel falsa legat taceat vel forte repente
> ante pios fratres lector in ecclesia.

---

[1] F. Novati, 'Di un' *Ars punctandi* erroneamente attribuita a Francesco Petrarca', *Rendiconti Istituto Lombardo*, Ser. II, xlii (1909), 83–118.

Thus quite early in the development of Latin minuscule not only was the earlier device of stichometry taken over, that ponderous system of punctuation by lay-out, or phrase grouping, to be seen for instance in the Lindisfarne Gospels, but special signs were beginning to be devised the better to sign-post written language. The places of insertion and the system of insertion followed primitive semantic and phonetic descriptions of speech originated by Greek rhetoricians eight centuries previously.[1] Paragraph, period, colon, comma, section (commation), first as label, then as signal, can have few rivals for length of continuity of usage in one context.

To return to Caxton. When he set up his press *c.* 1473, was there a local or even an international system of pointing ready to be taken over? Certainly punctuation as we know it today is more the invention of the printer than the author. The printer must be credited – at least till the invention of the typewriter – with refinements of pointing, because willy-nilly he, or his compositors, have been responsible for the consistent, final formalization of formally prepared written language, first within individual printing offices ('the style of the house'), and then within larger definable linguistic or geographical areas. An early printer, such as Caxton, substantially took over an established system of signalling, not necessarily an established system of signs or of sign usage that the theoretical system called for. One of the founders of descriptive bibliography, William Blades, tells us that Caxton's No. 1 type had only three signs of punctuation: the oblique (shilling mark, 'comma'), the colon, and the full point. He adds that 'they are used arbitrarily as to power, and in numerous varieties of combination'.[2]

This theoretical system was Aristotelian. The unit was the period, and this was subdivided into colon ('limb') and comma ('slice'; 'piece'). In early Latin minuscule script all signals were made, it would seem, with the same sign, usually the round dot

---

[1] Cf. Aristotle, *Rhetoric*, 1409b; Cicero, *Orator*, 62, 211; Quintilian, 9, 4, 22.
[2] *The Biography and Typography of William Caxton* (2nd edn, 1882), 111.

(point), and the class of signal differentiated by the positioning (*positura*) of the dot, according as it was on the scribe's blind ruled guide line, slightly above it, or higher still, in ascending order of importance. Hence the labels *subdistinctio* (comma), *media distinctio* (colon), and *distinctio* (*periodos*). This basic tripartite system long persisted, but signs and labels altered from area to area and from time to time. Those interested in such byways may fill out this picture from articles by Thurot, Novati, and Schiaffini.[1]

To this system English and continental printers adhered, at least in theory, until the 1560's and 1570's. The source of this change of system can be seen in reasonable perspective, but precise information as to the identity of the prime mover in the dethronement of the ancient scheme is not known. In 1561 a new system was promulgated under the authorship and imprint of Aldus Manutius, the younger, the *Orthographiae ratio* (Venice), reprinted 1566, 1575, 1590, 1591 and later in Italy, and in 1564 and 1579 by Christopher Plantin, Antwerp. The new system is quadripartite. An additional signal and sign, the semicolon, is interpolated between comma and colon. The virgula with a point above it, first used by printers as an abbreviation for *ue* (e.g. q;), now becomes its sign, and the signal, or rhetorical value, is a distinction, or pause, greater than that of the comma and less than that of the colon. Later theorists correlated the pauses with an ascending proportional scale from one to four.

Equally indefinite is our knowledge about the introduction of the semicolon as a signal in English punctuation. McKerrow, in a brief note, states, following Ames, that the semicolon 'seems to have been first used in England about 1569, but was not common until 1580 or thereabouts'.[2] Neither Mulcaster nor Hart uses the word. The sign is labelled 'sub-distinctio' by

[1] Charles Thurot, 'Notices et extraits de divers mss. latins pour servir à l'histoire des doctrines grammaticales au moyen âge', *Notices et extraits des manuscrits de la bibliothèque impériale*, XXII, pt 2 (1868), 1–592; Novati, loc. cit.; Alfredo Schiaffini, 'Punteggiatura', *Encyclopaedia Italiana*, XXVIII (1935), 546–8.

[2] *An Introduction to Bibliography for Literary Students* (2nd edn, 1928), 316.

Ben Jonson in his *English Grammar* (1640),[1] a later version of
an earlier manuscript attempt destroyed by fire in 1623, and
'sub-distinctio' and 'comma' are erroneously equated with
comma and colon, as traditionally used. The earliest appear-
ances in English of 'semicolon' would appear to be 1633[2] and
1644.[3] In the heavily edited 1692 edition of Jonson's *Grammar*
comma and semicolon are printed instead of 'sub-distinctio'
and 'comma'.[4] By then the semicolon had arrived in England
to stay, as a sign, though later to take over the colon's signal,
at least rhetorically. The theoretical, prescriptive quadripartite
system is advocated in two grammars long current, Robert
Lowth's (1762–1804) and Lindley Murray's (1795–1874); perhaps its last classical exposition is in John Wilson's *Punctuation*
(Boston, Mass., 1856). Wilson was of British origin, and himself
a compositor. Today supersession of the quadripartite system
in English usage is almost complete. As Lord Beaverbrook is
reported to have said to an unnamed leader-writer: 'No colons;
no semicolons.'

The commonsense minimal pointing of today would appear
to vindicate the elegant self-sufficiency of the ancient Greek
tripartite analysis of the period. When the colon is used today
in English, disjunctively or co-ordinately within a lengthy
'period', it is used according to the preceptive regulations of
Ben Jonson's *English Grammar* (1640). Jonson, it should be
noted, derived his punctuational precepts from de la Ramée
rather than from Aldus junior, even if much of his writing has
not been pointed by the compositor in the way that his own
Grammar might require.[5] The fact that the paragraph, and not
the period, is the functional unit in written language has only
just begun to be recognized and appreciated.

Was Aldus Manutius senior the originator of the quadripartite scheme? It is indeed possible; but Orazio Lombardelli,

---

[1] See *Works* (ed. Herford and Simpson), II (1925), 431–2; VIII (1947), 552.
[2] Charles Butler, *English Grammar*.
[3] *NED*, Richard Hodges, *English Primrose*.
[4] Cf. Jonson, *Works*, II (1925), 424–8; XI (1952), 208–10.
[5] Cf. Jonson, *Works*, XI, 208–10.

in his *L'Arte del puntar gli scritti* (Siena, 1585),[1] makes the general statement that punctuation in Italy came to be regularized by the printers Aldus Manutius senior and junior, the Gryphii, Gabriel Giolito, and Vincenzo Valgrisi. That printers should wish to regularize punctuation as a matter of craft discipline is understandable, but why, as humanist printers, should they have wished to 'improve on' a classic system? Was a quadri-partite system required for the phonetics of sixteenth-century Italian, and then superimposed on Latin? In theory, no Renaissance scholar would have wished to point an ancient text with other than its own system.

Such data as are now available suggest that there is little correlation between contemporary preceptive punctuational practice and the phonetics of any Western European language. Stopping for the ear and pointing for the eye are only vaguely analogous, nor has any system of pointing been genuinely 'logical'. If the new scheme was not due to a printer, could it have been devised by a writer equally interested in the classics and the vernacular, for example Pietro Bembo? The comma – the nicest point – has traditionally been eschewed by lawyers for reasons of their own, but this is not to say that commas, or punctuation, are unimportant. Even bibliographically a minute alteration in typographic style may occasionally be decisive. William Blades,[2] for example, dates Caxtons printed in Type 4 by changes in punctuation. The short comma (*virgula*) is alone used, 1480–1482, is then found occasionally in 1483 with the long comma (shilling mark), and finally disappears. Perhaps the casual discovery of a scholar delving, for the nonce, into a field not his own, will ultimately reveal the paternity of the semicolon.

DAVID B. THOMAS

[1] pp. 32, 42.   [2] Blades, op. cit. 117.

17 · A Note on the *Landdísir*

In his *Bidrag til en historisk-topografisk Beskrivelse af Island* I (1877), 581 note, P. E. K. Kålund quotes a note written by an Icelandic clergyman for the Royal Commission for the Preservation of Ancient Monuments (Den Kongelige Kommission for Old-sagers Bevaring) in 1818.

According to this note, there were, in a number of places in the Ísafjarðarsýsla, stones or rocks called *landdísasteinar*. These stones were held in deep veneration. There must be no joking near them, children must not play, and no grass must be torn up or mown. If any of these things were done, a calamity would befall. The reason is plain enough; these stones were the home of the *landdísir*.[1]

The *landdísir* are not mentioned in any early text, but there can be little doubt that they survived from pagan times, and filled a certain place in religious life, or at least in the lower religion. They might in some ways be comparable with the *landvættir*, the protective spirits of the land. Like the *álfar, huldu-fólk*, and other figures of lower mythology we may suppose that the *landdísir* were better able to survive the Conversion than the greater gods, who were first reduced to demons and then vanished from popular belief.

Living in their rocks, the *landdísir* may remind us of the *spámaðr* (prophet) who, according to the *Þorvalds þáttr Víðförla* (Ch. II),[2] lived with his family in a great rock at Giljá in

---

[1] Similar conceptions may underlie Norwegian and Swedish place-names, such as *Disarøys* (cf. ON *hreysi*, 'pile of stones'), *Diseberg*. See M. Olsen, *Hedenske Kult-minder i norske Stedsnavne* I (1915), 181 ff.; J. de Vries, *Altgermanische Religions-geschichte* (second edn, 1957), II 297 ff.

[2] Important editions are published in *Bps.* I 35 ff. and in B. Kahle, *Kristni Saga*

Vatnsdalr, where he was ardently worshipped by Koðrán, the owner of the farm.

Friðrekr, the first of the missionary bishops, reached Iceland about 980, and was conducted to Giljá by the Christian Þorvaldr, the son of Koðrán, who hoped to convert his family.

Although he entertained the Bishop and his party for the winter, Koðrán did not at first wish to adopt the Christian religion, or to desert the *spámaðr*, whom he had worshipped for so long. In the end, however, he agreed with his son that if the Bishop, whom he called Þorvaldr's *spámaðr*, proved stronger than his own *spámaðr*, he would adopt the new religion.

On the next day, the Bishop sprinkled holy water on the rock and all around it. In the night, the *spámaðr* appeared to Koðrán in a dream. He was gloomy and trembled with fear, and complained that Koðrán's guest had been pouring boiling water over his house, scalding his children so cruelly that their screams were hard to bear. The Bishop took his holy water to the stone again on the next day, and again the *spámaðr* appeared to Koðrán in a dream. This time he was even more gloomy than before and, instead of the fine clothes which he used to wear, he was dressed in a poor leather jerkin. He urged Koðrán to drive his guests away, but said that he would never leave his home, hard as it was to put up with all the discomfort and ill treatment.

The Bishop sprinkled the rock again on the third day, and in the night the *spámaðr* appeared for the last time. Now he was angry. He accused Koðrán of disloyalty; the wicked Bishop had ruined his house and his clothes, and there was nothing for him to do but go out into the wilderness. All was over between them.

The syntax of the *Þorvalds þáttr* suggests that it was first written in Latin.[1] Reference is made twice to the authority of Gunnlaugr Leifsson, the monk of Þingeyrar (died 1218). If the

---

(1905), 59 ff. References in this paper are to the latter edition. The version given in *Flb.* I 268 ff. appears to be much abridged.

[1] Cf. Kahle, op. cit. XVI ff.

o

þáttr was not written by Gunnlaugr himself, we may be satisfied that it was written by one of his school and, as topographical
interest shows, in the neighbourhood of Þingeyrar.[1]

Apocryphal as it is, the *þorvalds þáttr* illustrates several things
in religious history. We are told that Koðrán worshipped his
prophet in the rock as a powerful god (*styrkan guð*). He had
conferred many blessings, telling Koðrán the future and looking
after his cattle. He was friendly, cheerful and dressed in splendid
clothes, but once the holy water was sprinkled, and he did not
receive the attention which he had received before, he was
broken down and depressed. The gods cannot flourish without
our help, any more than we can get on without theirs.[2]

This same story of Koðrán is told in much shorter form in the
Kristni Saga (Ch. II).[3] The prophet is there called the *ármaðr* or
'year-man', and that was probably his original title. His chief
function was thus to secure the welfare of the crops and the
cattle, just as this was the chief function of Freyr, who was
called the *árguð*.[4]

The story of Koðrán may also help us to understand other
problems in Norse religious history. The veneration of stones
was widespread in the Germanic world, and in the Celtic as
well.[5] Examples are recorded both from the Middle Ages and
from modern times. According to a clause often quoted from
the Swedish Uppland laws, no one must 'believe in' groves or
stones (*a lundi ællr stenæ troæ*).[6]

Veneration of other inanimate objects is also recorded widely.
According to the *Guta Saga*,[7] the Gotlanders of old believed,
not only in heathen gods, but also in woods, burial-mounds,
holy places, and enclosures (*a hult oc a hauga, wi oc stafgarþa*).

---

[1] See Finnur Jónsson, *Den oldnorske og oldislandske Litteraturs Historie* (1920–24),
II 399 and the references there given.
[2] Cf. Folke Ström, 'Gudarnas Vrede', *Saga och Sed* (1952), 32, and especially his
'Tro og Blot', *Arv* VII (1951), 30 ff.
[3] Kahle, op. cit. 6 ff.   [4] *SnE* 98.
[5] Numerous examples are quoted by A. Olrik and H. Ellekilde, *Nordens
Gudeverden* (1926–51), I 339 ff.
[6] F. Ström, *Arv* VII (1951), 23.
[7] H. Pipping, *Guta Lag och Guta Saga* (1905–7), 63.

According to an early Norwegian law,[1] it was a heathen superstition to believe that *landvættir* dwelt in groves, mounds and waterfalls.

Records of Iceland contain several stories of settlers who worshipped inanimate objects. It is told of one that he brought sacrifice to a grove, while another sacrificed to a waterfall.[2] The story of Koðrán and the clause just quoted from the Norwegian law suggest that it was not really the groves and waterfalls themselves which these men worshipped, but rather the deities who dwelt in them. In other words, these passages provide no evidence of nature-worship or of any kind of pre-theistic belief.

In Icelandic sources we read of the veneration of mountains and hills, such as Helgafell in the Breiðafjorðr[3] and Krosshólar by Hvammr.[4] Stories are also told of the veneration of *haugar* or mounds in various parts of Scandinavia.[5] In such cases it is often plain that the objects venerated were believed to be the abode of dead ancestors, who had been raised to the status of gods, as Grímr Kamban, the settler of the Faroe Islands,[6] or else, like Ólafr Geirstaðaálfr in eastern Norway, had come to be worshipped in their burial-mounds as elves.[7]

Indeed, the female *landdísir*, dwelling in their rocks, were probably not far removed from the masculine elves. We learn comparatively little about the cult of elves from Old Norse literature. According to Sighvatr's *Austrfararvísur*,[8] an *álfablót*, or sacrifice to the elves, was held in Gautland in the late autumn. In the *Kormáks Saga* (Ch. XXII), it is told how the blood of a bull, which had been slaughtered as a sacrifice, was smeared on a hillock where the elves lived, and a feast was made for them of the meat. In return they healed a wound which their worshipper had suffered in a duel.

[1] Later Gulaþing Law in *Norges gamle Love* II 308.
[2] Finnur Jónsson, *Landnámabók* (1900), 237, 355.   [3] *Eyrbyggja Saga*, Ch. V.
[4] *Landnámabók* (1900), 158. There are many other examples.
[5] See M. Olsen, *The Farms and Fanes of Ancient Norway* (1928), 304 ff.; Olrik and Ellekilde, op. cit. 500 ff.   [6] *Landnámabók* (1900), 12.
[7] *Flb.* II 7.   [8] *Heimskringla, Ólafs Saga Helga*, Ch. XCI.

In the story of Ólafr Geirstaðaálfr, the purpose of the sacrifice to the dead King is explained; it was *til árs*, i.e. for fruitful
harvests and prosperity. The same should probably be said of
the *álfablót*, to which Sighvatr alludes. It was held in autumn,
the time when sacrifice was held in honour of the god Freyr[1]
and the extraordinary veneration of the phallic Vǫlsi took place
in Norway.[2]

It is noteworthy that the *vetrnætr*, the late autumn, was also
the time of the *dísablót*, the sacrifice to the *dísir*, as is plainly
stated in *Viga-Glúms Saga* (Ch. V) and in the *Heiðreks Saga*,[3]
and is probably to be read between the lines of the *Þiðranda
þáttr*.[4] In that story, no tribute was paid to the *dísir* at the
'winter-nights', but they took their revenge, killing the favourite
son of the house. It seems, therefore, that the *dísir* were fertility
goddesses, and this is borne out by the nickname *Vanadís* (*dís*
of the Vanir) applied to Freyja, the supreme fertility goddess.[5]

Both place-names and traditions suggest that in eastern
Scandinavia the cult of the *dísir* was more public than it was in
the west. In the *Ynglinga Saga* (Ch. XXIX), Snorri mentions a
dísarsalr, probably in Uppsala, where King Aðils fell from his
horse and died. In the *Historia Norvegiæ* this same building is
called *Ædes Dianæ* (G. Storm, *Monumenta Historica Norvegiæ*
(1880), 101). The *Disting* (earlier *Dísaþing*), which was held in
Uppsala and survived into Christian times as a fair, must also
have been a public festival. Place-names, such as *Disevi* (Temple
of the *Dísir*)[6] in Östergötland, also suggest that the *dísir* were
patrons of a central place of worship. In the west, on the other
hand, the *dísir* seem to be more intimately linked with a family
or a group, as is emphasized in the story of Þiðrandi, where
they are identified with the attendant spirits of the family
(*fylgjur yðrar frænda*).

---

[1] As in *Gísla Saga*, Ch. XV.   [2] *Flb*. II 331 ff.
[3] Ed. Jón Helgason (1924), 91.
[4] On the interpretation of this text see especially Dag Strömbäck, *Tidrande och
Diserna* (1949); also F. Ström in *Arv* VIII (1952), 77 ff.
[5] *SnE* 38.
[6] See de Vries, op. cit. II 298 and references.

In the Greenland *Atlamál* (Str. 28), the *dísir* are said to be 'dead women', and they appear in a dream, calling the doomed Gunnarr to join them. Similarly, Bjǫrn Hítdœlakappi seems to speak in a verse of *dísir* who appear in dreams warning him and calling him home.[1]

The ring seems now to close. As dead female ancestors, the *dísir* assure the prosperity of their descendants, the fertility of their crops and their cattle, and perhaps of their women. But when the time is ripe, they call those whom they have protected to join their own ranks. According to the *Víga-Glúms Saga* (Ch. XIX), a woman fell into a swoon when her husband left the house. She saw dead people coming to meet him, and she knew that his time had come.

From these very short notes we may conclude that the *landdísir* of the Ísafjǫrðr were dead women ancestors of the people who lived there. They had come to be venerated, being goddesses at once of death, fertility, and rebirth.

G. TURVILLE-PETRE

---

[1] *Bjarnar Saga Hítdœlakappa*, Ch. XXXII. The passage is discussed by Strömbäck, op. cit. 24–5, who shows how the *dísir* came nearly to be identified with the guardian angels.

18 · The Orthography and Provenance of Henry Machyn

Henry Machyn, merchant-tailor, of the parish of Trinity the Little by Queenhithe, died in October 1563. His Diary begins in August 1550, and the last entry is for August 8, 1563. The various events mentioned in it were evidently not always described immediately after they had taken place, since the date was often left to be filled in later, and this has not always been done. Only rarely does Machyn refer to his own affairs: the burial of a brother on Nov. 30, 1550, his age, 56 on May 16, 1554, but 66 on May 20, 1562, and the baptism of a daughter on Sept. 27, 1557. In addition, he enjoyed, with other neighbours, a banquet provided by Mistress Lentall on Twelfth Night, 1556, was present at an oyster breakfast on July 30, 1557, acted as witness at the payment of money on Sept. 15, 1557, and on Nov. 23, 1561, had to do public penance for slandering Veron, the parson of St Martins, Ludgate. Most of the entries deal with public events, but so cautiously and discreetly that it is not often possible to see where the author's sympathies lie. More particularly Machyn shows an interest in funeral furnishings which suggests that the provision of them was his particular speciality, an impression confirmed by a memorandum on the first page of the manuscript concerning Lady Mason's bill for arms and a hearse, as also by the occasional mention of orders for such things in terms which suggest that he had provided them.

The manuscript itself suffered in the fire among the Cotton manuscripts in 1731. As a result one or more lines are missing at the top of each page, along with a varying number of letters at the beginning and end of each line for part of the way down the page, though as a rule not many letters are missing in these latter positions, and often enough the word that originally stood there is fairly obvious. The manuscript was edited for the Camden Society by J. G. Nichols and published in 1848.[1] He reproduces the matter adequately enough, but linguistically his edition leaves much to be desired. A number of errors in transcription are listed by Dr A. Wijk,[2] who also points out that Nichols often supplies missing words, either from Strype who used the manuscript before it was burned, or by deducing the missing word from the context and the remaining letters, but that he too often omits to mark the fact that these forms are not actually present in the manuscript. Since they are sometimes in a different spelling from Machyn's usual one, their presence tends to make his orthography seem even less consistent than it is. Apart from the damage done by the fire, the manuscript is quite legible, though *e* and *o* are sometimes difficult to distinguish, as also *a* and *o*, and less frequently *s* and *r*.

Earlier scholars, naturally enough, assumed that the Diary would provide them with an example of the language of a middle-class Londoner of the period, though their use of the evidence was not always well considered, partly because of the inadequacies of the printed text, and partly because of a tendency to make use of isolated forms which were not in fact characteristic of Machyn. Then, in 1937, Dr A. Wijk, having collated the text in Nichols's edition with photostats of the manuscript, published an excellent description and analysis of Machyn's orthography. Unfortunately his localization of the dialect hardly follows from the evidence he provides, though it appears to have been widely accepted.[3] Beginning with the

---

[1] J. G. Nichols, *The Diary of Henry Machyn, Citizen and Merchant-Taylor of London, from A.D. 1550 to A.D. 1563* (Camden Society 42, 1848).

[2] A. Wijk, *The Orthography and Pronunciation of Henry Machyn, the London Diarist. A Study of the South-East Yorkshire Dialect in the Early 16th Century* (1937), pp. 3 ff.

[3] See, for example, F. Mossé in *Études anglaises* iii, 373–4, and E. J. Dobson, *English Pronunciation 1500–1700* (Oxford, 1957), 571 n. 3, 776, n. 4.

assumption that Machyn is a distinctively Yorkshire name, he concludes that 'the Diary is written in a practically pure se. Yorks dialect' which he would further localize to 'the marshland between Holderness and the Ouse, Ellis's district number 30[4]' (p. 15). Machyn may or may not originally have been a distinctively Yorkshire name; at present we know too little about the subject for any certainty to be possible, but by the sixteenth century it was certainly widespread, as can be seen from the examples given by Reaney.[1] In any case, Wijk's methods are suspect; for his knowledge of the Yorkshire dialect he must rely almost entirely on Ellis,[2] and since the two sources are separated by more than 300 years, we can have no certainty that the distinctions characteristic of the dialect in Ellis's time were also characteristic of it in the sixteenth century. In the intervening period, too, the dialect has been subjected to influences from the Midlands and from the standard language which would tend to bring it closer to London English and may have obliterated differences which earlier existed. Moreover, Ellis is describing a spoken dialect whereas we know only the written form of that used by Machyn, and the result is a general assumption of values for the spellings to indicate the provenance required. The assumptions may or may not be correct; we have no means of knowing, but must, to some extent at least, assume a northern provenance which the evidence of the spellings is then being used to prove. A further argument often used by Wijk, that Machyn's forms could not have been the ancestors of the modern standard English ones, assumes for the period a uniform London speech from which the modern language has descended. But recent investigation, more particularly by Dobson, has shown clearly that at a much later date there was a good deal of variety within the London speech, and the existence of a uniform dialect in sixteenth-century London with its population drawn from various parts of the country and its differences of class is in any case inherently unlikely. Certainly,

---

[1] P. H. Reaney, *A Dictionary of British Surnames* (1958), 216.
[2] A. J. Ellis, *On Early English Pronunciation. Part V* (1889).

the statement that 'the Diary is written in a practically pure
se. Yorks dialect' is hardly supported by the repeated explanation of disagreement between the two as due to the influence of
London English on Machyn or of standard English on the
Yorkshire dialect.

Apart from the assumed northern origin of the name, the
only external evidence brought forward to show Machyn's
'interest in and familiarity with those parts' is a list of execu-
tions which took place in various Yorkshire towns in connexion
with the seizure of Scarborough castle in April 1557. It is a
mere list, such as might well have become known from official
sources, and it is difficult to see in it any indication of a detailed
knowledge of this part of the country.

This evidence, however, is not stressed, and Wijk depends
mainly on internal linguistic evidence for his localization. It is
impossible to deal in detail here with all his points, but in
general it may be said that his precise localization of particular
forms assumes a knowledge of sixteenth-century dialects which
we are far from possessing. Many of the orthographical features
need indicate only that Machyn was untrained in current
scribal traditions, and similar spellings are in fact to be found
in the private letters of the period, where, admittedly, they are
not used so consistently as in Machyn, but allowance must be
made for the difference between a work of more than 160
folios written at regular intervals, and the writing of occasional
comparatively short letters. Machyn himself is often incon-
sistent, especially at the beginning of his work, and in many
cases only settles gradually to the fairly consistent use of a particular spelling, while for words which are infrequent and were
probably unfamiliar to him, he often has a wide variety of
forms, e.g. *condutt, condut, conduyd, condytt, condyt, condyth*. Wijk
would probably agree that his points are not of equal importance, but would perhaps argue that their evidence is cumulative. In the following pages, the evidence of some of the more
obvious orthographical peculiarities will be examined, and if
it fails to support the assumed northern origin, the cumulative

value of the remaining ones must diminish sharply in signifi-cance. But it must be emphasized that only when the number of examples is large enough to be statistically significant is it safe to use them as evidence. Occasional spellings may or may not be significant; no use can be made of them because we can never be certain that their explanation is linguistic and not psychological.

Perhaps the most striking feature of Machyn's orthography is the use, especially in certain words, of the spellings *ay, ey, oy*, for ME *ā, ē, ō, ū*. With *ay* for ME *ā* we have: *gayff* 87,[1] *gaff* 2; *grayff*, *Grayffesend* 11, *graff* 1; *stayffe* 17, *stayffes* 98, *staffe* 4; *Baythe* 7, *Bathe* 6. In addition, with too few examples to be statistically significant, are *mayd* 'made' 8, *mad* 190; *Rayff* 1, *Raff* 12.[2]

With *ey* for ME *ę̄* are *cheyff* 61, *cheff* 2, *chyff* 2; *shreyff* 79; *theyffe* 5; *Cleyff* 'Cleves' 5; *Steyn* 'Stephen' 5. The spelling also appears in *beyffe* 'beef' 3; *beyn* 'been' 2, *bene* 43, *byne* 10; *betweyn* 1, *betwyn* 52; *cheysse* 'cheese' 2; *feyld* 2, *feld* 27; *hey* 'he' 1, *he* frequent; *heyde* 'heed' 1, *hed* 3; *qweyns* 1, *quen* 334; *weypons* 1, *wepons* 2; *Cheyke* 1, *Cheke* 1; *Seythin lane* 1. Here again, even when *ey* is the only spelling, the number of occurrences is too small for any con-clusions to be safely drawn.

For ME *ę̄* both *ey* and *ay* appear: *beyr-* 'to bear' 31, *bayr-* 32, *ber-* 6; *beyrar* 2, *bayrer* 3, *berer* 5; *gayre* 6; *leyff* 'to leave' 5; *treysorer* 7, *trayssorer* 1, *tresorer* 24; *Beycon* 6, *Becon* 2; *Leydenhall* 5, *Ledyn-hall* 10. The spelling also appears in *beyt-* 'to beat' 3, *bett* 3; *breyke* 1; *conterfeytyng* 4, *-fett* 3; *deyken* 1, *decon* 6; *deyn* 1, *dene* 53;

---

[1] Here and elsewhere the spelling given is that which is most commonly found, and variation in letters other than the essential ones is ignored. For example, the 87 examples of *gayff* are made up of *gayff* 78, *gayffe* 6, *gayffes* 2, *gayf* 1. My own figures are derived from a microfilm of the manuscript provided by the British Museum. There are occasional slight discrepancies from those given by Wijk, but the differences do not seem to be significant and are easily enough explicable in a work running to 312 pages in Nichols's edition and containing many mutilated forms.

[2] Some of these, e.g. *gayff* 3 sg. pt. ind., *stayffe, Baythe*, should have a short vowel in Middle English. Presumably it is assumed that they are to be derived from analogical forms with a long vowel. This may well be the case, but so far as this text is concerned, the only evidence for a long vowel is the assumption that *ay* is used as a spelling for *ā*, an assumption which these forms are then used to prove.

deyth 2, *deth* 30; *feymall* 1; *leydyng* 'leading' 1; *leyftenantt* 3; *mayntyme* 1; *meyll-* 'meal' 1, *mell* 5; *reyme* 1, *rayme* 4, *reaym* 1, *reme* 2; *say* 'sea' 1, *see* 23; *seyll* 'seal' 2, *sayll* 1, *sell* 9; *seyryd* 'cered' 1; *seysenyd* 'seized' 1; *sheyffes* 1; *speyres* 1, *spayrers* 4, *speres* 15, *spares* 1; *theys* 'these' 3, *thes* 18; *treysun* 1, *tresun* 10; *veyver* 'weaver' 1; *wayr-* 'to wear' 3, *wher* 7; *Beymont* 1.[1] In addition, the various spellings for 'Sweden' may perhaps be significant: *Swaythen* 4, *Swaynthen* 1, *Swaynland* 1, *Swaythland* 1, *Sweythen* 1, *Sweth-* 1.

For ME $\bar{\varrho}$ *oy* appears in *doyst, doys, doysse* 'does'; *loysse* 1, *losse* 1; and *uy* is found in *chuysse* 2. Here, *doyst, doys, doysse* are suspect since the *y* may be part of the ending, and in general such spellings for ME $\bar{\varrho}$ are so rare that their significance is doubtful.

For ME $\bar{\varrho}$ *oy* appears in *boyth* 'both' 93, *bowth* 7, *both* 3; *cloyffe* 1; *cloyth* 2, *cloth* 68; *cloythyng* 3, *clothyng* 9; *oythe* 4, *othe, owth* 6; *sshroyff* 4, *shrowffe* 1; *thoys* 'those' 2, *thos* 2.

ME $\bar{u}$ is represented by *oy* in *aboyff* 17, *abuyff* 1, and *uy* is found in *tuyffes* 'tufts' 1. In addition, *oy* appears for ME *o* before *ht* in *boythe* 'bought' 1; *broyth* 'brought' 2, *browth* 67; *doythur* 11, *dowther* 30; *foyth* 'fought' 2, *fowth* 3; *noythy* 'naughty' 3, *nothe* 2; *wroyght* 1, *wroght* 7; and 'self' appears as *seylff* 19, *selff* 1.

By listing such spellings under orthographical as compared with phonological characteristics, Wijk to some extent pre-judges the issue, since he thereby assumes that they are to be connected with the distinctively northern representation of long vowels by the addition of *i* or *y*. But if this is the case, it is diffi-cult to see why they should appear regularly in some words and be rare in others in which they might equally well be expected. Their regularity before certain consonants leads to the suspicion that we are here concerned, not with a traditional ortho-graphy, but with a sound-change, whether one in some way connected with the monophthongization of the *ai, ei* diphthong

---

[1] Wijk also includes *deseyffe, deseyv-* 6; *deseyt* 2; *eygyll* 1, *egyll* 1; *pleyssur* 1, *plesur* 7; *reseyff, reseyv-* 16. But these could be from French forms with *ei, ai,* and so are better omitted.

in early modern English, or whether with a diphthongization before *f* and *r*, and perhaps also before *th*, it is impossible to say. The *seylff* forms are explained as due to loss of *l*, lengthening of *e*, and subsequent representation of *ē* by *ey*. If the *l* has in fact been lost, presumably we have here merely another example of the change before *f*, but the evidence for loss of *l* in Machyn's dialect is slight, and the change may also have taken place before *lf*. In the North the use of *y* to represent long vowels appears to have originated in the monophthongization of the *i*-diphthongs. In Machyn there are occasional examples of the representation of ME *ai, ei*, by *a, e*, but the only cases in which they are sufficiently numerous to be significant are *aganst* 23, *agaynst* 40; *mare* 'mayor' 109, *mere* 13, *mayre* 107; *pent* 'to paint' 11; *penter* 13; *proclame* 15; *wettes* 'musicians' 21, *waytes* 2, *weyttes* 1. In most of these cases other explanations are possible: *aganst* may represent an earlier unstressed form, *proclame* is regular in Middle English, and *mere* and *wettes* could be from alternative French forms in *e*. In any case, since similar spellings are found not infrequently in the private letters of the period written by non-northerners,[1] it is difficult to see how these *y* spellings can be used as evidence of northern provenance. The spellings are not used as regularly as in Machyn, and if they do in fact indicate a sound-change their evidence would suggest that it occurred before other consonants than those we could safely assume from Machyn alone. Certainly, when we get away from the scribal texts, such spellings are sufficiently frequent to make it clear that they were not necessarily northern by the middle of the sixteenth century.

A further group of possibly significant forms in Machyn is made up of words with ME *ē* for which the spelling *y* is common: *brykyng* 3, *bryke-* 1, *breke* 4, *-breyke* 1; *pryche* 235, *prychyd*,

---

[1] See H. Ellis, *Original Letters illustrative of English History* (1825–46), and especially those by West (born at Putney) I, i, 66 ff., Pace (born near Winchester) I, i, 108 ff., and Pery ('certainly a Cockney', Dobson, p. 571) II, ii, 140 ff.; and compare also the spellings in an account of the expedition of 1544 written by a steward who lived at 'lydingetone' (Liddington, ?Wilts, ?Rutl.) (*English Historical Review* xvi (1901), 503 ff.).

-yng 13, *prechyd, -yng* 22, *preychyng* 2; *prycher* 10, *precher* 7; *spyke, spykyng* 18; and in addition *betwyn* 52, *betweyn* 1; *byne* 'been' 10, *bene* 43, *beyn* 2; *forfyt* 1, *-fett* 2; *yche* 'each' 1; *myllman* 'mealman' 1, *meyll-* 1, *mell* 5; *myter* 'metre' 1; *qwyne* 15, *quen* 334; *syne* 'seen' 2, *sene* 54. Some of these, e.g. *betwyn, byne*, may perhaps be from un-accented forms. The others Wijk would explain as 'due to a tendency to shortening in front of consonant combinations or certain final single consonants' (p. 98). As Dobson points out (p. 631), it seems probable enough that the spellings represent short *i*, but he also shows that such forms are not uncommon in other southern texts, and there seems no reason at all for ascribing them to Machyn's supposed northern origin.

Machyn also has a number of spellings of ME *i* with *e*, of which the following appear to be significant: *belettes* 6; *cete* 23; *dener* 254; *deprevyd* 10; *deleuered* 30; *epocras* 6; *emages* 33, *ymages* 1; *leverey* 37; *menyster* 15, *mynysters* 1; *pelere* 101; *pelers* 5, *pilers* 1; *pennys* 'pinnace' 10, *pynnes* 2; *pete* 'pity' 3, *petest* 1, *petevsly* 2; *presun* 12, *presunmentt* 1, *presoner* 16; *preve* 18; *theder* 10; *trenete* 11; *veker* 5, *vycker* 1; *veseters* 9; *vetell, -ar* 9. The spelling is found also in *fegur* 1; *melener* 'milliner' 1; *phesyke* 1; *rebyn* 2; *reches* 1, *ryche* 32, *rychely* 4, *rychest* 1; *rever* 'river' 1; *sester* 1, *syster* 19; *tepytt* 1.[1] It appears in place and personal names: *Belyngatt* 6; *Chechastur* 6; *Eslyngtun* 2, *Yslyngtun* 3; *Medyllsex* 2, *Mydyllsex* 1; *Demmoke* 1, *Dymmoke* 2; *Gefford* 1, *Gyfford* 3; *Necolas* 17, *Nycolas* 1; *Necolles* 5, *Nycolles* 1; *Phelype* 9, *Phylype* 1; *Recherd* 36; *Recherdsun* 6. In addition, Wijk includes *reseduw* 10, in which the *i* is in an un-stressed syllable, as well as *bedyll* 4, *evyll* 1, which have OE *y* and can only be included here by presupposing the northern origin that the spellings are to prove. Wyld's theory, that such spell-ings were due to a general lowering of ME *i* to *e* which took place in the speech of certain social classes in London as well as in the East Anglian dialects, is objected to on the ground that if this were the case we should expect such *e* spellings to be evenly distributed between close and open syllables, whereas

[1] Some of these words, e.g. *pelere, trenete*, may of course represent alternative French forms in *e*.

they occur mostly in open syllables. This, of course, might only mean that Wyld has not defined precisely enough the conditions under which the change took place, but this possibility is disregarded, and it is claimed that the true explanation of such spellings should 'be based, partly on the northern lowering and lengthening of ME *i* to *ę̄* in open syllables, and partly on the substitution of [*ī*] from ME *ę̄* for French *i* in open syllables in such words as were adopted in the northern dialects after the transition of ME *i* to *ę̄* to *ī*' (p. 113). But Wyld had at any rate the support of similar forms in works of non-northern origin, e.g. Greyfriars Chronicle, *sheppes, wenter, sheppyd, dech, reche, drevyne, wettelles*; Verney Papers, *wretyn, geven, geving*; Mary Tudor, *hether, sens, wretten, gewyn, prences*, &c.[1] Such spellings in fact are by no means uncommon in southern texts of the period. However we may explain them, and whatever may have been the sound intended, their presence means that similar spellings in Machyn can only be accepted as northern if his northern origin can be conclusively proved on other grounds, and without accepting these spellings as part of the evidence.

ME *ǭ* normally appears in Machyn as *o*, with *oo* only in *good, goodly*, and *oy* in *loysse* 1, but also with a certain number of *u* spellings: *blud* 3; *bredurud* 1; *butes* 'boots' 1, *butt-* 1; *chusse* 5, *chuysse* 2, *chosse* 1; *dune* 'done' 1, *done* 79; *fulles* 'fools' 1; *gudes* 2, *goodes* 8; *kukes* 'cooks' 1, *cokes* 3; *shumaker* 1; *shut* 'shot' 1, *shott* 4; *shut* 'to shoot' 4, *shutyng* 17, *shottyng* 1; *skulles* 'schools' 1, *skolle* 8; *sune* 'soon' 3, *sone* 6; *thudur* 2, *thodur* 28. Some of these occur only infrequently and may be omitted from consideration, while *bredurud* is probably due to lack of stress. But the *u* spellings for 'shoot', 'choose', and perhaps also those for 'blood' and 'soon' are likely to be significant, though exactly what sound is intended is doubtful. Such spellings are not uncommon in other

[1] J. G. Nichols, *Chronicle of the Grey Friars of London* (Camden Society 53, 1852), 5, 11, 13, 21, 27, 28, 46, &c.

J. Bruce, *Letters and Papers of the Verney Family* (Camden Society 56, 1853), 39, 46.

H. Ellis, op. cit. I, i, 121, 124, 125.

writings of the period, e.g. Wriothesley, *chuse, fluddes*; Expedition, *shuyt, shutyng*; Longland (born at Henley), *gud, gudnes*; Lords of the Council to Mary, *bludd, bludshede*, &c.,[1] and Wijk in fact explains some of them as 'due to influence from the London pronunciation [*ū*] (or [*u*] when shortened) for ME *ǭ*' (p. 142). In that case the spellings for 'shoot', whether indicating a long or a short vowel, could equally well be due to London influence, and it is not easy to see why they should be listed as phonological features speaking against London.

But if some of these spellings are to be ascribed to London influence, then Machyn's forms for OE *y* might similarly represent a London dialect of the period. The usual result is *i*, but *e* and *u* forms also appear in significant numbers: *beld* 'to build' 6; *bedyll* 4, *Bedyll* 4; *bere* 'to bury' 2, *berehyng* 43, *bered* 574, *bured* 1; *bereall* 2, *buryall* 1; *besenes* 4; *chyrche* 175, *cherche* 28, *cheyrche* 5, *churche* 1; *evyll* 1; *furst* 74, *forst* 3; *kechens* 1; *mere* 'merry' 6, *merele* 1; *pet* 'pit' 1; *shurt* 7; *thurd* 3; *Crepullgatt* 15. The *e* forms are explained as due to the northern change of *i* to *ę̄* or to Machyn's habit of writing *e* for *i* in open syllables, the *ur* forms to the fact that *er, ir, ur*, have fallen together in *ǝr*, while *beld* is said to indicate a development of the ME combination *īld* that was chiefly characteristic of various northern dialects (pp. 122–3, 33). Some of the *e* forms may, of course, represent a lowering of earlier *i*, though these would not necessarily be northern, and we can hardly be certain of the exact phonetic value at this date of the combinations *er, ir, ur*. But the range of forms is not unexpected in the London dialect of the period, the preponderance of *e* forms for 'bury' and 'merry' perhaps reflecting the fact that these have become the standard ones. Moreover, since Wijk considers that the 'exceptional *ur*-spellings in *Fanchurche* 1*x, bured* 1*x, buryall* 1*x* are perhaps best explained through London influence' (p. 124), there seems to be no reason why other *u* and *e* spellings should not be similarly explained.

[1] W. D. Hamilton, *A Chronicle of England* (London, 1877. Camden Society NS. 20), 114, 130. *English Historical Review* xvi, 503 ff. H. Ellis, op. cit. I, i, 180, 181; II, ii, 243.

The spelling *yerle* 117, as compared with *erle* 9, is taken as a phonological feature speaking against London. Such forms are certainly found in the modern Yorkshire dialects, but they also appear in many of the southern ones, and place-name forms show that already during the Middle English period some of them had evidently developed a [j] before an initial vowel. In addition, they appear frequently enough in southern writings of the period, e.g. Greyfriars Chronicle, *yerth-qwake, yerle*; Pery, *yendinge, yentrede, yorne* 'iron', *yend*; Stafford (born at Penshurst, Kent), *yerly* 'early',[1] so that they can certainly not be used as evidence of a northern origin.

Most of the other orthographical features which have not been mentioned, the rareness of *ea* for ME *ę̄*, of *oo* for ME *ǭ*, Machyn's use of single and double consonants and of final *-e*, his representation of *i* by *y*, of ME *iu* and of French *u* by *u* or *uw*, of *ght* by *th*, his consistent use of *e* in *pepull*, his fondness for initial *ff, ss*, and the frequent use of *h* in hiatus, can all be paralleled from the private letters of the period, and bear witness only to his comparative freedom from the current southern scribal traditions. Of more interest is the use of *ff* in positions in which we should expect *v*, e.g. *gyff, gaff, gayffe; graff, grayff; shreyff; aboyff*, &c. Wijk connects such spellings with the northern unvoicing of final *v*, but since they are found also in medial positions where the *f* sound is unlikely, e.g. *gayffelyn, shreyffes, stayffes, wyffes*, and in some cases with the spelling *ffv, ffw*, it seems clear that Machyn merely used *ff* as an alternative spelling for *v*. Nor is it difficult to see how this may have come about; the plural of nouns is formed regularly by the addition of *-es* to the singular, and since in such words as *wyff, stayff*, this results in the change of *f* to *v*, it may well have led Machyn to use *ff* as an alternative spelling for *v* in other words.

So far as the phonological characteristics are concerned, evidence for the retention of OE *ā* appears only in *gahyng* 2, as compared with *gohyng* 18, and because of the occasional

[1] J. G. Nichols, op. cit. 5, 53, 54, &c. H. Ellis, op. cit. II, ii, 140, 142, 151, &c.; III, iii, 111.

difficulty of distinguishing *o* and *a* these examples are hardly sufficient evidence that Machyn may have known the pronunciation [*æ*] for OE *ā* (p. 150). Spellings such as *dee* 'to die' 4, *ded* 130; *he* 'high' 31, could be northern, but West has *dee*,[1] and it is difficult to be certain that they could only be northern at this date. The northern lengthening of *u* to *ǭ* is unlikely to be represented by Machyn's *aboyff* 'above' 17, and in any case Ellis's forms do not agree and have to be put down to the influence of standard English. Nor is the northern shortening of *ū* before *nd* likely in *bond* 'bound' 1, *bone* 2, *bune* 1; *grond* 'ground' 11; *hond* 'hound' 7; *wond* 'wound' 1, since the spelling is regular also in French loans before *n* plus consonant, and would point either to a general shortening of *ū* under such conditions, or to the use by Machyn of *o* as a spelling for *ū* in such words. The assumption that in the combination *al* plus dental, the *l* had been lost, depends on too few examples for it to be a safe one: *alderman* 7, *altherman* 56, *arderman* 1, *artherman* 1; *aldermen* 14, *althermen* 121, *artheralthmen* 1; *fasshele* 'falsely' 1; *halters* 7, *harters* 1; *salter* 5, *sarter* 1; *swone* 'swollen' 1; *shuldurs* 1, *shuder* 1. Moreover, his exceptional *Awdborowr* 'Aldborough' (Yorks), would indicate that the northern development was different from that which appears in his own forms. On the other hand, the change of *d* to *th* in such conditions is well evidenced, but since it is found just as frequently in Machyn's London street-names, e.g. *Aldermare* 2, *Althermare* 6; *Aldersgatt* 2, *Althergatt* 8, there seems no reason for not accepting it as a change in, at any rate, some varieties of London English.[2] Machyn also has numerous *s* spellings for *sh* in unstressed syllables, but it is clear that the *s* in such cases stands for *sh*, not for *s*, so that this should not appear as a phonological characteristic (p. 30). Again, spellings with *ct*, *kt*, for ME *ght* are too few for any safe deduction that 'there was still something left of the spirant in his pronunciation' (p. 30), as also the forms *elther* 1, *eldest* 4; *chyltheryn* 1,

---

[1] H. Ellis, op. cit. I, i, 73.
[2] The *d* forms of such words are usual up to f. 33; they are then gradually replaced by *th* forms which become regular after f. 51.

P

chylderyn 44; *Elthertun* 1, *Eldertun* 1, for the assumption that *d* had become *th* after *il, el*, though in view of the frequency of such spellings as *altherman* it is likely enough. The forms *drahyns* 'drawing' 1, *drane* 21, *drae bryge* 1; *straberes* 2, may well suggest that in Machyn's dialect *au* had become monophthongized before a consonant, but would not support his northern origin since they do not agree with the later southeast Yorkshire forms. The development of the definite article to *t* is frequent enough in northern dialects, but it is difficult to believe that the isolated *de duke* 2, *de devyser* 1, are really sufficient evidence to point 'to a plosive consonant' (p. 34) in Machyn, especially when the following word begins with *d*. Nor is it easy to see why the frequent appearance of the *th* spelling in *thodur* should be 'a plain indication that he pronounced the definite article as *t*' (p. 34). The falling together of *wh* and *w*, and the loss of initial *h*, are common enough in southern dialects, and the fact that we are uncertain when the latter took place in the south can hardly speak against London unless we have definite evidence that it had not taken place there until much later. Machyn's spellings for 'devil, devilishly', *dulle* 2, *duwll* 1, *duwylles* 1, *dullvyll* 1, *duyllyll* 1, *dullysly* 1, are difficult to explain, and their nearest parallels certainly appear to be northern, cf. Towneley, *dwill*, Dest. of Troy, *dule*. On the other hand, the representation of ME *eu* by *u, uw*, is not uncommon in southern texts, e.g. Wriothesley, *drue, slue, overthrue*, &c.; if *myche* was 'distinctly dialectal in London even before 1500' (p. 36), it is surprising to find it used regularly by Thomas Pery who 'was certainly a Cockney'; *shreffys* is usual in the Greyfriars Chronicle,[1] so that the form with syncopation of the first syllable is not peculiar to Machyn; and since *frer* was 'fairly common in southern 16th Century texts' it should not appear as 'a dialectal feature speaking against London' (p. 38).

The grammatical features give little help to the attempt to localize Machyn in the north. So far as the verbal inflexions

---

[1] W. D. Hamilton, op. cit. I, 83; II, 111, 146. H. Ellis, op. cit. II, ii, 140 ff. J. G. Nichols, op. cit. 2, 7, &c.

are concerned Machyn normally uses the preterite; there are comparatively few examples of the present, and it is not always easy to tell whether the indicative or the subjunctive is intended. Apart from the verb 'to be', there are 18 examples of a 3rd sg. pr. ind. in -*es*, -*ys*, -*s*, along with *has* 39, and three, or perhaps four, examples in -*yth*. For the 3rd pl. pr. ind. we have *calle* 2, *comys* 3, *do*, *folowes*, *hange*, *hanges*, *has* 2, *have* 5, *kepys*, *longes*, *longyst*, *pute*, *say* 2. These give no support at this date to the presumed northern localization, and it is admitted that Machyn's 'grammar had been somewhat more susceptible than his pronunciation to the influence of the London language' (p. 41). The use of *wher* 'were' with a singular subject, and of *was* with a plural subject, are not unexpected in lower-class English of any locality. Wijk's objection that though the usage is common in modern vulgar London English 'whether it was so common in the 16th Century, as is indicated by M.'s usage, seems rather doubtful' (p. 43), is matched by the fact that his evidence for its use in the particular Yorkshire dialect comes from Ellis in the late nineteenth century, and we are equally ignorant of whether it was common there at an earlier date. So far as the nominal inflexions are concerned, the use of the *s*-less genitive was certainly not peculiar to the north; there are plenty of examples of its use in the London churchwardens' accounts of the period, and it appears also in private letters by non-northerners.

The only syntactical point mentioned is Machyn's use of *the wyche* in various constructions, but similar ones are used by Fox, London, Scrope,[1] and others, so that the constructions were evidently not obsolete in southern English of the sixteenth century.

It seems clear that most of the points brought forward as proof of Machyn's northern origin are at the best suspect; only occasional isolated words and forms remain which might be explained as due to the author's northern provenance, but

[1] H. Ellis, op. cit. II, ii, 4 ff.; I, ii, 81; I, ii, 238. London was born at Hambledon, Bucks, but Fox at Ropesley, near Grantham.

they are far too few to provide satisfactory evidence of this. Most of the phonological and orthographical characteristics can be paralleled in southern writings of the time, though it is true that many of the examples given above are taken from nineteenth-century editions whose accuracy may be suspect. On the other hand, most of the spellings exemplified occur frequently enough to allow for occasional mistranscriptions and still retain value as evidence. Dr Wijk has provided an excellent descriptive account of Machyn's language, and he rightly emphasizes the caution that is necessary in any attempt to use the evidence of the forms, but there appears to be no reason whatever to accept his conclusions with regard to Machyn's origin. He may have been a northerner; but there is practically nothing in his language to show this, and on the whole, the earlier view, that Machyn's Diary is written in a middle-class London dialect of the period, still seems the most acceptable.

R. M. WILSON

19 · Wing Commander A. H. Smith, O.B.E.

An Aberdeen store, looking back in 1949 at its fifty-five years of existence, described in a commemorative brochure its one war incident:

> It happened in 1941, in the spring of the year after the Battle of Britain had been lost by the Germans. That made the enemy more venomous. So, in the evening of 13th February, about seven o'clock, a bomb was dropped from the air and landed not a hundred yards away.

The vision of a frustrated Goering seeking his revenge on Britain by an attack on the redoubtable store of Mr Isaac Benzie is a happy one to contemplate. Unfortunately, I cannot claim such a direct interest by the Reichsmarschall in my first meeting with Hugh Smith, beyond remarking the coincidence that this happened after the Luftwaffe had failed to demolish Mr Benzie's emporium.

In the autumn of 1941 I was telephoned just before lunch one day by a Flight Lieutenant Smith, who said that there was something that he wanted to discuss with me, and that it could be suitably broached over lunch in the 'Thatched House', a club which, as he put it, was noted, in double contradistinction to the Athenaeum, for its high living and plain thinking. When I met the Flight Lieutenant, who quickly became my very good friend, Hugh Smith, he explained that he was in danger of being invalided out of the R.A.F., owing to a combination of a motor-cycle accident and a duodenal ulcer, and he had decided that despite this he could be of value in my department. He had previously been an Intelligence Officer in France in 1940.

He thought that we must get many damaged German documents to examine from crashed aircraft, and that these would provide scope for the techniques that he had developed to detect the forgeries in the Anglo-Saxon Chronicle. Actually, I doubted whether we had many documents suitable for this treatment, but I was so impressed by the ingenuity of the argument, the excellence of the lunch, and the liberality of Hugh and Helen Smith's subsequent hospitality at Alstone, that I was happy to secure the posting of Hugh to my staff towards the end of 1941. Thereafter he and Charles Frank (now Professor F. C. Frank) and I shared an office throughout the war; and the unusual experiment of appointing a Reader in English to the staff of a department responsible for anticipating the German applications of science to warfare turned out to be thoroughly rewarding.

The success of Hugh's appointment was immediate. He took over the task of pinpointing the increasing number of German radar stations from photographs and other information, and the preparation of the appropriate target dossiers. By the end of the war we had located seven hundred and forty stations, leaving no more than six to be discovered by our ground forces. Hugh's skill with his hands was very valuable to us, because he also took over the drawing of our diagrams. Figure 8 shows his map of the Bruneval raid of 27 February 1942, where there was also included, for the sake of completeness and inspiration, the track of a somewhat older and larger raid. This latter was in fact the route of Edward III from Bosham Harbour to Crecy (which is about as near to medieval studies as we shall get in this memoir), plotted in the same way as an R.A.F. reconnaissance sortie would have been plotted. We duly received inquiries from a Squadron Leader, asking when this raid had taken place.

On the same map, we pointedly marked the position of Swanage, the dangerously exposed site of the Telecommunications Research Establishment, with the hint that it might be selected by the Germans for a reprisal. When we found, shortly

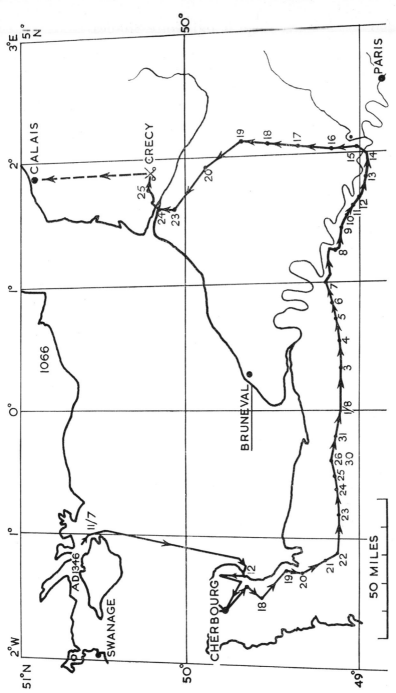

Fig. 8. The location of the Radar Station at Bruneval, raided 27 February 1942. Intelligence Report map drawn by Hugh Smith

after the Bruneval raid, that a German parachute unit had in fact moved up behind Cherbourg, Hugh and I visited Swanage and underlined our faith in the information by carrying pistols and tin hats. The Establishment was rapidly removed to Malvern where, as the Royal Radar Establishment, it still is.

Hugh had developed a method of perspective drawing from elevation and plan diagrams, with results such as that shown in Figure 9, which is one of his drawings of German radar equipment.

We had occasional problems in photography and in the copying of documents. Hugh went along to discuss one of them with the chief photographer at the Foreign Office; it involved either ultra-violet or infra-red photography, and the Foreign Office man said, 'The best advice that I can give you is to read an article about it by a chap called Smith!' – who was, of course, Hugh himself.

Apart from these specialist activities, Hugh made a great contribution by his personality. As a group of scientists who had not especially cultivated the social graces, we sometimes found it difficult to get our way when we wanted extra facilities or accommodation, and Hugh quickly became our liaison officer in such matters. It was amazing what he could charm out of a Quartermaster Officer over a drink in the 'Thatched House'. One day we even persuaded the Firearms Officer that we wanted a firearms certificate for a fictitious 25-pounder gun that we had installed near Hugh's house in Gloucestershire and which we used with proximity-fused shrapnel shells to shoot rabbits. I think that we told him that our biggest bag to a single round had been two hundred and forty-three, and we left a brace in his office as a token. We also persuaded the Photographic Reconnaissance Unit to take a photograph of where we said the gun was emplaced, and the Firearms Officer much admired our skill at camouflage, because the photograph showed absolutely no trace of the gun, or of any tell-tale tracks.

Hugh's great manual skill was invaluable in another way: he had a hobby of making model railway engines. In June 1943 it

Overall height 28 ft
Frames (together) 21 ft × 17 ft
Cabin 7 ft × 7 ft

Fig. 9. 'Freya' early warning radar apparatus, used by the Luftwaffe and drawn by Hugh Smith, 1942

became clear that when we were finally allowed to drop 'Window', the aluminium foil strips intended to confuse German radar, the person who would be most blamed if the device failed was myself. I was therefore most anxious that the bomber crews should be as well informed as possible about the principles of the device and its manner of use. I knew that there was sometimes a lack of proper information at aircrew level, and I therefore wanted Hugh Smith and Edward Wright (Professor of Mathematics at Aberdeen), as two of our most skilled lecturers, to go and lecture at all our bomber stations. Unfortunately, I also knew that Bomber Command much disliked any direct contact between the subordinate formations and the Air Staff, and that we were therefore likely to encounter much resistance. Fortunately, I remembered that the Deputy Commander-in-Chief's hobby was model railways, because I had in October 1942 spent an amazing half-hour after lunch playing trains with him in his bedroom. I therefore telephoned him and explained that I was most anxious that two of my officers should visit his stations and talk to the aircrews, because I thought that we did not attach enough significance to their combat reports. As expected, he said that this would be difficult because the C.-in-C. did not like members of the Air Staff visiting his stations. I remarked that this was a pity, because Smith and Wright were two very good chaps, and that Smith had as a matter of fact made a remarkable No. 1 Gauge coal-fired and superheated model of a G.W.R. 'County' class tank engine, and that if the Deputy C.-in-C. could call at my office next time he was in London, we would let him run it. 'Oh,' he said, 'that makes it quite different. If Smith is as good a chap as that, I think that it would be safe to let him talk to our aircrews.' And so Hugh and Edward Wright had *carte blanche* to visit any stations they liked; I believe that they gave about forty lectures each in about a fortnight. And I am sure that 'Window' was used by the aircrews with much more enthusiasm and understanding than would ever have been possible without Hugh's model locomotive.

As we entered 1944, it became obvious that we ought to send a party to the Continent with the invasion forces. We therefore formed the A.D.I. (Science) Overseas Party, and Hugh was given the rank of Wing Commander and appointed Officer Commanding. Notwithstanding his rank, he was apt to drive a three-ton lorry at the slightest opportunity. Very quickly he discovered that the Americans, with their written constitution, had an enormous respect for paperwork and that if you possessed an authorization headed 'Orders' they would allow you to do anything that was written thereon. Hugh therefore drafted, as befitted his profession, a masterpiece for my signature. On Air Ministry notepaper, it was merely headed 'Subject: Orders', and it stated that the bearer was an officer of my staff, and that any British or Allied Officer was asked to give him all the facilities that he might request, including free access to all targets and all necessary transport. I was very sceptical about the efficacy of the document until I myself had to travel with an Air Commodore who had the official British Authorization – he encountered much trouble from American guards, while my 'Orders', drafted by Hugh and signed by myself, produced an immediate salute.

The adventures of our Overseas Party merit a book. More than one German town surrendered to a single A.D.I. (Science) Officer – we were sometimes the first to enter. M.I.5 spent quite a time trying to catch a large black market gang ranging over Germany and Austria, and using an unbreakable W/T code, but sometimes lapsing into *en clair* obscenity. The Commander-in-Chief of the British Air Forces of Occupation lost for about two months most of his transport reserve – eighty three-ton lorries – and five armoured cars, which were all commandeered by the A.D.I. (Science) Overseas Party. Ultimately, this event was correlated with the black market gang, but the Overseas Party rode serenely over the inquiry, and emerged with the C.-in-C.'s promise that if they ever wanted even more than eighty lorries, he would see what he could do.

For the week-end after V.E. day, I was with Hugh at his home in Alderton; there was to be a church parade of the local forces, and the Royal Observer Corps came to us to seek aid in their fight with the Home Guard as to which should take precedence in the parade. The arguments on both sides were ingenious but indecisive, until we had the happy thought of telephoning Hugh's former colleagues in the Air Ministry who had to deal with problems of protocol and ceremonial. They welcomed our query as a matter of precedence that had never been raised before, and they spent most of the time arguing the case with the War Office. On the Saturday evening a ruling was given, which would have forced the Observer Corps to second place, but they had in the meantime decided to settle the matter by cutting the preliminary parade, and sitting in the front pews at the Church.

This was only one of many hilarious events that had flowered under Hugh's encouragement at Alstone and Alderton throughout the war. One of our colleagues, who was as near a full-blooded Secret Service man as one is likely to meet, came to spend a week-end at Alstone. Hugh and I thought that he might be embarrassed if we undisguisedly met him at Evesham, and so we adorned ourselves suitably with false eyebrows and moustaches cut from one of Helen's cast-off furs, and with other stratagems such as mutilated hats, clay pipes, and string tied round our trouser legs. Our success was such that the Secret Service man failed to recognize us; so did Hugh's landlady; and so, most impressive of all, did the landlord of 'The Hobnails'. There was some local curiosity about our Secret Service friend; but everyone was satisfied when Hugh let it be discreetly rumoured that he was a defrocked naval chaplain, and this was deemed, by the understanding people of Gloucestershire, to explain everything.

Several of us will be always grateful to Hugh and particularly to Helen for the relaxation which Alderton provided. Helen had two children of her own, and had two locally stationed officers permanently billeted with her, and yet she sometimes had my wife and family to stay for holidays for two weeks at a stretch. Looking back, and remembering rationing and the other restrictions, we wonder how she did it.

In October 1945, Hugh returned to University College, having been awarded an O.B.E. for his many services. In the following twelve months most of the rest of us had left, mainly to come back to the Universities. What we had done in the war is now a matter that in our flowing cups may be remembered with advantages; but all that I have said here, however improbable it may have sounded, is true – and, leaving the advantages to 'The Hobnails' and 'The Marlborough', we were permanently enriched by having had Hugh Smith as a colleague. It is a pleasure to salute him with gratitude on his sixtieth birthday, when, perhaps – as his daughter, Greta, prematurely put it on his fortieth birthday – he is entering the Middle Ages.

R. V. JONES